Studying Children

Studying Children:
A Cultural–
Historical Approach

Mariane Hedegaard
and
Marilyn Fleer
with
Jytte Bang and Pernille Hviid

 Open University Press

Open University Press
McGraw-Hill Education
McGraw-Hill House
Shoppenhangers Road
Maidenhead
Berkshire
England
SL6 2QL

email: enquiries@openup.co.uk
world wide web: www.openup.co.uk

and Two Penn Plaza, New York, NY 10121—2289, USA

First published 2008

A catalogue record of this book is available from the British Library

ISBN-13: 978 0335 234783 (pb) 978 0335 234 790 (hb)
ISBN-10: 0335 23478X (pb) 0335 234798 (hb)

Typeset by Kerrypress, Luton, Bedfordshire
Printed and bound in the UK by Bell and Bain Ltd, Glasgow.

Fictitious names of companies, products, people, characters and/or data
that may be used herein (in case studies or in examples) are not intended
to represent any real individual, company, product or event.

The *McGraw-Hill* Companies

Contents

Acknowledgements

The special beginnings of this book took place in December 2005 when Marilyn Fleer invited Mariane Hedegaard to visit Monash University for three weeks and discovered that our research interests were very closely aligned. Together we embarked on a project within the cultural historical frame that we have defined as a wholeness perspective on children's everyday activities, life within the family, and across different institutions. Mariane's colleague's Jytte Bang and Pernille Hviid then joined the project. The following May 2005 Marilyn Fleer came for a short visit to Copenhagen, where our discussions continued and led us to agree to write a research methodology book that would capture the cultural historical ideas of Vygotsky and Leontiev. This book builds on our earlier work and has informed our research into children's everyday lives within the family and across institutions.

Mariane has for several years worked on the theoretical aspect of such an approach and Marilyn's recent research fits well within these ideas. This collaboration became the background for the development of the book, with Jytte Bang and Pernille Hviid joining the writing process as they too shared our theoretical and practical research ideas. We have had very lively discussions via the internet on the content of the book and by early 2008 we had completed half of the manuscript. The last contribution to the writing process took place in April 2008 when Marilyn stayed in Copenhagen and worked in parallel with Mariane, a wonderful but exhausting experience! We enjoyed this month of shared work immensely, and would like to thank Jytte Bang and Pernille Hviid for the great discussions we had over the content of this book and for their valued contributions.

The research which Mariane has drawn upon for the development of this book has built up over the past 20 years. The work that Marilyn sites in her chapters has been undertaken over the last four years together with her two PhD students Avis Ridgway and Gloria Quinones. An Australian Research Council Grant (Discovery) and the Margaret Trembath Research Scholarship provided funds for these projects. Through these research collaborations with our colleagues, we have put into practice a number of the methodological ideas of both Vygotsky and Leontiev and we want to thank them for their contribution to these projects. We would also like to thank Professor Ray McDermot, School of Education, Stanford University who has critically commented on the first four chapters of this book. Furthermore we would like to thank the commissioning editor, Fiona Richman, for her support and for her helpful comments on the chapters.

Mariane Hedegaard and Marilyn Fleer
August 2008

Figure 1.1 Louise at group time in her childcare centre.

1 Researching child development – an introduction

Mariane Hedegaard, Marilyn Fleer, Jytte Bang and Pernille Hviid

Introduction

Our premise is that in order to understand children we must be cognisant of the social, cultural and historical practices in which they live and learn. That is, we need to be aware of the *social situation of children's development*. Finding ways of effectively researching childhood learning and development across children's everyday lives, at home, in the community, in preschool, and as they make the transition to school or other places, is the central theme of this book. We begin this chapter with a series of visual examples taken from research that focuses on children's development and learning.

Figure 1.1 shows Louise (2 years old) in her childcare centre at group time. The teacher is reading a story. The children are seated on cushions on the carpet. The cushions have been specifically placed on the carpet with the intention of defining the area for whole group 'story reading'. It is just before lunch and most of the children are restless or yawning, some are talking and most are wriggling. However, the children generally look towards the teacher and stay within the designated area for story reading.

In the first frame of the filmstrip, we see Louise lying on the carpet. Within the 7 minutes of observation taken of Louise during story reading, she makes seven almost 360-degree body turns. She actively uses more space than the other toddlers, and maintains this activity throughout the observation period. However, she does not move away from the story-reading area.

In the second frame of the filmstrip, we see Louise focused on her sandal. Throughout the observation period, Louise feels her sandal, plays with it and even attempts to put it on her foot. She also plays with the teacher's shoe and makes numerous advances towards the shoes of the child sitting immediately next to her.

In the final frame of the filmstrip Louise is shown squatting. During this observation, Louise positions herself into a squatting position and looks intently at the teacher, raises her body into a standing position and immediately returns to the squatting position each time the teacher asks her to sit down. The interactions appear to be mischievous and fun for Louise. One of the toddlers sitting next to her looks intently at Louise as she moves up and immediately says 'Sit down' in an authoratative voice. Louise ignores this and continues to look towards the teacher, but remains standing. Louise is again asked to sit down by the teacher and she responds by immediately squatting down while warmly smiling. Louise appears to 'tease' the teacher and the other children through her 'standing up' and 'sitting down' game.

The routine in this childcare centre is for children to sit on the carpet area, aided by the cushions, in order to listen to the teacher reading a book. The children are expected to look towards the teacher, listen to the story and not interfere with other children. The focus of attention is on both the teacher and the storybook. The children are given lots of reminders when they do not conform to the teacher's expectations in relation to these practices. Children are verbally reminded, and physically moved back to the cushions, when they move about or face the wrong direction. When we focus on the *teacher's perspective* we note that the conditions for learning are centred on the book and on the teacher's mediation of its contents to an 'all listening group of children'. However, if we take the *perspective of the child*, we see other things happening during this teaching practice.

In this observation of Louise, we notice that she has generated her own activities within group time – that is, Louise plays a mischievous 'standing up' and 'sitting down' game which is directed to the teacher. In addition, within the teaching practice of story reading, she has also created her own activity of 'exploring shoes'. Finally, we observe that Louise enacts a vertical and horizontal physical movement activity, but confines this within the boundary of the story-reading area. Although she takes more room than the other children, she is permitted this latitude. We notice all these activities when we take the *perspective of the child*. The conditions for learning are framed by the teacher in a particular way, but Louise has created her own activities within the 'schooling' practice.

Louise expertly shows that she understands the practice tradition in the centre and at the age of 2 can also generate her own activities within this practice. We can only examine the activities of the child if we also observe the practice traditions in the childcare centre. The standing up and sitting down activity that Louise has constructed can only be understood as a game if we also pay attention to the teaching practice in the centre. Similarly, we can only understand the teaching practice if we observe the children and teacher interacting – the practice tradition of teaching is only a practice when there are participants (i.e. children and a teacher). Teaching practice is meaningless without children and children's activities are meaningless without teaching practice. The perspective of the teacher and the perspective of the child are both needed for researching the social situation of Louise's development. This is the dialectical view of research that underpins the methodological material discussed in this book.

In this book, we specifically examine the perspectives of children, teachers and researchers through actively considering the relations between all these perspectives. It is only through this dialectical–interactive view of research that we can understand the social situation of children's development. This dynamic methodology for researching follows a cultural–historical tradition. In this book, we not only critique the traditional approaches to researching children by discussing limitations and strengths, but we also build a new methodology for researching children's development and learning in ways that include the child's perspective in research, alongside the cultural and historical practices in which they live and learn (e.g. teaching practice; family practice) and the researcher's motives and goals for the study. This chapter introduces the themes within the book and provides a 'road map' for the content that follows.

Beginning the methodological journey

The psychological research tradition of developmental psychology has been influenced by the positivist traditions of medicine and the natural sciences, especially physics, where Cartesian logic has dominated thinking (Lewin, 1946; Bronfenbrenner, 1977; Burman, 1994; Latour, 2003). For example, some researchers following this tradition have been interested in looking at specific variables such as 'cognition' and will test children about what they know using standardised tests. Their focus of attention will be 'what's in the head'. Evidence can easily be found when textbooks of developmental psychology are examined (see Cole, Cole and Lightfoot, 2005; Berk, 2006). Objectivity in the form of researcher reliability and measurement validity, as is found in the natural sciences, has influenced the principles for doing research in developmental psychology. For example, observations are given to two separate individual 'coders' who are employed to categorise the observations. They are usually blind to the research question and are asked to code particular behaviours. They have a coding sheet that explains exactly which behaviours fit within a particular category. The two coders will then compare their results to ensure that the coding is reliable. When the coders agree with their categorisations, the coding is deemed reliable enough to use.

Ideas of objectivity in the form of hypotheses testing and experimental approaches have led to research of very limited psychological functioning without taking into account the social conditions.

In developmental psychology, critiques of this approach have been undertaken from a range of perspectives. Marx Wartofsky (1983) has given a critique from a philosophical perspective and Erica Burman (1994/2007) has given a critique from a psychological perspective. Both scholars have pointed out that the 'great theories of developmental psychology' have not taken the societal conditions, norms and values into consideration in their conceptualisation of child development. Critiques from sociologically oriented research have demonstrated that psychology has constructed children as abstract entities. Anthropologist and sociologists have argued that one has to consider the various conditions that different societies give for creating childhood (James and Prout, 1993; Corsaro, 1997; James, Jenks and Prout, 1997). Researchers within an anthropological tradition have outlined methodologies that have inspired our cultural–historical approach (Christensen and James, 1999; Gulløv and Højlund, 2003). The methodological principles recommended by childhood research about locating research in time and space creates problems transcending the historically specific settings in which children are studied. The risk is that the research will only focus on children growing up in specific historical settings such as America, Italy, or Great Britain without theorising on the conditions generally applicable to children's development. The tension that emerges can be seen between how specific or how general one must be when doing research, and when creating new theories of children's development.

Working within the cultural–historical tradition formulated by Vygotsky, the authors of this book agree with these critiques from philosophy, and from childhood research, and support the view that childhood research should be explicitly anchored in historical settings. However, as pointed out by Burman, developmental psychology should also be very explicit about the aim of research and about what and for whom development research is valuable (i.e. what are the values that guide ideas of development). We argue furthermore that it is not enough to focus only on the societal conditions and values, we must also have a methodology that will allow both theory and research about child development to be generated. Such a methodology must be anchored in a concrete historical setting and at the same time contribute towards an understanding of the *general conditions* that support child development.

In this book we ask an important question: How should we conceptualise the object of our study – children's development – and formulate a methodology for studying children's development? In the chapters that follow, we put forward a new methodology that will allow researchers to study children in their everyday lives within a particular historical setting, using *concepts* that can transcend these settings.

Some of our preconceptions about child development have been inspired by Leontiev (1978), Vygotsky (1998) and Elkonin (1999). In addition, our preconceptions have also been influenced by the phenomenological tradition of Schutz (1970) and the ecological tradition of Barker and Wright (1954, 1971) and Gibson (1966). Taken together, we find it is important to study children's everyday settings in order to gain insights into the social situation of their development. An important dimension of the methodology discussed in this book is the acknowledgement of the various institutions in which children participate and which influence their everyday lives. It is only through studying institutional traditions (family, kindergarten, school) that we begin to see the social situations of children within and across these institutional settings. In drawing upon Schutz's theory, we find that we are able to examine the validity and reliability of data generated across settings as we analyse children's everyday activities. For us it has been important that Schutz has argued that the everyday naive world of the acting person becomes the basic reference, even in scientific descriptions across settings.

A methodology for studying children's development in everyday settings has to use methods that are different from those of natural science and medicine, where the research is on human functioning. Instead, we argue that our methodological approach is in line with Vygotsky, Elkonin, Leontiev and Schutz, where the methodology focuses on children's motives, projects, intentional actions and interpretation. These concepts are discussed further in Chapters 2, 3 and 4.

In the 1980s, Hedegaard (Hedegaard, 1984; Hedegaard and Hakkarainen, 1986) formulated the 'Interactive Observation Method' which is based on a critique of Eriksson and Piaget's 'synoptic' research approach (i.e. that children's development is seen from a synoptic viewpoint, where neither the child's nor the researcher's perspective is taken into consideration, and no account is taken of the social interaction in the research situation). We will continue this line of development for the formulation of a series of practical methods for researching children's development in everyday activities in their historical (local) settings (see Chapters 5 to 11). It is important to include the child's perspective in a research methodology as this will enable researchers to investigate how children contribute to their own developmental conditions. At the same time it is also important to include other perspectives that can illuminate the societal and the institutional conditions that create a child's social situation. It is children's intentional activities and the interactions in which they take part in their everyday social situations – and how other participants contribute to these situations through their interactions – that should be studied.

We build on Vygotsky's concept of the social situation of development, as this integrates the child's perspective and competencies at different developmental ages in relation to social reality. We integrate this with Hedegaard's broader view of developmental potentialities for children – societal, institutional and personal *perspectives*. When bringing these perspectives together, it is possible to analyse how a child develops through interaction with other participants in institutional practices and to examine the conditions that the institutions can give for different kinds of interaction. This is discussed further in Chapter 2.

In recent years, anthropological methods have significantly influenced psychology. This is in line with the new area of childhood research that has developed in relation to the study of children's development (i.e. by Corsaro, 1997; James, Jenks and Prout, 1997; Christensen and James and 1999. We are also inspired by the critique and methodology from this approach, and find it important to use the qualitative methodology of field research. This approach allows researchers to gain different perspectives and to interact with participants in the research study. This approach also gives researchers a new way of researching children's motives, projects, intentional actions and interpretation.

Contents of the book

The first question we raise in this book is: How can we as psychological and educational researchers formulate a methodology and undertake research in ways that focus on the social situation of children's development that are conditional both by the institutional traditions and the specific practices? This will be the first theme in this book. The second theme will be how to make that transition from a collection of observations and interviews in the research field to interpretations of these observations and interviews. Through using a systematic approach to this conceptual progression, we can still talk about reliable and valid research results.

The four contributors to this book have developed their own versions of a cultural–historical research methodology, and case examples are provided. However, we share the basic theoretical considerations about child development and knowledge epistemology and these are illustrated in the forthcoming chapters as principles that we advocate for researching children's development.

This chapter has given an introduction to developmental psychology and childhood research. In the next chapter, Mariane Hedegaard introduces a model for learning and development that focuses on societal conditions, institutional practices and the motives and intentions of children in everyday activities. When Hedegaard's model (Figure 2.1) is used for framing up research it focuses the researcher's attention on how to gain insights into the developmental conditions from societal, institutional and individual perspectives. Through this expansive view of development, a more holistic approach to research is afforded.

The methodological implications for using cultural–historical theory for researching childhood are the focus of Chapter 3. In this chapter, Mariane Hedegaard introduces a dialectical–interactive research approach through a series of case examples. These examples underpin the theoretical constructs needed for understanding the dialectical approach to researching children's development that is introduced in the second section of this chapter. A critique of traditional methods is given in the context of a dialectical–interactive approach.

Chapters 2 and 3 provide a methodological discussion for framing research of children's development from a cultural–historical tradition, while Chapter 4 exemplifies the observation protocols. Mariane Hedegaard discusses, in detail, how a researcher following a cultural–historical approach enters the field and begins a dialogue with children. In a dialectical-interactive approach, as discussed in Chapters 2 and 3, the researcher as a person as well as a researcher are conceptualised as part of the research. Chapter 4 highlights the significance of the position of the researcher in research. Mariane Hedegaard points out in this chapter that although the researcher has to be open towards the research aims, the preconceptions influence those issues to which the researcher pays attention and records. She argues that when following a cultural–historical approach to childhood research, the intentions of the various people being observed offer the opportunity to gain insights into the different perspectives of the participants in the study. In the latter part of Chapter 4, Mariane Hedegaard provides a detailed account of how researchers can generate interpretations. She outlines the differences between writing protocols and generating different forms of interpretation: common sense interpretation, situated practice interpretation and thematic interpretation.

In Chapter 5, Marilyn Fleer illustrates the methodological principles of a cultural–historical approach to researching children's everyday lives in a case example. Through introducing a study of science learning in preschools across three different contexts, Marilyn Fleer discusses how the institutional perspective can be gained, how conflicts between different staff perspectives can be illustrative of important conditions for learning and how interpretations of the protocols generated through this study can be made. The mechanics of undertaking a cultural–historical approach to research are given in this particular chapter. In the final part of this chapter, Marilyn Fleer discusses the role of the researcher in the study and how the positioning of the researcher influences the way in which the observations are framed.

A further example of a cultural–historical approach to research is given in Chapter 6. Marilyn Fleer introduces examples of observation protocols and interpretations that focus on the child's perspective within the context of the family and in the context of the school traditions. This chapter shows how the values and motives of the institution influence the conditions for learning for the participating children. These values and motives are historically embedded and are re-presented through the teaching practices of the staff in the particular institution. The chapter gives examples of how the institutional values are preserved, discussed by staff through their own professional learning activities and enacted through institutional teaching practices. In this particular example, it is possible to see how a wholeness approach to researching childhood development can illustrate far more than when only one perspective is taken in researching the conditions of development for children.

In Chapter 7, Marilyn Fleer shows how digital video observations and computer technologies can be used in a cultural–historical approach to childhood research. This chapter shows, by practical examples of the techniques used, how the dialectical–interactive approach can be realised through digital video recordings of children and their families. It is shown how digital observations can be logged, arranged, interpretations made and analyses undertaken, through the aid of a computer. The iterative and open nature of a cultural–historical approach for research is shown through the examples of digital video interpretations given in this chapter.

In Chapter 8, Jytte Bang discusses how potentials for development embedded in the activity setting and the developmental moments over a long time span can be considered as the 'relation between small and great novelty'. Central in this discussion is the concept of 'affordance'. In using the concept of affordance in relation to activity settings, she shows how cultural–historical researchers can conceptualise the environment of the child. Jytte Bang gives a range of examples of interpretations that have been generated through the explicit examination of the environmental affordances.

In Chapter 9, Pernille Hviid introduces the research method of interviewing following a cultural–historical approach. Pernille Hviid critiques and builds upon previous methodological writings on the interview method. She begins her critique with Piaget's clinical method and shows how dialectical logic takes the interview process further than Piaget had conceptualised. Importantly, this chapter also shows how the researcher can enter children's activity settings and undertake an ethical interview with children in relation to their development. Through case examples, she is able to illustrate how children can learn the interview script and can act as interviewers in research

– both 'with' the researcher and 'for' the researcher. The chapter provides a strong methodological argument for a cultural–historical approach to interviewing.

Chapter 10 specifically examines how to generate a questionnaire that reveals the demands for children's learning in school and children's perspectives on their own activity setting in school. Jytte Bang and Mariane Hedegaard specifically discuss the methodological constructs needed for framing a questionnaire from a cultural–historical perspective. They show how societal traditions for education can inform instrument design and explicitly demonstrate how these can become the focus of attention for observations of schooling practice and, through this, create a tool that supports both the child's perspective and the needs of the school.

In Chapter 11, Mariane Hedegaard shows how an educational experiment can be conceptualised and implemented following a cultural–historical approach. In this chapter, she illustrates, through a case example, the dynamic nature of a dialectical–interactive research methodology. There is transformative interplay between the pedagogy and the children's social situation as they generate models about the concepts they are exploring. In this evolving and dynamic educational experiment, the dialectical–interactive approach seeks to capture the perspective of both the teacher and the child.

In Chapter 12, Mariane Hedegaard provides a reflection on the role of researchers following a cultural–historical tradition. Because few people have written both methodologically and practically about how to undertake research on children's development and learning following a cultural–historical tradition, it was deemed important to examine the researchers' role. This, the final chapter, makes visible some of the challenges that researchers face when undertaking cultural–historical research in children's learning and development.

2 A cultural–historical theory of children's development

Mariane Hedegaard

According to our theoretical standpoint, developmental psychology and childhood research need to embrace the child as an individual person and see the child as a participant in a societal collective interacting with others in different settings. A child develops as an individual with unique distinctiveness, and as a member of a society where different institutional practices are evident.

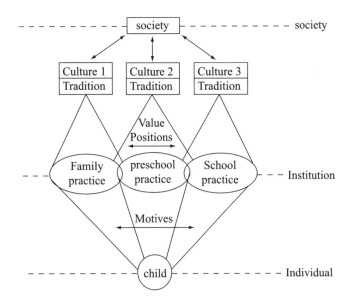

Figure 2.1 A model of children's learning and development through participation in institutional practice, where different perspectives are depicted: A societal, and institutional, and an individual perspective (Hedegaard, 2004).

The model in Figure 2.1 illustrates a situated dynamic where a child concurrently participates in several institutional settings and arenas in his or her everyday life, for instance home, day care and extended family, or home, school and community peer group or after-school activities. It can also be seen as a developmental pathway in Western industrialised/information societies, where the dominant institutions in a child's life change from being at home, to day care/infant school, to school. In the following sections, these conceptions of children's development will unfold in relation to three different perspectives: a societal perspective, an institutional perspective and a person's perspective. A wholeness approach to studying children should encompass daily life across different institutional settings and arenas from all three perspectives.

Important conceptions to describe children's development from a societal and cultural perspective are:

- Children's development takes place through participating in societal institutions.
- Institutional practice and children's development are connected to a conception of what constitutes a 'good life' and these vary within the different types of institution and even among those who participate in the practices found within these institutions.
- A child's development can be thought of as a qualitative change in his or her motive and competences. Development can also be connected to the change in the child's social situation (i.e. when the child moves from one institution to the next or as a result of change in a particular practice within an institution).

A societal perspective that relates to qualitative changes in development

Differences in how children are brought up are reflected in their developmental competencies. Descriptions of such differences can be found in anthropological literature. These are richly illustrated by Barbara Rogoff (2003) in her book, *The Cultural Nature of Human Development* and in Rogoff's (1990) longstanding research documented in *Apprenticeship in Thinking*. Margaret Mead (1956) has also nicely shown how cultural differences in upbringing can differ radically even within the same small society over a generation. In her anthropological research on *New Lives for Old: Cultural Transformation – Manus 1928–1953*, a radical change took place in adult work culture in this period. The American troops in the the Second World War contributed to a fast change in material, cultural and religious traditions in the Manus society, which in turn influenced both work relations and everyday social relations between adults. Mead writes that cultural traditions that were central in the old Manus traditions – for instance, sharing of goods – lived on in children's peer relations longer than among the adults and could be found even after they were abandoned by the adults. The change in Manus traditions influences the way children grow up. In connection with this study Mead points out that 'Every new religion, every new political doctrine, has had first to make its adult converts, to create a small nuclear culture within whose guiding wall its children can flourish …' (1956, p. 150). She writes further, 'Such changes in adult attitudes come slowly, are more dependent upon specially gifted or wise individuals than upon wholesale educational schemes' (1956, p. 151). According to Mead, the adult community creates the conditions for children's development.

Cross-cultural research provides us with a broader understanding of beliefs and expectations of children's development. For example, in some parts of West Africa the principle underpinning child development is social rather than biological, as noted by Nsamenang and Lamb in their study of Nso children in the Bamenda Granfields of Cameroon, West Africa:

> [C]hildren are progressively assigned different roles at different life stages depending on their perceived level of social competence rather than on their biological maturation.
>
> (Nsamenang and Lamb, 1998, p. 252)

Assumptions about development as constructed in one community do not necessarily transfer to other communities. Critically examining one's assumptions about development is important for researchers interested in studying the development of children as anchored in concrete historical settings, institutional practices and the general everyday living conditions of children and their families.

Developmental pathways

In a cultural–historical perspective on children's development, the focus of attention is on the person and the caregiver's perspective in relation to life opportunities and possibilities. In this approach, the formulation of possible trajectories has been very important, although I prefer the concept of pathway, because it surpasses the 'bird's eye' view on children's development and anchors what happens in the person's activities. The conception of developmental pathways takes the focus away from a particular course of development and gives room for a forward-directed approach where children can influence their own developmental pathways . Developmental trajectories have been formulated as an opposition to the 'course–reason' description of children's development and also have this forward-directed perspective.

Klaus Riegel (1975), in his critique of the more traditional theories, formulated the concept of developmental trajectories as an alternative to a more simple environmental influence and pointed to four inter-acting trajectories: the inner biological, the individual psychological, the cultural–sociological and the outer physical. Riegel showed how conflicts or harmony between the different types of trajectories in a person's life could lead to either a positive or a negative development, where timing is a central factor. Examples of conflict between biological lines and individual psycho-logical lines can be found when girls in some culture, get married very early or between individual psychological and cultural sociological developmental lines, when girls become underage mothers while still at school or when boys become soldiers in war zones.

Riegel argued that, in development, it is the dialectical interaction between inner biological/individual psychological factors and cultural–sociological/outer physical factors that is important.

Glen Elder (1998) has also outlined how a person's lines of develop-ment can be represented as social trajectories within families, education and work. Central to Elder's theory of a person's life course development is his conceptualisation of the historical aspect of societal trajectories and their change over generations. His conceptualisations, based on longitudinal research, show differences between children/youth growing up during the depression of the 1930s and children/youth growing up during the Second World War. How these conditions work together with economic hardship is influenced by timing. An example of timing is when children and youth enter education and work. Here, Elder points out that timing has a greater influence on a person's life trajectory than socially and culturally different life conditions. The relations between people have also been shown to influence how a person's life course will develop.

Elder's and Riegel's concepts of developmental trajectories and life course are structural theories that can be applied to, but not anchored in, practice in institutions and therefore even though they specify how interac-tion between conditions can take place, they cannot identify how new social relations are formed or what characterises the child's concrete social situa-tion.

Vygotsky (1998) also introduced the concept of developmental lines, but the meaning is quite different to that of Elder and Riegel. Vygotsky points to the importance of taking the child's social situation of development into consideration. A child's social situation of development changes in relation to different periods in his or her development. The social situation of development indicates that the child's personality and social environment at each age level are in a dynamic relation.

The structure of the child's personality appears, and is formed, in the course of the development of critical time periods. Vygotsky also talks of developmental lines as structural, but he places them within the child's development of personality and consciousness, where the structural changes are related to the development of central functions such as a child's speech. Such developmental lines of function can be diagnosed in relation to the child's social situation of development. The relation of the whole to the part, such as language development, is important at each age level. Vygotsky put forward the view that the developmental lines become central, or peripheral, according to their relationship to the child's developmental age. For example, at the age of 2, speech is a central line of development, while the exploration of fingers and toes is peripheral. During school age, the continuing development of a child's speech has a completely different relation to the central neo-formation of this age (e.g. where the focus becomes written symbols for learning to read), consequently, speech must be considered as a peripheral lines of development when at school in relation to learning to read and write (Vygotsky, 1998, p. 197).

In Vygotsky's terminology, developmental lines cannot be separated into biological, environmental and psychological, but rather they are woven together. The environment in this relation must not be conceived as something outside the child, as an aggregate of objective conditions, without reference to the child and how they are affecting him or her by their very existence:

> ... at the beginning of each age period there develops a completely original, exclusive single and unique relation, specific to the given age, between the child and the reality, namely the social reality, that surrounds him. We call this relation the *social relation of development* at the given age.
>
> (Vygotsky, 1998, p. 198)

The social environment is the source for the appearance of all specific human properties that have been gradually acquired by the child. It is the source of a child's personality development that is grounded in the process of interaction of 'ideal' and 'present forms' form of properties. In different periods different developmental lines dominate and these can be thought of as the 'social relations of development':

> Toward the end of a given age, the child becomes a completely different being than he was at the beginning of the age. But this necessarily also means that the social situation of development which was established in basic traits toward the beginning of any age must also change since the social situation of development is nothing other than a system of relations between the child of a given age and social reality.
>
> (Vygotsky, 1998, p. 199)

Vygotsky writes that the child's chronological age cannot serve as a reliable criterion for establishing the actual level of development. Determination of the actual level requires research that can diagnose the child's development, and to do this one has to focus on reliable traits or functions that can be used to identify the phase and stage of each age of the development process. In my interpretation, this must mean that one has to formulate ideals of child development that interweave biological lines as well as cultural–historical lines of development, so that caregivers and educators can formulate ideals of cultural development that are specific for a cultural tradition.

In combining Vygotsky's conception of developmental lines and the social situation of development with Riegal and Elder's conceptions of trajectories and life courses into a conception of developmental pathways, this concept can be seen as highlighting the ideals for children's development. But it also highlights that there are several ideal pathways for the development of each child. This is in line with Vygotsky's conception of how the child's social situation is created.

Further, I think it is important to combine the concept of institutional practice, as well as a person's activity, with the concept of developmental pathways.

Learning and development through entering institutional practices

The societal perspective is a macro perspective that perspectivates the conditions for the practices in which children can participate, in home, education and work. Changes in children's relation to the world are first and foremost connected to qualitative changes in what are the dominant institutional practices in a child's life. Entering a new institutional practice, such as going to school, can be viewed from a societal perspective. How a child participates in these different institutional practices, and what he or she learns from these experiences, can lead to developmental changes in a child. These changes need to be analysed in relation to the child's social situation.

Children's efforts and motives are usually directed towards successfully participating in the practice traditions of particular institutions. Children also create their own activities in the specific activity settings within these practices. As such, children's engagements and motives has to be seen in relation to both the traditional practices of the institutions and the activities they generate for themselves in the institutions. The concept of setting is inspired by Roger Barker and Herbert Wright's description of *One Boy's Day* (1954). They use the concept of behavioural setting to describe the context of the boy's activity. The setting is the cultural–material conditions that take the form of city architecture, material characteristic of the institutions, room size, furniture, all sorts of materials including books, TV, etc., that are available to the child. Barker and Wright use the term *behaviour* to describe their *meaning* of the boy's activity. They write that: 'All that is concerned with objectivity of this record must face two facts. One is that behaviour without feeling, motives and meanings is of little significance for the student's personality and social psychology. The other is that motives, feelings and meanings cannot be observed directly' (1954, p. 8).

I agree with Barker and Wright when they state that in order to get a child's perspective on what is meaningful to them, one must focus on a child's activities in everyday practice and differentiate between the different institutional activity settings within which children's everyday activities can be found. Instead of behaviour, the authors of this book use the concept of *activity*. Activity is a concept developed by Leontiev (1978). This term foregrounds the person's perspective by focusing on the person's intentions and motives in the practice being studied. Conceptualising what is going on in an institutional practice from a person's perspective, we prefer to use the concept of activity, a concept that is defined in relation to its 'motive goal'. An example of the relevance of this differentiation can be seen when a child is playing in a preschool activity setting. The traditional practice in the preschool is for staff to provide a spacious setting with the possibility for using different play materials and for supporting children to play together. The children's activity can be described as play when their motive is directed towards imagining activities such as when a child is imagining driving a car or being a mother taking care of a baby. It is through the focus on the child's engagement in 'make believe actions' as he or she plays with other children or plays with special toys that the child's activity, and not the institutional practice, is foregrounded. Here, the research takes the child's perspective. Had the focus of attention been on the materials and the space, then the institutional practice would have been the focus.

Practice and activity are related concepts: We will use *practice* when the institutional perspective is taken and *activity* when the person's perspective is taken (an overview of the conceptual relations can be seen in Table 2.1). Children develop through participating in institutionalised practice that are characterised by communication and shared activities. These forms of practice not only initiate but also restrict children's activities and thereby become conditions for their development. A child's participation in a kindergarten's activity settings such as meals and play lead to different activities for the child in kindergarten than in the home, since the kindergarten setting and its practice traditions give different conditions for learning and development than home traditions for these activities.

Learning activities such as mathematics, eating lunch and playing are done within the practice tradition of the schools. In school, neither meals nor play are expected to be the dominant activities; but learning subject matters, such as mathematics, are seen as the dominant activities in school practices. In kindergarten, however, play is seen as the dominant activity (for many countries such as Denmark, Australia, United Kingdom, USA, etc.).

Table 2.1   Levels of analyses

Society	Tradition	Conditions
Institution	Practice	Values/Motive objects
Social situation	Activity setting	Motivation
Person	Activity	Motives/Engagement/Intentions

To describe and understand the conditions for development, one has to ask:

- What kind of institutional practices do children in modern society participate in?
- What activity settings tend to dominate the institutional practices of modern society?
- What demands do these dominant practices put on children?
- What possibilities for activity are generated and how do children act in these activity settings?
- What kind of conflicts can occur between different demands?
- What kind of crises will children meet through conflicting demands and motives (i.e. moving from one institution to the next, appropriating the orientation and competence required by these institutions)?

Children's development seen in relation to values and norms

Development should also be seen in relation to values and norms. For instance, development should be viewed as a process that integrates a person's development of competencies with values. In order to enable caregiving persons and educators to evaluate what competences and motives children have appropriated, they need a set of descriptive norms for children's development. However, valuable competencies and motives are connected with what is seen as a 'good life' by the caregivers or educators who surround the child and who focus on developing the child.

Conceptions of a 'good life' are anchored in the norms and values that are interwoven in the different cultural traditions in the institutions where daily life is lived and daily activities take place. They are expressed through interaction as well as through the material conditions available to children, such as the type of food, way of dressing, where to live, how to give space to children's activities, environmental designs and the financial costs associated with having a child. Ideas of how to create a 'good everyday life' for children are not so simple, because children participate in several institutional practices every day (i.e. in family, kindergarten/school and perhaps religious institutions, sport and leisure time activities) and also in community life. In such a variety of places, there can be different practice traditions and different values and sometimes these values and traditions are not compatible. For example, some refugee families find that there are multiple 'instances' of what constitutes a 'good life', particularly when families experience institutional traditions in their new society (i.e. school, workplace and community in general) that are different to those known and found in their original home community (Hedegaard, 1999, 2003). Even within an institution, there can be different opinions of what is good practice and a good life. For example, this can be found even among teachers at the same school and can sometimes be noticed explicitly between members of the same family.

Change in institutional practice

Elkonin's (1999) theory of child development especially focuses on the importance of social practice in different institutions. These social practices mark important qualitative changes in children's development. Elkonin describes three periods in children's development and outlines how these are related to the dominant practice traditions in Western industrialised society. I especially draw upon Elkonin's formulation of the dialectic between competence and motives throughout a child's development, as seen within different age periods. I have to state very clearly that a concept of period or stage in a child's development has to be understood in relation to the different types of institutional practice and the activities this affords to children. Through participation in institutional practice a child acquires specific motives and competencies. But it is also important to state that in a shared activity setting with other people, the child's engaged activity is central to what he or she may learn. Parents/teachers/educators evaluate a child's competence and motive appropriation in relation to their ideas about what such participation in institutional practices should lead to – either directly or indirectly. That is, as children participate in the institutional practices, their involvement or activity are oriented towards certain goals and their successful appropriation of these 'goals' is then used to evaluate their competence and motive development.

The child's perspective

When we consider the child's perspective, the activity setting in which the child participates is known as the child's 'social situation'. In the child's social situation, demands from caregivers and the possibility for realising their own intentional activity leads to the appropriation of competencies and motives connected to the activity setting.

In order to take a child's perspective as they enter a new practice, one has to focus on the motives inherent in the activity settings. One has also to relate the activity settings in which the child participates to the projects in which the child is engaged, and the intention the child shows through his or her actions.

The easiest way to understand a child's intention is to note when there is a conflict where the child cannot do what he or she wants to do and cannot realise the projects in which he or she is engaged. As such, a cultural–historical methodology needs to focus on the conflicts between the child's intentions and what he or she is unable to realise. It is important, however, not to over-evaluate conflicts. In the first instance, conflict should be seen it as a way to understand the child's motive and to see what he or she is oriented towards. Conflicts also allow the researcher to note the ways in which a child interacts with his or her surrounding and this gives greater insight into the child's perspective.

To be able to take a child's perspective one has to focus on the intentions that guide the child's actions and from the patterns of actions and communication, interpret the projects and motives in which the child engages.

Children's intentional orientation, projects and motives

Since intention and motives are central in a methodology focusing on the child's social situation, a short overview of how the author understands these concepts will be presented. Inspiration will be drawn not only from Leontiev (1978) and Elkonin (1999), but also from Bruner's (1972) research into children's intentional activities in infancy.

Through shared activity, the child becomes aware of his or her own needs and goals and it is through this interaction that the child's biological needs are transformed into societal needs. That is, the biological needs becomes attached to a cultural 'motive–object' (Leontiev, 1978). For example, when we follow an infant's development we usually note how the child's biological needs turn into cultural needs and become the child's motives. According to Bruner (1972), from the very first moments of an infant's development, the child is intentionally oriented to its surrounding and from this orientation springs further development of the child's dynamic and cognitive orientation to the world. Building on the cultural–historical approach of Leontiev and Elkonin, one has to conceptualise a child's intentional orientation or projects as a relation between the child's motives in an activity settings and the demands in the institutional practice – i.e. between the motives of the child and possibilities for activity. The child's motives have to be seen in relation to his or her experience and competence and the possibility for realising the child's motives in an institutional practice. Meaningful motives are created for the child through experience and through gaining competences when participating in new activity settings.

Leontiev (1978) states that a child's development can be viewed in relation to his or her 'hierarchy of motives'. A child's motive hierarchy has to be understood in relation to what is considered to be the most important activity for the child. A child's motive hierarchy changes over time because he or she appropriates new motives and also because practice changes. When practice changes, children are given new possibilities for participating in important activity settings. A motive becomes a leading motive when the activity connected with this is the most meaningful activity for the child. The leading motive in a child's life is related to what is the dominating institutional practice in which the child participates, in a given life period. This means that, for a school child, the dominant practice in school would result in a motive for 'school learning'. When a child's leading motive in school is connected to a meaningful activity setting then it should result in academic learning. This holds in most cases, but it is not always the activity in the school practice that the teacher has in mind that becomes the most meaningful, and thereby the leading motive, for the child. The motive complex related to school practice (as well as to other institutional practices) is complicated because so many activities are going on in school between subject matter teaching, peer group activities, teacher–student relations, student–student relations and all the extra curricular activities.

To take a child's perspective in research is to ask: What different practice is the child taking part in? What activity settings is the child engaged in? What characterises the child's motives and activity settings in relation to these different practices and what projects does the child engage in across different institutional practices? Is it possible for children to engage intentionally in activity settings that are meaningful for them and realise their motives when interacting with others who participate in the same everyday activities?

The child's motives are not always in line with the expectations of caregivers – for instance, when a child is playing and is not happy when other children take his or her toys but the caregivers believe it is important to share. In this example, the caregivers and educators should support the child to accept that other children will interfere with his or her play. If, by the same token, the caregivers accept that each child will have his or her own special toys, such as a special teddy bear, then the caregivers should also help the other participants to respect the child's wish not to share this toy. Conflicts can arise between children during shared activities and it is important to recognise that a shared activity setting can contain different projects for different children, depending upon their engagement and understanding of the activity (an activity can be motivated both by several motives of the single person and by different motives from several persons). From a child's perspective, the child can have a special motive which can be seen as a project or an interest that transcends different activity settings or even practices. This can, for instance, be seen when a child is aiming at the same type of play in different settings or wanting to be with his or her best friend in different activities or both. Trying to see an activity from a given person's perspective gives the possibility for understanding how this person both learns from and contributes to shared activities.

During play the different motives and projects of children intersect. How motives and projects influence each other can be illustrated by an extract from an observation of three children, where the eldest child sets the scene for their play, but the two younger children, who do not really understand the theme of the play 'disturb' the older child's ideas by introducing simpler play themes.

Torben (5½ years old), *Jorn* (3 years old), *Louis* (3 years old)

Torben announces that he is Superman and says directly to Jorn: You are Peter Pan.

Torben: Come on Superman and Peter Pan (Torben does not ask Louis to participate). Jorn goes with him.

Louis: Can I be in?

Torben: Do you know what you can be? You can be our friend. I am Superman.

Torben runs away to look at the other children, Jorn and Louis watch him.

Louis (to Jorn): Can I have a cup of coffee?

Jorn: Yes, here you are. [He pretends to pour the coffee in a doll's cup and Louis pretends to drink it.]

Jorn (to Torben who has returned): Look, a small child.

Torben: No, we aren't playing that! (He laughs.)

Jorn: Yes we are!

Torben: No! Because he is Superman's dog and we don't have babies with us.

Torben walks away again.

Jorn: So I can be a baby.

Jorn: Look, I am a small baby.

Louis: Then I can be the mother – now the ship is sailing.

Jorn: Yes we can play dad and mum.

They look for a short moment on what the other children are doing and sit quietly next to each other.

Torben comes back and says to Jorn: No! This is not part of it [the play].

Torben kicks at the things the two small boys have played with.

Torben (to Jorn): Do not become so scabby, you should not be a baby but Peter Pan.

The children separate and play by themselves.

Jorn walks towards Torben.

Torben: Now I pour poison on your head.

Jorn: No! Now I can be Peter Pan's dog.

Torben: No! Do you know what you have to be? Superman's dog!

Jorn: Can I just have a cup of coffee?

Torben: Here! [He throws the imaginary coffee onto Jorn's head. Jorn is grinning.]

All three are now together. Louis looks at the other two and is grinning. They are having fun it seems, because Torben goes on playing that he is throwing coffee at Jorn's head. Jorn goes away and Louis also runs away. Torben runs after them and now he acts as if he is shooting Jorn. Jorn drop down on the floor.

Torben to Louis: Come here, here you will be safe.

Torben builds a fortress of pillows.

Jorn approaches them.

Torben is shooting at him.

Louis is looking with his mouth open.

Torben is shooting and shooting and Jorn is running, Torben runs after him, they end under a big table, where Jorn drops down as though he were dead.

The *theme* of Torben's play is superheroes. The *leading motive* in this activity setting for Torben is to be the leader of a shared play and he tries to organise the play in a different way in order to achieve this. He starts out with a play project that he cannot realise but ends up being the one that sets the theme of play by dragging the two younger children into a shooting activity. But he first has to act in relation to Jorn's play and this he does by threatening Jorn in a playful way and keeping the two younger boys apart by protecting Louis and making the play very simple.

For the two younger, children the *leading motive* is to play together. Jorn is the key person to keep the three boys together because he wants to play with both Louis and Torben. Louis proposes an activity of drinking coffee, in order to play with Jorn. This can hardly be called a play project as it is more an act that he proposes. Together Jorn and Louis construct a play theme of being a baby and playing dad and mum in opposition to Torben. They do not succeed with this for long, because they do not really know what to do; they just sit together and also because Torben interrupts them.

Problems and conflicts in children's everyday activities

Problems between a child and other persons can arise. For instance, conflicts can occur between an infant and first-time parents when establishing day and night rhythm. Problems between a mother and child can also arise in relation to breast feeding, such as when the infant will not take the nipple or will not drink as much as the mother wants, resulting in more frequent breast feeding. Later when the child has to be weaned from breast milk, this can create serious frustrations for some parents and their child. But problems like this, or that turn up later in a child's development, such as the conflicts described in the play above, do not have to be seen as negative because they are also an indicator of how the child is developing within a particular cultural tradition. It is the way in which caregivers tackle the problems and help the child to solve these conflicts in the social situation that is important, as they can be positive or problematic.

A child's engaged involvement in activities that seem to promote problems is also a sign that the child is acquiring competences within a certain domain. The caregivers can therefore make positive use of the problems that turn up in a child's everyday activities to help to develop a child's competencies within the domain to which the problems are connected. This can often be done by providing conditions that enable the child or children to solve their own problematic situations instead of the caregiver making direct interventions into the child's activity. Unfortunately, adults sometimes become upset when seeing children struggle in new activities and they frame these struggles as problems and conflicts. This happens when a social situation is viewed as a problem-creating confrontation between the adult's intentions and the child's intentions. In this situation, the adult does not always help a child to find relevant action possibilities in a shared activity to master the problems. Parents may see their small children as being naughty. Eva Ullstadius (2001) found that mothers change their reaction to their infants over the first year of the infant's life. In following a group of 17 first-born infants through weekly visits from the 1st to the 56th week, asking mothers questions related to the infants' 'difficultness' and the mothers' feelings of impatience and irritation towards the infants, she found that mothers' expression of irritation changes with the age of the infant, reflecting her growing demands on her infant. She used three categories: (1) infant crying/fretting/clinging, (2) sleeping problems, (3) protest/disobedience. The last kind of activity was the one that upset the mothers most from the 9th month, culminating around the 12th month. Ullstadius noted that mothers who were influenced by the Swedish childcare authority's child-centred ambition to fulfil the infant's wishes, were not as irritated by the baby's crying/fretting or by sleeping problems. Clearly, the mothers' demands were mediated by the social conditions of middle-class culture as expressed through the mothers' particular personal and social values of what to expect from an infant. Open conflicts and clashes appeared around 1 year of age, indicating a general crisis as described by Vygotsky (1998). But how this crisis took form can be seen in relation to the cultural tradition, where in this Swedish sample, crying and sleeping problems did not upset the mothers as much.

An adult who does not take the child's perspective or who cannot see the child's motive, may end up in more permanent conflict with the child (i.e. conflict may then show up recurrently in activities such as meals and night-time routines). When they cannot 'understand' the child's intention or motive, caregivers often interpret the child's motive/need in a cultural way and try to establish an interaction on this basis. If the interaction is not successful, it may lead to ongoing conflicts during social interactions when establishing day and night rhythms, when eating and around personal hygiene. If caregivers have to find a way to solve these problems, they have to find a way out of the problematic interaction patterns that they themselves are part of. But if the adult interactions with the child are not productive, then these difficult interactions may form a permanent pattern. As another example, a child may be so interested in other children that he or she pushes or hits them to get their attention. Usually caregivers help the child by developing a better interactional pattern (more acceptable in the institutional culture setting) in order to realise his or her motive to be with other children. But if the child is punished instead, this activity pattern around the content of everyday activities can gradually be reflected in the way the child begins to see itself and may result in a self-conception or self-perception of being incompetent or even 'bad'. The way children learn to realise their motives influences the way they develop motives, conceptions and morals in relation to practices in their everyday lives.

Developmental crises

Vygotsky has introduced a special variation of the 'concept of conflict' known as the 'concept of crises'. This concept directs attention to important developmental events in children's development.

Vygotsky conceptualised his ideas of crises as events that alternate with stable periods in a child's life. A developmental crisis is characterised by three parts: deconstruction, construction and mastering (Vygotsky, 1998, pp. 191 ff). The last part is characterised by what Vygotsky calls central neo-formation, which is the stable part in the dominating activity at a new developmental stage.

Crises have been part of other developmental theories, i.e. Piaget (1968 – disequilibrium) and Eriksson (1950 – psychic conflicts). In these theories, crises have been located in the child as either functional–cognitive or emotional. Vygotsky's conception of crises is that they must be viewed as being located in the social situation that the child experiences. The first part of Vygotsky's description of crises in a child's social situation – deconstruction – has not been formulated as part of other theories (i.e. Piaget's or Eriksson's theories). What is important here is the deconstruction and reconstruction of the social situation, where we note that the child's competence and motives for development are allowed to proceed. Those dominating conflicts in a child's social situation can be seen as a way forward and not as a drawback. These kinds of conflict, among others, are those that toddlers have when they want to do everything themselves and do not want the parents to help and at the same time cannot handle the problem by their own activity (i.e. as when a 3-year-old wants cross a street without holding a parent's hand).

A dominating conflict can also be a drawback when the conflict does not proceed to a solution for the child, leading to neo-formation of his or her social situation, but instead becomes a fixed negative interaction pattern for the child in the social situation. An example of a long-lasting conflict can be seen when Western families become fixated on eating behaviour and make strong demands on children. The parents worry that their child does not eat enough or does not eat healthy food and the child object to the parents' demands and sometimes even turns the eating situation into a power game.

A child's individuality

In the 1970s (Bruner, 1972, 1999) a great deal of research was focused on early infancy where scholars began to acknowledge that young infants were actively and intentionally orienting themselves towards the world. Individual differences between infants also became an important topic (this can be seen in the development of the Brazelton test for newborn infants, see Brazelton and Nugent, 2000).

This research into early infancy shows differences between infants in relation to such things as sleep patterns or sucking patterns. Wolfe (in Schaffer, 1979, p. 46) studied infants' sucking patterns and showed that newborn infants had an individual regularity and individual pattern in nutritional sucking, allowing researchers to predict when each single child would start sucking and how long it would last. Even when a child was given a pacifier, which was then removed, the child continued to make sucking movements according to his or her pattern. But the sucking process can be influenced. The sucking rate increased with an increase in the milk stream and nipple size. Bruner (1972), referring to a range of experiments done with colleagues on infants' sucking patterns, showed that from birth onwards infants are in active interaction with their environment. In some experiments done by Kalnins (Bruner, 1972, pp. 23–24), they were able to show that infants intentionally influence their surroundings through sucking, starting around 6 weeks. Some of these experiments showed that infants (3 months old) could make a picture of their mother clear by sucking on a pacifier connected by a device to the picture. In the sucking process, there is an in-built competence for adaptation that makes it possible for an infant, at a very early stage, to discover a way of interacting intentionally with his or her surroundings.

From the beginning of a child's life his or her sleeping pattern, sucking pattern and digestion rate influence the infant's interaction with the mother and other caregivers. How the caregivers experience this influences their interaction with the infant (see Ullstadius, 2001) and this in turn influences the baby's experience. This interaction influences the way in which the infant's primary needs start to find its objects and are cultivated into motives.

In the long run, it is the availability of the possible developmental paths that has the biggest influence on children's development and their experience and appropriation of capacities through imitation and activity with others are very important (Vygotsky, 1998, pp. 2002–2003). A child's biological dispositions are in play as threads in a rope and are easier to see in the early months of the infant's life – e.g. digestion, sleeping rhythm and sucking rate. But later these functions become integrated in the child's activities. It will never be the child's disposition for bowel function or disposition for language that have the decisive influence for the child's relation to hygiene training or appropriation of language, but instead it will be the experience the child gets through his or her activity, starting at the first trials with bowel function and language communication in interaction with other people. Each child's development can be viewed historically and in this history the child's biological disposition is an important part; however, they are *not* frames, but aspects that change and develop together with the child's psychic development.

Each child's specific experiences become the foundations for its motive and competence appropriation; therefore one could expect that a developmental description would be specific for each child. But shared characteristic evolve in children's development because they participate and engage in a shared community and in the same type of cultural events in its institutional practices. A local community is also based on a common and shared material world, which means that most children in a shared community share the same type of experience. In the Western tradition, this can be sleeping arrangements, eating arrangements, the use of a pacifier, types of baby food, objects to play with, kind of cloth and values such as the elderly members of Western families (e.g. the grandparents) living apart from their adult children and their grandchildren.

A description of a child's motives, knowledge and competencies demands a description of the activities that are central in children's development. To find the central activities in children's development, it will be relevant to describe children's everyday life in relation to a content description of the activities in which children engage in institutional practices in a society; and how these influence their everyday lives.

Implications for researching children's development

The conceptual ideas about children's development discussed in this chapter have led to the following consideration about cultural–historical oriented research:

- The practice traditions of the institutions in which the child lives his or her everyday life.

- Children's appropriation and display of motives and competencies through entering activity settings and sharing activities with other people within a particular cultural practice tradition.
- Demands in upbringing and education that children meet in these shared activities.
- Norms and values that are explicated by caregivers and educators as demands in the everyday practices they share with children.
- Demands in upbringing and education have to be viewed from the child's perspective, i.e. related to the child's projects and intentions.
- The interaction and conflicts between the child's projects and parents/educators demands point to what is happening developmentally for the child.
- The trouble that the individual child has with realising his or her projects and intentions and at the same time considerations for the demands and wishes of his or her parents and educators/teachers' can result in developmental learning.

Some researchers believe that the researcher has to go 'native' in order to be able to study children in their everyday social situations. Those that argue this position suggest that the researcher has to become 'childlike' and 'enter' the children's world to 'play' with them (for a critique of this, see Gulløv and Højlund, 2003). Instead, I want to promote an idea of the researcher and the researched as communication partners. From this position, one would think that spoken language would be the prime medium, but I would argue that this implies a much broader research approach than can be found through interviews and informal conversations – especially when one does research *with* young children.

To research a child's social situation the researcher has to be a participant in the child's social situation. But the researcher is not a full participant in the everyday activities, because the researcher's social situation is also a research situation. A social science researcher both enters the everyday activity settings of a person with the intention of being a communication partner in the researched person's social situation and enters with a special intention of her own as related to the research aim of the project. A fuller discussion of what specific type of social situation a researcher enters into can be found in Chapter 3.

Summary

In this chapter, a theoretical discussion of what child development means from a cultural–historical perspective was given. In the next chapter, the methodological implications for undertaking research following the ideas introduced in this chapter will be further elaborated.

3 Developing a dialectic approach to researching children's development

Mariane Hedegaard

The aim of this chapter is to outline the methodological implications for researching children's development as they participate in everyday activity settings within different institutional practices. In cultural–historical research, the researcher is positioned within the activity as a partner with the researched person. In this way, it is possible to examine how children contribute to their interactions with adults and other children within the family, community and educational institutions in which they are involved. The aim is to understand how children create their activity within the institutional practice of the home, school, day care and after-school activities. At the same time it is also important to examine how society gives conditions for adults within communities as this influences the way they can be parents, caregivers and educators who have responsibility for children's upbringing. Research that is culturally and historically framed takes into account all of these multi-dimensional elements of children's participation in everyday life.

Two examples are given in this chapter to illustrate these developmental concepts. The first is connected to societal change and the new norms and demands that refugee children meet when entering a new country where everyday life and its institutions are quite different from anything they have previously experienced. The second example shows how demands and expectations in different institutions can influence a preschool child's activity and motives and how these may create crises in the child's social situation.

The refugee boys

For my research into refuge boys who had problems in participating in the Danish schooling system, it became important to form a new theory that could encompass both societal change and crises in children's development.

The children in this project came from refugee camps in the Lebanon and Palestine prior to attending school in Denmark. In this setting, they had developed strategies for surviving and protecting themselves and their families. These strategies created problems in the Danish school. The boys had difficulty concentrating while at school and after 4–6 years they had not learned the elementary skills of reading, writing or other school competencies. They had also caused so much trouble in the comprehensive schools that they had been rejected by several local schools. The municipality had a responsibility to ensure that these boys could attend some form of school education and conceded to the introduction of a new type of experimental day school for these boys. The boys who were assigned to this particular school had in one way or another been in contact with the police as a result of shoplifting, pick-pocketing and other minor criminal acts. I became attached to this experimental school project as a consultant and researcher with a responsibility to develop an alternative teaching system that could improve the childrens' learning and competence in school subjects and support their learning in an environment that would lead them away from criminality (Hedegaard, Frost and Larsen, 2004). In order to realise new motives in the school, a different perspective had to be introduced.

From the children's perspective, their difficulty was not a learning problem, but one of finding strategies to survive in a new societal context. They had learned in the war zone to mistrust authorities and saw them as enemies. They had not built realistic expectations for their future. The most important aspect of the children's lives was the people they knew and cared about. Therefore, from the children's perspective, their social activities – being together and doing things with their friends – seemed relevant only in relation to what they cared about.

From the Danish society's point of view, children who come from war zones and become young criminals are seen as having inadequate development. It is not enough to say that they are intelligent and function socially with their friends, when they cannot read or write Danish and when they transgress the laws of society.

From the schools' perspective, they were teaching disabled children. From this perspective their competencies were not seen as age related, and their antisocial activities were seen as obstructive; they were classified as having behavioural problems. Their social motive of caring for friends was not seen as a positive activity; it was instead interpreted as gang activity where the central aim was to protect members from any form of authority.

This need to take into account the children's social situation, and to integrate this perspective into the new context, is not only pertinent for these boys from Palestinian refugee homes, but is the case in general for children who are considered to be troublesome and difficult to control. Instead of marginalising them as children with behavioural problems, it might better to see them as children in developmental crises. The institutional values and pedagogy do not match the children's own strategies and wishes. For some children, such crises are more obstructive to school and community than for other children, as in the case of the boys from Palestinian refugee homes who were obstructing their Danish school.

This example illustrates the problem of how to research and evaluate the development of motives and competencies. We need a developmental theory and a methodology that can handle societal and institutional change in relation to the child's perspective. Through integrating the perspectives of society, institution and the child, it is possible to understand that crises for children and young people can be caused by societal change, by change in the child's social relations in a new institution, and by his or her biological maturation.

The preschool child

Extract from observation of *Jens* (4 years, 6 months)

Jens attends a Scandinavian kindergarten with 30 children, aged from 3 to 7 years. The children are separated into two groups of 15. The group to which Jens belongs has three pedagogues.[1]

The observer is M.H.

It is late afternoon and several children have gone home. The observer is with Jens and is taking field notes. Jens is riding a small bike.

Jens: I have to write a letter.

The observer shows him how to write JENS on a piece of paper and invites him to write below her writings. He begins the task, but writes JES. He inserts an N when the observer shows him how one can write an N by drawing two straight lines and combining them with a diagonal line.

The pedagogue, Anita, comes back into the room where the observer and Jens are writing. For the second time she asks Jens to come into the reading room and join her and Christina (a girl the same age as Jens).

Jens folds his paper with his name and says it is for his daddy.

The observer enters the room with Jens.

Anita puts her arm around Jens and Christina while reading a fairy-tale.

Jens: My dad will be angry.

The pedagogue continues to read without listening to Jens.

Jens: Do you hear, my dad will become angry if you read that book.

He jumps up and runs around in the small room. Anita wants to put her arm around him again, but he becomes agitated when she touches him and runs out of the room.

The pedagogue runs after him. They come back and Jens sits down reluctantly next to Christina so that the pedagogue cannot put her arm around him.

The observer asks Jens to listen so that he can explain to her what Anita (the pedagogue) is reading. This book is about whales and is rather technical.

The pedagogue says that this is not such a successful choice for a book, but continues reading.

Jens is concentrating hard and when Anita points at a picture and says: This is a baby.

Jens comments: That is not how a baby looks.

Anita: Yes whales!

Jens: Not baby whales! (Jens corrects the pedagogue to show that he knows they are talking about whales).

If we take the societal perspective, the traditions in Scandinavian kindergarten are to give children room to play and to care for them, focusing on their social skills. Academic teaching is postponed until the children enter school at the age of 6 years.

The pedagogue's perspective in this observation builds on the premise of what to expect from a pedagogue in a kindergarten. She wants to build close and tender relations to Jens. In the observation, the pedagogue wanted to calm him down by putting her arm around him, since, in the kindergarten, Jens is viewed as being too energetic and disruptive, and not acting in a socially acceptable manner. She is also aware of the observer's evaluation of her as a pedagogue.

From the child's perspective, it seems that Jens was oriented towards learning and appropriating 'a school child's competences' and not being 'a small child'. Jens orients himself to the academic competences of reading and writing and play is no longer viewed as an accomplishment. A child who is oriented towards entering school wants to perform 'real school activities' and that is what Jens is demonstrating, perhaps influenced by parental values at home – by his dad, who, he says, will not appreciate the 'childish' book the pedagogue chose initially as a reading text. When the pedagogue takes a 'school like' book about whales, Jens is able to sit calmly and listen and concentrate.

It is not that Jens did not want closeness. Rather, closeness should take another form and be subordinated to the dominant motive–orientation to learning (as is demonstrated in his relation to the observer). He therefore became angry when the pedagogue held him like a 'small child'.

These two examples show the importance of the three perspectives of society, institutions and persons for understanding how traditions in a society influence the conditions for children's activity and the norms and values of those adults who have responsibility for guiding, supporting and restricting children's activity.

In our cultural–historical activity approach to researching children's activities in everyday life, our methodology must focus on children's activities within the institutional practices that are also inscribed within societal traditions and values, as depicted in Figure 2.1. It is the child's activities in social practice that are of interest. With this focus, the task is to conceptualise the everyday activity settings from the three different perspectives. In this approach, we especially focus on the perspective of the different people's viewpoints. Our research methodology must allow for the participation of several people in an activity setting, all with different viewpoints. To understand a specific child's social situation, it may be necessary to take the perspective of several people into consideration, as well as the institutional practice tradition.

The difference between dialectical–interactive research and hypotheses testing or descriptive methods

A methodological dilemma faces researchers interested in psychological research into children's development. On the one hand, it is desirable to avoid rigid operationalised sharpness and certainty and to avoid the position in which answers and results can be deduced in advance. Experimental research in the hypothesis testing tradition can only support or reject what the theory outlines. On the other hand, a non-theoretical participant observation approach is equally unproductive. Without a theoretical frame empirical research results only in a collection of 'objective' facts. These research approaches – traditional experimental research of child functioning or the descriptive approach – are shown in Table 3.1 and are contrasted with a cultural-historical research approach where a dialectical–interactive method is used.

Table 3.1 Main difference between a hypotheses testing or a descriptive approach and a dialectical–interactive research approach

Research method	Research principles	Knowledge form	Knowledge content
Hypotheses testing/ Descriptive methods			
Laboratory experiment	Control groups Blindtest design	Empirical	General laws of children's psychic functioning
Observation	'Fly on the wall' One-way screen	Empirical/ narrative	Description of children in actual, local situations
Interview	Non-leading questions/ clinical interview	Narrative	Description of children's perspective
Dialectical–interactive methods			
Experiment as intervention into everyday practice	Theoretical planned interventions into local practice	Dialectical– theoretical	General conditions for children's activity in local situations
Interaction-based observation	Participation in shared activities Activity partners	Dialectical– theoretical	Diversity in conditions for children's activity in local situations
Interview as experiment	Leading and provoking questions Communication partners	Dialectical– theoretical	Relations between conditions and children's perspective

In the dialectical–interactive approach, the aim is to research the conditions as well as how children participate in activities. This allows the conditions and the child's development to be conceptualised as a whole. Thereby the research problem becomes connected to how well the researcher in his or her conceptualisation can handle the different perspectives. In order to catch the child's perspective, the researcher has to enter into the everyday activities of the child.

In the classical hypothesis testing research, the problem has been how the researcher can operationalise and measure the child's psychic functioning as behavioural reactions. Hypothesis testing research has been criticised by hermeneutic and narrative approaches, (see Flick, 2002). In hermeneutic and narrative approaches the focus has been on creating new methods and discursive techniques for generating meaning and understanding of the researched persons. Within early childhood developmental research these approaches have had less influence because it has not been easy to study young children through interviews or discourse analysis. Children had, however, been interviewed from early preschool age, as in Piaget's research (1968). Piaget used and argued for a clinical-oriented interview method where the researcher follows the child's ideas and answers. Using the clinical interview, the researcher becomes a communication partner. The cultural–historical approach to interviewing children described in Chapter 9 takes a step further than the clinical and hermeneutic approaches indicate, not only by entering children's activity setting but by inviting children into the researcher's activity setting. The concept of reliability thereby has to be changed since a research interview is seen as a shared communicative activity, where the interviewed persons also appropriate the aim of the research and are not seen as having a neutral standpoint about what is communicated. (This changed conception of research reliability will be discussed in a later section in this chapter.)

Observational studies have been developed to study children in their everyday life activities (Medinnus, 1976). The aim of traditional observational studies has been to make descriptions without necessarily reflecting upon how the researcher and his or her theory is a central factor in constructing the description. This tradition has been renewed by the anthropological tradition, where researchers have now started to express concerns and thoughts about whether the researcher with his theoretical orientation, is part of the research situation (Corsaro, 1997; Corsaro and Molinari, 1999; Gulløv and Højlund, 2003; Pellegrini, Symons and Hock, 2004). These new anthropological approaches to observation are relatively close to the approach we outline. However, one important difference is that they have not yet solved the problem of the relations between the specific situation and the general conceptions of their thematic studies. This is the focus of the discussion in the following section. A research methodology that takes the child's perspective into consideration has to be reformulated in relation to how general theoretical conceptions relate to situated descriptions and how one can move from societal conditions and institutional practice to a general understanding of children's development. How a dialectic–interactive approach tackles this problem will be discussed in Chapter 4 with the specific content of field reports and interview protocols and their interpretation. The following section will outline the epistemology that leads us to characterise these methods as dialectical–interactive.

An epistemological outline of a dialectical–interactive study of children's everyday activities

To formulate an epistemology that gives a theoretical foundation for integrating different perspectives, this section will draw on the dialectical epistemology formulated by Iljenkov (1977), Davydov (1990) and the relation between everyday knowledge and scientific knowledge formulated by Schutz (2005).

Theoretical–dialectical knowledge

Conceptual knowledge is the core of scientific knowledge, but what is conceptual knowledge? This has been a central problem in both philosophy and psychology. In drawing upon the philosophies of Hegel and Marx, Iljenkov (1977) argues that the dominating epistemology of objects and events as the basis for knowledge representation always leads to difficulties. Instead, he argues that the *activity* of humankind has to be seen as the foundation for knowledge. Throughout the history of humankind, people have produced objects, and objects embody the activity of production and of knowledge. For example, a house embodies centuries of labour knowledge. Activity embodied in knowledge can be transformed, it is not easy to follow how the knowledge has evolved. Iljenkov draws on a classic example from Karl Marx, where the concept of money is seen as the objectification of labour knowledge. To understand how the currencies of different countries can be exchanged, one has to focus on the activity of exchange values of labour. It is not the object or artefact in itself as a £10 note or a $10 note, but the products of human labour activity that can be exchanged for this money that define the pound or dollar notes. Iljenkov argues that in a theory of knowledge it is the product of activity that has to be in focus and these products are embodied as generalised labour (ideal activity) in objects and artefacts. Iljenkov characterized this generalised labour as ideals or concepts.

An object/artefact is from this perspective united with ideals of activity and has to be seen within this activity or practice perspective. This dialectic can be expressed as follows: an object/artefact contains the concept or ideal of activity and, at the same time, the ideal activity cannot exist without its artefact/object. The ideals of activity or concepts that are connected to concrete objects/artefacts can have affordance character that can initiate a person's concrete activity.

Davydov (1990) draws on Iljenkov's theory of concepts as ideals of activity that are connected with concrete events and objects and in using this basic principle he has formulated two different types of knowledge: empirical and theoretical dialectical knowledge.

Empirical knowledge or concepts are related to objects and events as facts without explicating the conditions for production of these facts – the relation of objects and artefacts to practices and activies as conditions for their existence is not explicated. Empirical knowledge has been outstanding in some science tradition and in school education (Davydov and Markova, 1983). Empirical thinking and knowledge are based on the idea of knowledge as a categorical system: where objects and events can be classified in relation to properties. The system is fixed so that new knowledge gives more information but does not restructure earlier knowledge. For example, scientists discovering new organisms will categorise the new creature based on a pre-existing classification system. The origins of the system of classification (i.e. why we divide organisms into 'animals' and 'plants' rather than some other descriptive categorisation) are assumed as a natural given base and not related to practices that have made these categories relevant.

Theoretical-dialectical knowledge is the type of knowledge that catches the dialectic relationship between production/practice and the ideals of activity/concepts that can be found in objects/artefacts (Davydov, 1990, pp. 231–301). Theoretical-dialectical knowledge is based on the idea that knowledge generalisation is connected to the content of the problem areas that have produced the knowledge. For example, in some indigenous cultures in Australia, organisms have traditionally been classified in relation to the plants and animals that can be harvested or are 'active' within the community and therefore can be readily found as sources of food. The classification system is based on the indigenous people's activity in relation to the seasons and food sources. There is a direct relationship between the classification system and the problem area of finding food in the environment. As such, objects/artefacts and activities must be understood as part of a connected conceptual system that has evolved from human practice and not as divorced and separate entities.

A key task within a knowledge area is to find the *core relations* that are fundamental between the practices that produce the basic artefacts, which, in turn, become the abstract ideals/concepts. Such abstractions are always related to the content of the human practices within the knowledge area and its evolution. Dialectical knowledge in this meaning includes categories of empirical knowledge, but also surpass these by relating the categories to the practice conditions in which they have evolved. Knowledge in a problem area should be able to relate back to the *core relations within the practice*. To keep these relations obvious, visual models should be formulated that depict the dependent and complementary core relations between the ideal activities and its objects/artefacts within a problem area.

Davydov exemplified this difference between empirical and theoretical knowledge with the difference between Linné's classification system for plants and Darwin's theory of the origin of species.[2] In Linné's classification system plant families are distinguished by essential properties. In Darwin's theory of the origin of species, he constructs a model relationship between the ideal concepts of species, ecology and population. It is impossible to define a species from properties alone, it must also be defined in relation to the production of new members of the concrete population and the conditions of the ecology in which it can be found, and if population or ecology change, this will eventually influence the characteristics of species (Gould, 1977; Mayr, 1980).

Iljenkov's theory of concepts as ideals of concrete events and activities connects the general and the specific and Davydov's extension of this theory focuses on modelling relations between 'ideal objects'.

It is important to point out that it is from analyses of the content of a problem area and by following how this has changed through the history of a subject area, that one formulates the core relations of a conceptual area. A core relation is never characterised with fixed attributes, but always has to be seen as a relation. A core relation depicts the foundational wholeness in a problem area. All further knowledge within a problem area should then be related to this core relation and thereby contribute to its evolution.

I will illustrate within the problem area of intelligence as a measurement of cognitive abilities, how a specific child's concrete intelligence score has to be related to the general conceptual relations on which the problem area builds.

A relationship between a general conception of intelligence and the concrete facts that a child has an intelligence score of 100 at the WISC (Wechsler Intelligence Scale for Children) has to be seen in relation to the general problem area of distinguishing between cognitive abilities. In a theoretical–dialectical approach, this problem area has to be looked upon as a whole. Intelligence neither as a concept nor as an individual score can stand alone as a fact; it has to be related to the whole procedure of the measuring activity, both as an activity of the researcher's construction of the test and as a test-taking event undertaken by the single individual. Therefore, a concept of children's intelligence has to be related to the specific problem area that, in the history of science, has led to the production of intelligence tests. Intelligence tests and scales are a result of researchers' activity of constructing questions and validating them in large population samples aimed at sorting children into different cognitive ability categories. A child's intelligence score does not say anything unless we relate it to the problem area that has resulted in the historically developed scientific conceptions. Originally, intelligence grew out of the problem of teaching children in school and the difficulties with a wide variance in children's age and competence in a concrete school practice (Sarason, 1976). It is in these relations of teaching and variance in children's competence and age, that it is important to place the concept as an idealisation of a practice. It has to be seen in comparison with other concepts that are related to the practice in this problem area and be seen as interdependent and complementary to such concepts. In a concrete case, a special measure of a child's intelligence score has to be related to other concretisations in the practice areas as a whole, such as the child's age and performance as well as educational aspects of the institution (i.e. the family or school practice) and a median score and age adequate test population. In this concrete case, a child's score is related to his or her placement in a population, the practice in school, as well as to his or her own activity in answering a set of questions. Here, it is found that if one element changes, such as the median score in the age population or school practice, the other elements, such as the child's activity and his or her intelligence score can also change. As such, the content of the theoretical––dialectical knowledge between school practice and children's performance/ intelligence can be seen as connected core relations. This model reveals a unity, but this unity is always related to the concrete and is always challenged, renewed or extended, as seen in the history of the concept of intelligence. The activity of research within the subject area of developing intelligence tests (the practice of research) within school practice, has to be seen as a condition for a child's activity in taking an intelligence test. A test score is an activity score that has to be set in relation to the general theoretical conditions for testing and is never a characteristic of the child outside this activity setting.

One has to realise that facts are not facts in themselves, but should be seen in relation to the practices as conditions for establishing facts. A child's intelligence score cannot stand alone as a fact, it has to be related to the whole procedure of measuring intelligence, both as an activity of the researcher's construction of the test and as an activity by the single individual child being tested.

The theories of Davydov and Iljenkov are epistemological theories that focus on how to combine general knowledge with concrete practices. In a research scenario, I find that it is also important to anchor a theory of knowledge in the perspective one takes on practice. This can be a perspective from a specific society, an institution with specific practices or from the perspectives of the participants engaged in institutional practices (see Figure 2.1). Schutz's theory (1970, 2005) of knowledge builds upon the same preconceptions as the cultural–historical approach, as discussed by Iljenkov and Davydov – that is, people are born into the practices of humankind and through this create their own relations to the world. Schutz's conception of the social world can be seen as 'something we have to modify by our activities and that modifies our activities' (Schutz, 1970, p. 73).

Perspectives as a fundamental aspect of research in social science

Schutz (1970, 2005) argues that the general aim of social science research is to explain the social reality as it is experienced and lived by humans in their everyday lives in the social world. The objective is, therefore, to study human activity and make common sense interpretation of social reality. In order to accomplish this, the social scientist undertakes analyses that include the conceptualisation of peoples' projects, motives and intentions.[3]

Schutz formulated the epistemological point that as people act in their everyday life they build knowledge of activities and he argues that people will construct different kinds of realities (1970, 2005). Basic reality can be thought of as an everyday immediately experienced reality. Other forms of reality include a scientific reality and a dream world reality. All these different forms of reality must relate to everyday reality. Schutz's concept of different forms of reality can also be considered in relation to different institutional practices, as these different institutional practices give different perspectives. These multiple perspectives need to be taken into consideration when approaching a research theme.

Schutz writes that the unconditioned experiences that a person has are present as typification. This means that the person will relate these experiences to earlier experiences, but will also be open to new experiences (2005, pp.27 ff). Preconditions for such typifications are:

- Interrelatedness of person's perspectives
- Social origin of knowledge
- The social distributions of knowledge.

Typifications for people centre on expectations of the world and its activities. Significantly, how will these be experienced and how will someone make sense of them?

According to Schutz, the acquisition of knowledge in everyday activity is very different to research activity. Everyday activity can never be completely rational. In contrast, meaning construction in research activity are seen as being systematic and coherent (1970, pp. 131–137). There are several degrees of rationality in the interactions that a person can have with other people. The social scientists' interactions and how they construct meaning are quite different to the meaning constructions of the actors in the specific everyday practices (2005, p. 25). A researcher's sense of typification, together with his rationality for seeking coherence and systematisation, constructs meaning of events that can be related into meaningful relations to other events, so that they connect into a subject area (Schutz, 2005, pp. 60–61).

Within the different science traditions, there are also differences. For the natural scientist, there is a structure of relevance that takes the form of finding/creating meaningful relations in his or her research material to the research goal. For the social scientist, there are two structures of relevance: one for the people that he or she researches and one in relation to his or her own research goal.

The social science researcher participates in two roles in the research situation: (1) as a social actor who enters into a social situation with other people where he or she understands what is going on as a participant in everyday practice; and (2) as a researcher researching the practice, where the meaning construction is related to the tradition in the scientific problem area. For the social scientist, it is the person's activity in everyday settings (with motives, projects and intentions) that is the object of study, but, as a scientist, the researcher must also conceptualise his or her own participation (motives, project and subjective interpretations) as part of the researched activities. These scientific demands, Schutz points out, imply a combination of general categories with concrete biographical events as well as with the collective practice tradition. According to Schutz, every concept in a scientific model of human activity should be constructed so that the actor and his or he colleagues can understand it from a commonsense and everyday perspective (2005, pp. 69 ff). There has to be consistency between conceptual constructions and social reality.

In drawing upon the theories of Schutz, Iljenkov and Davydov, I argue that the researcher must construct a model of the studied practices and activity settings. Based on both Iljenkov's and Davydov's cultural–historical approach and Schutz's phenomenological approach, I argue that human science has to build on theoretical–dialectical knowledge visualised in core models. This is what I have shown in Figure 2.1. In this model, I have visualised how the conceptualisation of societal values and demands have to be seen as conditions for, as well as influenced by, both practice in institutions and biographical aspect of a person's activity. The importance of the person's projects and motives are also seen as central in this conceptualisation. The validity of the conceptual relations in a core model has to be found in how well it can be used on concrete lived activity of the persons being studied.

Valid research: clear theoretical preconditions and model formulations

The methods described in classical experimental child research are aimed at being tools for objective description of children's ways of functioning (thinking, memorising, perceiving, talking) or analyses of children's age adequacy reactions to demands from parents and educators in educational settings (i.e. kindergarten and school). In this type of research the child is isolated as an object, and interactions with the child's surroundings is technified so that it can be described as exactly as possible. Claims for validity are made in relation to the objective measurement of the children's functioning.

In the dialectic–interactive approach that is advocated here, validity is not an operationalisation of delimited functions, events or phenomena into measurable units. Neither is it aimed at objective descriptions of local events. Instead, it is a conceptualisation of the studied practice and the social situation of the research participants in relation to the different perspectives. Validity is not the operationalisation of the child's reactions in relation to different inputs, as is common in classical experimental designs. Rather, the focus of a dialectic–interactive approach is on the practices, activity settings and activities. Neither can triangulation of different results, as in herme-neutic approaches, be accepted as research validation from a dialectic–inter-active approach because content and methods in the dialectic–interactive approach are always seen as defining each other. This means that one will get incompatible but complementary results using different methods within a research area.

The dialectic–interactive research based upon a conceptual model conceptualises children's activity settings in relation to practice traditions, where it is possible to follow changes in practices and activity settings over time and identify qualitative changes. In this type of research, the validity is connected to how well the researcher can explicate the historical tradition of the practice and the preconditions that are anchored in the values that integrate and specify different perspectives. The validation question for studying children's development is: How can we conceptualise children's participation in everyday activities as the basis for understanding and guiding practice? The answer depends upon how well the model being used can catch the different perspectives of the participants in everyday practices, and how they are contributing to the conditions for children's development.

Reliable research: distinguishing between the researcher's perspective and the re-searched person's perspectives

In the classical experimental tradition, which is based on the natural science research tradition, researchers obtain reliability and achieve a truthful description independent of the describer, through the elimination of the researcher's influence by specifically using devices that will not influence the participants' views on the phenomena being studied.

In the traditional classical experimental designs in psychology, an attempt is made to eliminate the influence of the researcher. For example, in observations and interview studies the observer is positioned as a fly on the wall and the interviewer must relate to the subjects using unambiguous non-leading questions. In this type of research, any potential deviation caused by the researcher in the research situation has to be eliminated so that the phenomenon under study can be interpreted independently of the researcher.

In a dialectical–interactive research approach, one has to conceptualise the projects of the researcher as different from the persons being researched and at the same time conceptualise the researcher as a partner in their activities. The researchers should find a balance in their interaction with participants, especially children, so that when they ask questions and react in a way that is relevant to the situation, meaningful insights are gained into what is being researched.

The interaction between a researcher and the participants can in practice take several forms. Interactions during interviews can be based on verbal communication, where the researcher can not only ask, but also answer questions from children as well as other people in the social situations. In field research using participant observations, the researcher can also communicate verbally with a child or children and adult participants. The researchers can also use other forms of interaction, such as participate in games (play football) or introduce a task that is mainly manual. The interaction can also be a form of interview around topics, mediated by pictures or drawings, or the researcher can participate without directly taking part in the activity, but he or she should always have a role in the activity setting, such as when the researcher is an observer.

Because the researcher's project is the scientific activity and not the project of the activity of those being researched, the concept of double relevance comes into focus. The researcher has his or her own life projects in line with the researched persons, but in the research activity, the researcher's dominating motive is the research project. The rationale for participating in the everyday activity with the researched person is the aim of the research. Thereby it becomes possible to distinguish between the researcher's project and the motives and intentions of the participants in the researched situation.

To be able to catch the difference in intentional orientation between the researched persons and the researcher, the researcher has to be very explicit about the research goals for the researched persons.

As the topic of the next chapter I will argue that the research process has to fall in two parts: (1) collecting material through the process of participating in the research situation (research protocols), and (2) leaving the research situation to interpret the research protocols.

Implications for valid research from a dialectic–interactive approach

In this chapter, the methodological aspects of using a cultural–historical approach to research were given. The implications for undertaking valid and reliable research following this theoretical tradition are summarised below:

- Theoretical preconcepts based on the research tradition within the subject area studied has to be formulated as relations.
- These conceptual relations should be visualised as models that depict these relations, so that change in one aspect can be seen in other aspects.
- The activities that create the changes have to be the objects of study.
- The perspectives in the field of research should be outlined. Here the participants in the social situation have to be specified so that interactions between them can be documented.
- At minimum, there will be two perspectives – a researched person's perspective and the researcher's perspective
- The institutional practices should be outlined as conditions for the social situation.

Notes

1   Kindergarten teachers in Scandinavia are called *pedagogues*, because their education is different from school teachers and they belong to a separate union that promotes other educational goals than those provided by the schools. In kindergarten, there is no fixed curriculum, the focus is on giving children the opportunity for play, social activity and experience of nature and the community.

2   Davydov, by using these two examples, does not clarify the difference between social science and natural science.

3   A conceptualisation that is very much in line with the cultural historical approach (see Leontiev, 1978) and can be found in Davydov's writings (1982, pp. 15–16).

4 Principles for interpreting research protocols

Mariane Hedegaard

In Chapter 1, we wrote that our aim was to study children over time in their everyday settings in order to capture their social situation and to follow children's development. I have argued that it is important to include in research the practice traditions of institutions when studying children's everyday life so that children's social situation can be seen as part of practices in institutional settings such as family, kindergarten, school and after school.

The first question outlined in Chapter 1 asked: *How can we as psychological and educational researchers formulate a methodology and undertake research where we focus on children's development, as related to societal conditions, institutional practice and children's social situation?*

The first step in the answer to this question was to formulate a theoretical conception of development based on people's activies in institutional practices that also included societal conditions. This conceptualisation of development was anchored in the cultural–historical approach, as elaborated by Vygotsky's, Elkonin's and Leontiev's theories of development. The second step was to outline an epistemology that was inspired by Iljenkov's and Davydov's conceptions of scientific knowledge and thinking. This epistemological approach gave the possibility of seeing *activity* as the central relations between knowledge and 'objects'. The third step was to introduce the ideas of Schutz of anchoring a methodology in a person's everyday social experiences. Through these steps one could conceptualise a research methodology that integrates different perspectives (the societal, the institutional and the personal) into a theoretical model for a particular problem area, while also paying attention to different people's perspectives, including the researcher's perspective. The researcher's perspective includes the research aim and a meaningful intentional interaction with other persons in concrete everyday practices. This led to considering the interaction between the researcher and the researched persons as a kind of communication where each one has to understand the activity in which he or she is participating. The interactive communicative aspect of a research methodology can result in different methods, such as experiments as intervention into everyday practice, interaction-based observation and interview as experiment.

The problems of validity and reliability were also reformulated from a dialectical–interactive methodological standpoint. The researcher's theoretical preconceptions, as well as the motives and meaning of both the researcher and the researched persons, are central for this reformulation. Examples of different research methods based on the dialectical–interactive methodology will be presented in Chapters 5 to 10.

The question in this chapter is then the second general theme formulated in Chapter 1: *How can collections of research protocols documented in the research field be turned into reliable and valid interpretations?*

To approach this question, I need to outline first how to collect protocols of children's everyday activities and to systematically document the experiences of participants in the field. Second, I will discuss how to proceed in this type of research when using the protocols, the established categories and the theoretical preconceptions outlined earlier in this book.

The social scientist has a research attitude when he or she, as a participant, researches other people's interactions. But the protocols from these observations have to be interpreted and it is here that the systematisation and model building become quite explicit. Here the researcher stands outside the research situation, transcending from the specific activity setting, in order to be able to say something about children in a broader historical time-frame.

Field research as the general methodology in researching children's activities in their everyday lives

The dialectical–interactive research formulated in 1984/1995 by Hedegaard, and built upon in this chapter, shares many of the same methodological demands and traits as the research field of anthropology. I have found two approaches especially inspiring: Martyn Hammersley and Paul Atkinson: *Ethnography: Principles in Practice* (1983) and Dorothy Smith: *Institutional Ethnography. A Sociology for the People* (2005). I will draw upon my previous discussions in Chapter 3 and will relate these two references to the following methodological discussion.

Hammersley and Atkinson present the same kind of dilemma in anthropology between naturalistic research and positivist research in psychology as was discussed in Chapter 3 (see Table 3.1). The positivist tradition leaves a very limited possibility for finding new knowledge because hypothesis testing leads to very limited possibilities for developing theory. Naturalistic observation, by way of contrast, often does not even consider developing theory. In an anthropological approach where observation methods mean being a fly on the wall, ideas can be built and results obtained without a theoretical orientation. However, Hammersley and Atkinson point out that a theoretical orientation always will influence the data collection and therefore the theoretical preconcepts have to be explicated so their implication for data collection can be understood before entering the field. Hammersley and Atkinson also differentiate between being in the field and analysing the research protocols. They see both activities as different processes. This difference should not be seen as a difference between non-theoretical data collection and theoretical generalisations. As we do, Hammersley and Atkinson point out that collecting research material is always guided by theoretical preconceptions.

The research methodology I have argued for in Chapter 3 builds on some of the same ideas that Dorothy Smith (2005) formulated in *Institutional Ethnography*. She wants to formulate a sociology for people – a sociology that includes women's perspective. Through this perspective, she argued that the practice traditions and societal conditions can be unfolded:

> 'Standpoint' as the design of subject position in institutional ethnography creates a point of entry into discovering the social that does not subordinate the knowing subject to objectified forms of knowledge of society or political economy. It is a method of inquiry that works from the actualities of people's everyday lives and experience to discover the social as it extends beyond experience.
>
> (Smith, 2005, p. 10)

With this book, we want to formulate a child psychology that includes the child's perspective and see this as anchored in a societal context of practice traditions.

We want to discover how children develop motives, projects and orientations through participating in institutional activities in their everyday lives. To do this we also need to map the social relations that characterise the pattern of interactions and follow how they change. Smith wants to study people's experience in her project to be able to map the ruling relations in institutions. This is 'two aspects of the same coin', where sociology focuses on the institutional aspects and psychology on the personal aspects. For us, the field research is oriented towards the person's perspective, the person's social life, motives, self-understanding and development and these we need to integrate with the institutional practices and the societal conditions. Although there are differences between Smith's approach and ours, we have tried to transcend the categorical approach of respective sociology and psychology.

The methodological considerations that have been argued for in this chapter concern all kinds of methods used in field research. Smith in her examples draws on the interview method, while Hammersley and Atkinson draw on participant observations. Of course, the different choice of preferred method leads to variation in the protocol material. For example, everyday activities are the focus of attention when undertaking observations, but when conducting interviews, it is people's formulation of their experience and conceptualisations that is being considered. These two methods focus on different kinds of knowledge, but in field research both methods can support each other. However, for some problems one method may be preferred over the other.

Interaction as communication between researcher and the researched children

The methodological approach that we advocate is based on the idea that research always implies some interaction and that every kind of interaction implies a kind of communication where meaning is created between the researcher and the researched persons in the social situation. For example, when there is interaction among all the participants in a particular context, the focus – depending on the aim of the research – may be on a child or a group of children, or the caregivers and a child, or the caregivers and a group of children. It is the researcher's meaningful understanding, as created through this interaction, that becomes the 'data' in this interaction. This interaction can go from being rather passive, to engaging in a dialogue, to the other end of the spectrum where children are given tasks and do activities together with the researcher. But even when the researcher is rather passive, he or she has to conceptualise himself or herself as part of the setting in which the children's activities take place.

A way to validate a rather passive participation in everyday activities is to use the commonsense interpretation. A common-sense interpretation is the first explicit statement made by the researcher in relation to what seems meaningful in an observation sequence. How this can be done can be seen in the following example:

> *Observation without direct intervention:* Research about pedagogy in day care institutions and the conditions for practice that allow young children to engage in quality learning and development.

> *Observing an infant, Fredrik (1 year, 4 month), in a nursery* (translated extract from Hedegaard, 1995):

> Other children: Anne Helle, Jens Sille, Nicolas, Rune (all children in the activity setting are between 1 year and 2 years old).

There are two separate sections in the nursery. Pedagogues in Fredrik's section are: Asta, Helen, Sanne (Lise is visiting from the other section)

Observer: Ulla, N. 14 February	*Common-sense interpretation*
14.15	
1 The observer helps Fredrik to eat at the lunch table and changes his diapers.	Interaction between observer and child that is followed by the child trying to contact the observer.
2 While I am sitting and writing, Fredrik seeks my contact; he pulls my hair, tumbles a plastic basket onto my head and tries to climb onto my lap. I continue to write and he goes to the shelves and utters sounds of dissatisfaction.	This is neglected and a pedagogue tries to involve the child in an activity that demands fine motor and eye–hand coordination as well as visual discrimination.
3 Pedagogue Helen places Fredrik at a low table and tries to get him involved in a puzzle.	
4 He starts but does not finish; instead he plays with the puzzle pieces.	
14.45	
5 Fredrik has moved away from the table, pushes the plastic basket towards a high chair and examines the lock mechanism at the chair while standing near the basket.	The child finds his own activity pushing big objects around and climbing onto them.
6 Pedagogue Helen tells him that he does not have to stand near the plastic basket.	His favourite pedagogue hinders his climbing.
7 He leans over a high footstool, lying on his stomach and starts to cry, then pushes the footstool towards Helen and further towards the door.	Even though he is frustrated and briefly cries, he finds another big object to push and continues with his pushing activity, which again is stopped by a pedagogue from the other section.
8 Lise enters, 'Hello you are blocking the door.' She puts the footstool back in place.	

9 Helen helps Fredrik to sit down at the table again and involves him in building a pyramid.	He is again being placed at the table with a toy where he has to collect pieces, coordinating visual discrimination with fine motor activity.

21 February (a week later)

14.05

1 Fredrik and Nicolas eat fruit soup.	He is able to handle eating using fine finger motor movements.
2 Fredrik is eating by himself with a spoon even though the soup is thin. In between he takes a piece of scone from the soup with his fingers. He drinks his milk from a mug which he holds with both hands (one hand is on the handle and the other hand supports the mug with the fingertips).	

14.30

3 Fredrik is sitting across a child-sized chair with his front towards the back of the chair. The chair stands next to the trolley with the food. He draws himself up on his knee and pushed the trolley around from his position on the chair.	Again he moves around and tries to handle large objects, crawling under a chair.
4 Lise enters and walks away again.	He examines his surroundings and seems quite happy.
5 Fredrik sits down on the chair and put one of his feet out under the back of the chair. He says 'Hey' to his foot. He gains eye contact with pedagogue Asta.	Uses language spontaneously for own activity.
6 Asta asks if she can get his pacifier.	Conflict about pacifier that he wins.
7 Fredrik climbs down from the chair and steps backwards away from Asta, while he is looking at her.	

8 Asta gives up.	
9 Fredrik crawls back onto the chair again and then up on the lower part of the trolley.	Concentrates to climb around.
10 Morten also crawls onto the lower part of the trolley.	Is imitated by Morten.
11 Fredrik crawls out from the trolley.	
12 Asta asks again if she can get his pacifier.	
13 Fredrik stands quietly listening with his back to her.	The conflict with Asta is repeated.
14 He again crawls up onto the chair and sits on his knees.	
15 Asta to pedagogue Sanne: 'He should not crawl up on the chair.'	Again he is hindered in his crawling.
16 Pedagogue Sanne lifts and helps him down.	
17 Fredrik lies down on the floor.	
18 Sanne asks if she can have the pacifier. She takes it and he lets her do this, but starts crying.	Pacifier conflict continues. He loses and starts crying.
19 He is inconsolable.	
20 Asta: 'This is just to get the pacifier back.'	Third pedagogue lets him get his pacifier back and he is placed at a table.
21 Sanne: 'Yes, but perhaps he needs it.'	
22 He gets his pacifier again and the crying dies away and he and Morten play together with the small table.	He is seated again at the table and is given a new small object to handle.

14.45

23 Sanne had taken Fredrik and Morten with her into the adjoining room to find some more interesting playthings.	
24 Pedagogue Helen is dressing Sille.	
25 Sanne, Fredrik and Morten enter the room.	

26 They come back with two wooden boards with holes in them so that different size plastic objects can be put through.	
27 Fredrik and Morten are sitting at each side of the small table, each with their wooden board game.	
28 Morten is very interested and tries to put the plastic object through from both sides (that is possible).	
29 Helen stands besides their table together with Anne and observes the boys.	
30 Helen walks away with Sille.	
31 Fredrik puts the plastic object into his mouth and is whimpering.	He is whimpering because his favourite pedagogue walks away.
32 Anne also starts to whimper	
33 Fredrik's wooden board has fallen down; the observer picks it up, Fredrik start to play with it …	Inspired by Morten he start to use the wooden board.
34 Now Anna wails wildly.	
35 Morten's wooden board falls down and he takes Fredrik's.	
36 Fredrik protests: 'Waah!' He takes the wooden board back and goes on to put the objects through.	
37 Helen comes back and lifts Anne up (she is still crying).	When Morten wants his wooden board he protests.
38 They walk away and Helen sits down on a chair with Anne. Anne calms down.	

15.00

39 Fredrik's wooden board has fallen down again, he plays with one of the small objects and puts them into his mouth and makes sounds: 'Lalala.' Climbs onto the table and then walks to the staircase and start to climb up.	He is satisfied by sitting at the table playing with the small plastic objects for a while.

40 Rune enters with his mother and older brother.

41 A walking cart is on the other side of the stairs. Fredrik stands at the stairs and tries to move the cart that is caught by the sack chair.

He then start his climbing, climbs under the stairs to get a walking cart free and then pushes this around.

42 He climbs down from the stairs and walks past Helen and Anne and tries from the floor to free the walking chair from the sack chair.

43 He climbs back onto the stairs and succeeds in pushing it from there onto the floor.

He succeeds in climbing the stairs and gets the walking cart loose. This is positively commented on by his favourite pedagogue. He smiles and leaves his activity.

44 Helen: 'So did you succeed Fredrik?'

45 Fredrik leaves the walking cart and walks around and smiles.

46 He runs back, takes the walking cart and runs it gently into the foot of Rune's mother.

Then he runs back and pushes the cart to Rune's mum to gets a reaction.

47 Looks up and grins.

48 Asta enters.

49 Fredrik drives the walking cart back and bangs into the door and grins. He looks all the time to see if somebody is watching him, nobody takes any notice now (except the observer).

There is no reaction. He drives around and looks for reactions but does not get any.

50 He goes and takes the wooden board puts it into the walking car. It does not fit, he takes it and bites into it, rolls the cart towards the door.

Takes his wooden board but does not succeed in fitting it into the cart.

51 Rune, his mother and his brother leave.	When Rune's mum leaves she does not pay attention even though he is blocking the door.
52 The mother moves the cart so they can get out.	

To participate in the researched persons' social situation and get some insight into the interactional patterns, the researcher has to be in this situation for some time and repeat his participation, so that the children continue to engage in their everyday projects (rather than be distracted by the observer).

In our interactive research approach we would recommend combining different methods. The methods that are adopted will be specific to the research aim (see Chapter 11 for an example). This does not mean a triangulation of methods, as this is not a valid approach for studying the everyday activities within children's lives. We believe that different methods will reveal different aspects of a child's everyday life.

The results of the research process can be written up as a research protocol, such as interview material or recorded observations. Other kinds of research material that can constitute a research protocol are: video, photos, children's drawings, children's writings and other symbolic products.

In the collecting of protocol material, the aim of the research as well as the theoretical preconcepts have to be explicated and reflected upon many times. When entering the research field, the aim and the guiding theory frame the ways interaction can take place between the researcher and the persons in the concrete research situation.

The general preconcepts for the research projects presented in this book are formulated in Chapter 2 in the model in Figure 2.1. This model depicts how the relations between societal conditions, institutional practices and person's activity can be conceptualised. How developmental change can be conceptualised is formulated in Chapter 2.

Based on these conceptions, the researcher in participating in the daily practice in activity settings with one or several persons gains insight into:

- the intentional orientation of the researched persons,
- the ways interaction occurs between the participants (interaction patterns),
- the conflicts between different person's intentions and projects in the activity,
- the competence and motives that the researched persons demonstrate during their interactions.

These four themes are basic categories and preconceptions of our research into children's development. How they are actualised when undertaking interpretations will depend on the research goal. These basic categories will also be used differently for different research problems (discussed further in the later sections of this chapter).

Interpretation of protocols

As outlined in Chapter 3, protocols need to be interpreted in a systematic way. There is a difference between being in the field doing research and being back at the writing table making an interpretation. However, this does not mean that there are no theoretical considerations and concepts invoked in the field research. There is no research without preconceptions, as described earlier in this chapter, and these have to be made as explicit as possible before entering the field as they influence the construction of the protocols.

The main differences between the description process and the interpretative writing become evident when considering both the time and place of these activities. The writing or creation of protocols takes place in immediate connection with the activities that are researched. The researcher's interpretation of the research protocol takes place later, in a setting other than the researched situation, most often by the researcher at his or her desk and at least away from the field where the protocol materials were collected. The collected research material thereby becomes an object for interpretation. There is no longer any personal relation to the activities and people involved. The aim is to explicate the theoretical concepts and transcend the specific situation. The research aim becomes the dominating interpretation frame (see Table 4.1).

Table 4.1 Main differences between protocol writing and interpretation

	Protocol writing	**Interpretation**
Activity	Interaction	Reflection
Mode of relation	Person–person relation	Researcher–text relation
Focus	The persons and their activities in concrete situations	Differentiate between the specific social situation and the general conceptual relations
Concepts	Preconcepts	Formulating conceptual relations in relation to the research aim

The frame for interpretation can be constructed when working with the protocols. But even although the protocol writing and the interpretation both have the same aims and theoretical foundation, they also depart on several points, as presented in Table 4.1 and further unfolded in Table 4.2.

Table 4.2 Main differences between protocol writing and interpretation

Protocol writing	Interpretation
The creation of protocols implies an interaction between the researcher and the researched persons that are based on the experience and relevance for both the researcher and the persons in this interaction	In the interpretation of the protocols, the researcher does not have contact with the researched persons. The researcher uses her reflection in relation to explicate categories or theoretical consideration used on the material in the protocol
The collection of research material implies a subject–subject relation	In the interpretation, the researcher seeks to distance herself from the specific situation and thereby treat the protocol as a text
In collection of protocol material, the focus is on the specific biographical aspects of the person's life world	In the interpretation, the researcher seeks to transcend the specific research situation so that more general relations can be formulated
In the research situation, the focus is on specific themes without forgetting meaningfulness of the whole situation	In the interpretation, the researcher tries to build and use a conceptual frame in order to create and understand the material in relation to the research aim

Different forms of interpretation

There can be different forms of interpretation. There can be interpretation close to a common sense level that is focused on the unique activity setting and there can also be an interpretation at an institutional practice level or a biographical level. The third form of interpretation I call thematic interpretation, where the interpretation is related specifically to a problem area and where new conceptual relations can be formulated. These three forms of interpretation are discussed below.

Common sense interpretation

A common sense interpretation is the first level of interpretation. It can be seen in the observation of the infant Fredrik in the nursery practice shown earlier, where the common sense interpretation is explicitly detailed in the right-hand column. In this column, the interpreter is commenting on his/her understandings of the interactions in the activity setting. This kind of interpretation does not demand explicit concepts, but some obvious relations stand out and the patterns in interaction can be seen. The interpretation 'objectifies' the person's interactions in the activity settings where the interpreter is not part of the shared activity settings. This kind of interpretation is useful in validating the observation with the pedagogues or others who have participated in the observed activities.

Situated practice interpretation

A situated practice interpretation is an interpretation that transcends the single activity settings and links together observations taken across several activity settings within the same project. Situated practice interpretations generally focus on an interpretation of the practice in an institution in relation to specific children and caregivers. Dominating motives, patterns of interaction and problems can be explicated at this level. The conceptual relations are used explicitly in analysing the concrete activity settings, and finding conceptual patterns. This kind of interpretation will be illustrated in the following example, using the same observation of the infant Fredrik in the nursery practice shown above.

The interpretation will here be based on the theoretical conceptions outlined in Chapter 2 about child development as they were formulated earlier in this chapter:

1 The intentional orientation of the researched persons.
2 The ways of interacting between participants (interaction patterns).
3 The conflicts between different person's intentions and projects in the activity.
4 The competence and motives that can be seen in the researched person's interactions in his or her social situations.

These four themes unfold differently in relation to the aim of the research. One model is demonstrated in the interpretation of Fredrik's everyday activity in the nursery. Another can be found in Chapter 11 of an experimental teaching practice and children's learning and development through participating in this practice.

Steps in the interpretation of Fredrik's everyday activity in a nursery

The observation is numbered to make the interpretation proceed more systematically in relation to the analyses of these four themes. The first step is for the interpreter to read through the whole observation and mark the places where Fredrik has taken the initiative or shown intentions and then write these up as 'under *theme* 1' (outlined directly above and illustrated below for Fredrik).

To interpret the second theme interactions and the third theme conflicts, the researcher must proceed in the same way as before: re-read the observations in relation to all the interaction patterns and write a narrative of this, then find the conflict and problems for both the child and the adult and write a narrative of this. The last theme to analyse is not only based on finding places where the child demonstrates competence, but is also based on conclusions from the third step of finding places with conflicts and problems, which can indicate that new learning and development can be expected. Unravelling the thematic areas is not an easy task, as there will be overlaps between the four thematic areas. For the interpreter, this unravelling of themes is a double process that leads to formulating, reformulating and the extension of the thematic categories and thereby leads to new insight both in the concrete analysis and the formulation of the ideals (the general concepts).

Fredrik's everyday activity in the nursery

1. *Independent initiative and contact approaches and understanding of demands*

Fredrik pays attention to the adult in his nursery room (14 Feb.: 5, 10; 21 Feb.: 7, 30, 45) and shows clearly that he wishes to draw adults into the activities he initiates (14 Feb.: 2; 21 Feb.: 46, 49).

What get his attention and absorbs him is the research of large objects and his own performance in relation to mastering these objects. He pushes and climbs on chairs (14 Feb.: 6; 21 Feb.: 39) explores the laundry basket (14 Feb.: 6) and tumbles to get the walking cart free from the sack chair (21 Feb.: 41).

The adults follow his activities but often hinder his projects by giving him an alternative task that demands that he is sitting down and using fine motor hand abilities: puzzle (14 Feb.: 5), pyramid play (14 Feb.: 10), wooden board, (21 Feb.: 27). Fredrik accepts the adults' demands but when the adults leave he goes back to the activities that were interrupted by the adults – that is, to explore large objects and his own competences with these objects (14 Feb.: 6, 8; 21 Feb.: 39).

2. Adult–child interaction and child–child interaction

The pattern of interaction between Fredrik and the pedagogues and other adults (Rune's mother) is that they primarily react in a restrictive manner to Fredrik's research activity. As an alternative, they initiate activities that demand that he sit quietly at a table. Fredrik willingly accepts the adult's alternatives; however, the adult does not enter into the activity and engage in an interaction with Fredrik about these more 'quiet' activities but leaves him to himself as soon as he is pacified and not tumbling around. Fredrik's initiative in contacting adults is also dismissed quickly (14 Feb.: 2, 9; 21 Feb.: 5, 46, 49).

The pedagogues do not try to get the children to play together or to make contact with each other. They are mostly concerned with having the children sit together doing parallel activities (21 Feb.: 27). In general, very limited talk is directed at the children or specifically at Fredrik; only one, Helen, comments that Fredrik's activities are positively viewed (21 Feb.: 44).

The children themselves do not interact with each other very much. Fredrik and Nicolas sit together eating soup (21 Feb.: 1–2). The contact that takes place between them is in relation to taking things from each other; Morten takes Fredrik's wooden board (21 Feb.: 35), Morten and Fredrik imitate each other (21 Feb.: 10, 36).

3. Problems and conflicts in Fredrik's everyday activities and how the pedagogues are handling these conflicts

Fredrik's research of large objects as it turns out is also an activity that creates conflicts with the pedagogues. Fredrik's other conflict is with his pacifier. He reacts differently in relation to the different adults. He tackles Asta's critique by continuing his activities. When Helen hinders his activities he starts to cry and also cries when she walks away (14 Feb.: 8; 21 Feb.: 7, 31). Asta turns her interaction with Fredrik into a power game about his pacifier, and when Fredrik cries she makes the conflict into a personal one and comments on his crying as a demonstration of his need to dominate. When Sanne hinders his activities he starts to cry and also cries when she walks away (21 Feb.: 6, 12, 15).

4. What kind of competencies does the child demonstrate and what is he appropriating?

Fredrik can eat by himself, even when it is thin soup; he drinks the milk nicely (21 Feb.: 1–2). He also starts to imitate Morten's wooden board activity (21 Feb.: 36). But first and foremost he tries to handle large objects and can balance on a stair pushing things around (tray, walking cart). It is here that he is challenged and starts to acquire new competencies. He is also learning where he can get help (Helen) and who he has to keep away from in relation to the pedagogues (Asta), thereby acquiring social competence.

Conclusion and indication of development possibility in Fredrik's everyday activities in the nursery

In general, Fredrik is an infant who initiates researching his surroundings and tries his strength on large objects. He is also exploring interactional possibilities in relation to adults. Even though the adults either restrict him or show passivity in relation to his activities, he shows great initiative.

It would be a good idea if the adults were a little more sensitive to his contact with them and paid more attention to what Fredrik's projects really are, instead of dismissing him or pacifying him with quiet activities. One could also wish that the adults talked more with Fredrik about what happened around him so that they opened up the possibilities for spoken contact about shared activities. Another wish would be that the adults in the centre should help the children to be more aware of each other and help them more directly to play together in pairs.

Interpretation on a thematic level

This third type of interpretation is directly connected to the aim of the research. Explicit relations are formulated by using theoretical concepts to find patterns in the situated complexity of the institutional practice level of interpretation. A reduction in the complexity of the material is needed in order to be able to formulate new conceptual relations within a problem area. Several cases will be analysed to see if any pattern is related to the theme of the research.

This generalisation is based on situated interpretation – not with an aim to find identical events, but to find meaningful patterns in relation to the research aim. The researcher starts with the preconceptions and through analysing the situated interpretations evolves these conceptions into a relational scheme of interpretation.

In Fredrik case, the aim was to study small children's everyday life activities in institutional caregiving practices and how children's motive and competence developed as related to both pedagogues' and the infants' self-initiated projects.

The category scheme that was formulated was based on this research and can be seen in Table 4.3. The departure was taken in the preconcepts, but these concepts evolved throughout the analyses.

The category system is developed as a dialectic between the aim of the research (i.e. what one wants to study), the theoretical preconditions and the concrete material. Through this process new theoretical conceptual relations can develop.

Table 4.3 Schema for analysing small children's everyday life activities in institutional caregiving practices

---

- The intentional orientation of the researched children

  (a) Towards what kind of activities

  (b) Self-initiated activities

  (c) Understanding the demands of caregivers

- The interaction between the participants (interaction patterns)

  (a) Who does the child approach and how?

  (b) How does the caregiver or adult react?

  (c) How does the child interact with other children?

- The conflicts between different person's intentions and projects in the activity

  (a) How do conflicts starts for the child?

  (b) How does this proceed?

  (c) How do the caregivers/adults support solutions?

- The competence that the researched persons demonstrates during their interactions in these social situations

  (a) What competence and motives does the child demonstrate?

  (b) What competence and motives is the child starting to acquire?

  (c) How dos the child handle social interactions and feelings?

In Fredrik's case, the aim has been to study young children's competence and motive development and self-initiated projects, so the scheme for analysing the protocols did not include the caregiver's perspective. In the following chapter, the caregiver's perspective will be central in relation to analysing young children's everyday life activities.

With other aims, the preconditions will lead to other interpretation schemes, as can be seen in later chapters. In Chapter 10, the aim of the study focuses on how children's self-evaluation are related to the aims and values found in institutional practices in school. In Chapter 11, the aim was related to an educational intervention in order to study the relation between teaching and learning practice in school. The basic conceptions in all the chapters presented here come from the developmental perspective presented in Chapter 2, but they are all developed in relation to the theoretical considerations and the research aims for the particular research projects. In each research study, the formulation of new theoretical insight is directly related to the interpretation scheme.

Methodological demands when researching within the dialectical–interactive approach

I will conclude with a resume of the demands for doing research from the perspective we have formulated in this book – the cultural–historical approach of Vygotsky and others:[1]

(A) *The methodological demands on the researcher participating in the research situation constructing protocol material*

- The research situation is, for the researcher, an experienced situation and is dependent on his or her communication, including tape or video recording.
- In a research situation, the focus is on the activities that occur in the everyday life of the researched persons.
- The researcher searches for meaning in the situation.
- The researcher has to conceptualise herself as an active participant in the research situation even though he or she does not intervene in the situation.
- Interaction between researcher and children can have many forms, from mainly verbal communication to bodily interaction around shared objects.
- The writing of protocols is the main technique.
- In the recording, it is important to describe the context of the research situation.

(B) *The methodological demands on the researcher interpreting the research protocols*

- The aim of the project should be clearly formulated.
- Preconcepts should be formulated as *category relations* about activities that can detect patterns in interactions.
- Through analyses, these *category relations* should become extended or reformulated.
- There should be different levels of interpretation, a common sense level, a practice situated level and a theoretical level.
- These levels build on each other.

In the following chapters, examples of research projects that illustrate these demands will be presented.

Note

1   A source book for qualitative data analyses – which has the same aims as we do to develop a systematicity in relation to analysing

qualitative data and can be related to our approach, though this approach is in no way contained here – is Miles and Huberman (1994), *An Expanded Sourcebook: Qualitative Data Analysis*, London, Sage.

5 Interpreting research protocols – the institutional perspective

Marilyn Fleer

Introduction

In order to study the development of children from a cultural–historical perspective a complex and dynamic methodology is needed. In Chapters 1 to 4, the epistemological and theoretical dimensions of such a methodology were detailed. In particular, three concepts were discussed. First, children's development takes place through participating in societal institutions, such as preschool or home. Second, the institutional practice is connected to children's development and must be researched if a child's development is to be fully documented and understood. Finally, the study of a child's development seeks to examine the qualitative changes in the child's motive and competences in 'relation' to the child's social situation – which continues to change over time. A dialectical methodology which draws upon these concepts examines children in their everyday settings and seeks to understand the social situation of children's development. In this chapter, a study of the social situation of children's development is illustrated through a case example which demonstrates the 'relations between' studying the child's perspective, examining the institutional perspective and highlighting the researcher's perspective.

The assumption that sits under this research methodology, and which is illustrated through the example in this chapter, suggests that a study must seek to document 'how children contribute to their own developmental conditions'. To do this effectively, we need to include the different practices that a child participates in through his or her daily life. In particular, developing an understanding of the societal, institutional and personal perspectives is important for conceputalising the developmental potentialities of children and, together, these perspectives give the possibility for analysing how children develop as they interact with other participants in and across particular institution, such as preschool, home and in the community. Similarly, documenting the institutional practices allows for a better understanding of the conditions that the institutions give for the different kinds of interaction and activity – thus influencing the 'potentiality' for the development of children.

In this chapter, I discuss the significance of documenting the relations between the different perspectives and outline specifically how the protocols were recorded and the interpretations were undertaken. In order to foreground the significance of the relations between perspectives, I will begin by providing an example of the child's perspective only, followed by the institutional perspectives, finishing on the researcher's perspective. Taken together, the documentation of the perspectives provide for a richer and more clearly articulated study of the social situation of children's development.

The child's perspective

In order to begin the process of documenting from a child's perspective, the researcher needs to develop observational protocols that foreground how a child enters the practice within the institution. In a cultural–historical approach to research, it is important to note how a child participates in the activity. Simultaneously, we need to document what is afforded by the institution and what motives are inherent within the particular activities that can engage the child. For example, in a study that sought to understand the nature of cognition in play-based contexts across three different preschools, I wished to engage the children in the research project and to establish protocols for how a child enters and participates in science activities. The focus for the research was the teaching of science in preschools, with special attention on noting how everyday concepts and scientific concepts were introduced and used at home and in preschool play. Three different sites were included in the study: Seaside Kindergarten, Bush Kindergarten and City Early Learning Centre. The Seaside Kindergarten is discussed in this chapter and the City Early Learning Centre is discussed in Chapter 6.

In this example, the specific aim of the research was to study the child's social situation in his or her everyday settings, where play was the main pedagogical approach used to support learning. The catalyst for commencing the study was a box of science materials that had been selected by the teachers and the researcher (Avis). Although the science materials were specific to each of the three research sites, they each afforded a play opportunity for science exploration. In Figure 5.1, the three contexts for observing children is shown (three preschools: Bush Kindergarten, City Early Learning Centre and Seaside Kindergarten; children are aged between 4 and 5 years). The observation protocol focused specifically on how the children enter the activity and what activities and motives are afforded by the materials in the three play-based contexts – as set up by the teachers and researchers. Figure 5.1 illustrates that although the teachers and researchers all set up science materials for the children, each site featured different materials for science play for the children.

Bush Kindergarten   City Early Learning Centre   Seaside Kindergarten

Figure 5.1   Different research sites.

Through introducing science materials and a display space into the preschools, I was able to create a similar context across settings that allowed observation protocols to commence in the same way – even though the materials were clearly very different (see Figure 5.1). But these contexts also allowed for the observation of how the children engaged with the materials and how the institution supported, directed or diverted the children's play activities. In this particular example, the observations occurred over several weeks, which enabled me to document the progression of activity within each preschool. Thus, allowing, in the research protocol, for the documentation of potential change or conflict in the social situation of development. Similarly, it was also possible to document and analyse the children's intentions, orientations, motives and perspectives in relation to the science materials.

Hedegaard states earlier in this book that 'one has to conceptualise a child's intentional orientation or projects as a relation between the motives of an activity settings and institutional practices and the child's motives'. This allows the researcher to map and analyse the different possibilities inherent in the activity at the same time as considering the motives of the child: 'The child's motives have to be seen in relation to the child's experience and competence and the possibility for realising her motives in an institutional practice.'

For example, in the science play observation below (Transcripts 5.1 and 5.2), we find two preschool girls in a sandpit. Their teacher is close by. She has given them peanut oil, vinegar and baking powder (real ingredients in their original containers). The teacher encourages the children to use the materials. On a shelf next to the sandpit are a range of empty plastic containers available for the children to use. The children take the ingredients and begin to mix them together with sand and water. The teacher is interested in encouraging the children to conduct a science experiment. The children have a different perspective. They frame the task as an imaginary situation. They move in and out of the idea of cooking meat.

Observer: Avis

Transcript 5.1: Observation example of 'cooking meat'

Observation	Common sense interpretation
Lead Teacher: It's Lana's oil experiment. [Lana pouring oil into a bowl, puts oil down, makes sure the lid's on and then turns the oil container so that the label is facing her.]	The Lead Teacher works hard to re-direct the children's attention from making meat to looking at the mixing of the oil, water and sand.
Lana: There [child picks up oil container and looks at the label]. Baking, oil experiment. [Puts oil container down and picks up container with mixture and walks to another area where Molly is playing. Lana puts sand into her container and swishes it around. Molly then gets up and goes to where Lana was. Lana then brings the oil back and starts pouring it into another container.] Oh this is working babe. [Lana looks up as she speaks walking back to where she started from.]	The children take note, but focus on 'making different oils'. The activity does not support scientific thinking, but rather provides the children with a playful event in which they expand their experiences of playing with cooking oil. Later the Lead Teacher asks the children to comment again on the materials in the mixture, but the response from the children indicates that they have reframed the experience in relation to cooking once more.
Molly takes an oil bottle over to her teacher and asks her to close the lid.	
Lead Teacher: Ah that is hard to shut isn't it? [Molly tries to push lid down.]	
Molly: Hard to shut.	
Lead Teacher: So what are you going to do with it?	
Molly: Shake it. [Child is mixing substances (ingredients) in a bowl.]	
Lana: I'm going to mix this, all the way to the bottom, to the end.	

Observation	Common sense interpretation
Lead Teacher: What does it smell like? *Lana:* Um, cause I'm making meat. *Lead Teacher:* You're making? *Lana:* Meat. *Lead Teacher:* Meat okay. [Lana stops mixing and pours oil in.] More oil?	
Lead Teacher: What can you see Molly what can you see? [Tilts container.] *Molly:* Oh water and oil.	Here the Lead Teacher is drawing the child's attention to oil floating at the top of the mixture.
Lead Teacher: What's this at the top? [Molly looking] Can you see how something's at the top and there's other stuff at the bottom and then? *Molly:* There's oil [points to top], there's water [points in middle] and there's sand [points to bottom]. *Lead Teacher:* Why do you think it does that? *Molly:* Cause I put it in there, I put them all in there. *Lead Teacher:* Yeah but why do they all stay layered I thought you shook it? [Molly starts shaking.] *Molly:* I couldn't shake it properly. *Lead Teacher:* You can't shake it properly well how about we shake it together [shaking together] here we go. We're doing really well together aren't we? *Lana:* Yeah we make some more different oil. *Lead Teacher:* Okay let's have a look at it. *Lana:* I make some more different oil. *Lead Teacher:* See we shook that didn't we Molly but it's still the same. *Lana:* I make some more. [Comes over to Molly and teacher and observes.] *Molly:* Yeah but it? [Pushes on lid.] *Lana:* I make some different oil. *Lead Teacher:* Okay you made some different oil. [Lana pours oil into bowl and Molly looks on.]	

Observation	Common sense interpretation
Lana: Put a little bit, a little bit more sand [grabs a handful of sand and puts it into bowl] little bit, mix it all around. [picks up handful of sand with other hand and puts it into the bowl]. Lots of sand. [Mixes then picks up oil and pours it into bow.] Lead Teacher: A different type of oil. Lana: [Puts oil down and grabs something else and puts it down next to the oil. Opens up oil and stands up.] Lead Teacher: How come there's all these spots of it? [Pointing in bowl, Lana leans forward and looks into bowl.] Lana: Oh cause that's my meat. [Stands up and walks away with oil.]	These observations and transcript reveals an interesting context. The children have framed the activity of mixing sand, water and oil within the context of cooking meat. Although the sandpit was embellished with additives, such as water bottles, a peanut oil bottle and also a bottle of vinegar, this child has tied these disparate materials together and generated a 'play event' of cooking.

The Lead Teacher draws the children's attention to the mixing process, commenting on the particular substances that are being combined. In the following part of the observation, the Lead Teacher's scientific knowledge about mixing substances is foregrounded.

Transcript 5.2: Observation example of 'cooking meat' (continuation)

Observation	Common sense interpretation
Lead Teacher: So you don't want to use the vinegar Lana? Lana: Yeah. Where's the vinegar? [Lana stops mixing.] Lead Teacher: It's over there. [Lana turns and goes and gets a 2 litre plastic container.] Lana: Vinegar, vinegar. Lead Teacher: Hope this doesn't explode. [Lana brings 2l plastic container back to mixing bowl and tries to take the lid off.] I don't know what happens with oil and vinegar [laughs].	The teacher does not know how the particular materials she has chosen for the science experiment will react with each other.

In the observation above, we see that the children are taking part in quite different activities to those intended by the teacher. Their focus of attention is in relation to cooking and not the mixing of substances. The children's engagement is high, but their thinking is not directed towards what the teacher intends. The motives are in relation to cooking and not to 'mixing substances'. The children have transcended the particular context and are thinking and acting as though they are in a kitchen cooking meat. As Hedegaard argues, 'Seeing an activity from a given person's perspective gives the possibility to see how this person both can learn and also contribute to the activity and sometimes develop the activity.'

If we examine Hedegaard's model in Chapter 2 (Figure 2.2) we note that the protocols discussed above allow for an analysis in relation to: Person; Activity; and Interests/Projects/Engagement/Intentions. Further, we can go beyond the immediate context or activity to examine the social situation, the activity setting and the motives. The first focuses on the child's perspective and the 'activity' is central to the analysis. In the last, the institutional perspective is foregrounded and the (pedagogical) practice is analysed. The methodology outlined in this book makes a clear distinction between activity (child's perspective) and practice (institutional perspective). This distinction is important when examining the observation protocols and making interpretations beyond the specific activity setting. The examples above illustrate this distinction clearly and the researchers have specifically observed and undertaken common sense interpretations with this distinction in mind.

As researchers using a cultural–historical methodology, it is important to consider not just the child's perspective in relation to the activity (person, activity, interest/projects/engagement/intentions), but also the institutional perspective (social situation, activity setting, motives). In this next section, the observation protocol in relation to the institutional perspective of the particular case example is given.

Institutional perspective

When constructing interview and observation protocols for the study of children's development, it becomes particularly important to ask what kinds of institutional practices dominate particular institutions. For instance, are there common practices to be found in preschool centres in which young children participate or which teachers privilege? How do particular pedagogical practices position children? What do they allow for children and what interactions and activities do they constrain? These are important question for researchers to ask when drafting interview questions, when developing interpretations and when generating conclusions that go beyond the specific research context being investigated.

In studying the social situation of development, it becomes important for researchers to generate protocols that provide valuable insights into institutional practices that shape or are shaped by children – diverting or supporting particular potentialities. In the case example of science activity discussed earlier, I specifically created interview protocols that would generate information on institutional practices, beliefs and values. The observer (Avis) took photographs and video recordings of children's play in the kindergarten each week and re-presented examples to the teachers in order to solicit information on their institutional practices and beliefs. This particular approach was important for generating a dialogue on pedagogical practice and on institutional norms subscribed to by the teachers. Through showing examples of play, the teachers could discuss their beliefs and practices in relation to the activities that the children had directly engaged in that week. Through the interviewing of both the Lead Teacher and the Teacher Assistant, it was possible to note consistencies or conflicts and through this gain greater insights into teachers' taken-for-granted practices.

Through clarifying the different perspectives of the Lead Teacher and the Teacher Assistant (known as Assistant throughout), it was possible for a richer interview protocol to be established. In the example below, the opposing opinions that arose during interviews centred on the framing of the interactions between the staff and the children. The Lead Teacher's project was for minimalist materials and teacher interactions, while the Assistant's project was for loosely defined play sites for active engagement with particular scientific concepts. The Lead Teacher was focused on the children framing the learning activities and the Assistant had in mind particular scientific concepts that could be introduced through the creation of everyday play activities. The latter was more in line with my research project. Consequently, the observer (Avis) provided room during the interview for further comments to be made in relation to the perspectives being reported (see Transcript 5.3). In addition, the observer also noted against the interview transcript (field notes), the teacher activities during the week that corresponded with the responses made during the interview. These additions to the interview protocol allow for a wholeness orientation to begin to emerge in the protocols.

Example of teachers beliefs, practices and values

Context: At the end of the second week of researching children's activities in the Seaside Kindergarten, the observer (Avis) sits with the Lead Teacher and the Assistant at one of the children's tables in the kindergarten and begins an interview with them about the teaching programme.

The observer invites the staff to comment on their goals and the goals and motives of the children. The teacher has been at the kindergarten for

2 years, and the Assistant has worked at the kindergarten for nearly 20 years, having taught many of the families of the children who are attending the kindergarten.

The Lead Teacher responds first and comments on a range of child activities that have taken place in the kindergarten. Of particular interest is the topic of potions, as this dominated the activities of the children throughout the whole week. Potions is a fantasy term used to describe the mixing of substances together for magic or for the creation of 'new scientific discovery'. Children were provided with a range of bottles, buckets, coloured water, siphoning equipment, herbs and other scented plants, oils, and several mortars and pestles for grinding scented leaves. In the sandpit were oil, vinegar and shaving cream. In the water trolley were plastic dinosaurs. Teacher thinking in relation to the activities being planned for the children are shown in Transcript 5.3 (the teacher's perspective).

Transcript 5.3: Teacher's perspectives on societal institutions (Seaside Kindergarten)

Interview transcript	Researcher's perspective – common sense interpretation
Lead Teacher: The parent's will find out that their children are learning more than just numbers and that, outside, they didn't call it potions and I actually heard them use the word stuff. I'd rather the children didn't say this is a potion; they didn't have a fixed word for it.	Jan [child] said this is stuff that you feed to worms. The Assistant introduced the word potion last week to the children.
Researcher: The potion play went on too. It all flowed from one thing to the next, from cooking to poisoning to siphoning [Avis].	Following through is not easy when there is indoor and outdoor flow; one staff member does not see what the other is really involved with staff are working as two separate entities co-teaching in different ways.
Assistant: It all just evolved.	

Interview transcript	Researcher's perspective – common sense interpretation
Researcher: So the potion could be anything. It's a non-specific word, generic, and assumes that transformations can happen. We had leaves today, the children went from cooking, to perfumes, and experimenting with water, smell, various sequences, but scientific words I didn't hear much [Avis].	There was no explicit conversational play by the Lead Teacher with these mixtures. She watched on and watched the yard overall.
Lead Teacher: [Interview continues – The Lead teacher discusses other areas of play.] There's children coming out and in, when they want. I really liked the independence. I did not set up one thing, the children did it all themselves and I was really pleased with that because I just think people set things up too much for the children.	She says this proudly and emphatically. It annoys her when the Assistant sets things up.
Assistant: But generally the children do set up. They do.	
Lead Teacher: No I don't think they do.	
Researcher: Those activities merge from the interests seen [Avis].	
Assistant: I'm amazed that you're saying that this year [addressing the Lead Teacher]. Only basic things are out; the children have been using their own devices. Can you think of something in particular?	
Lead Teacher: Putting sheets out each day you've gone out and set things up you set up the potions, and you put the bottles in a specific area. What I'm saying is you put it in a specific area.	

Interview transcript	Researcher's perspective – common sense interpretation
Researcher: The teacher is thinking of the provocation. It provokes some extra play, in my experience it is good to put out a provocation, like the elastic, we all work like that [Avis].	
Assistant: I can't think of what you mean [addressing the Lead Teacher]. I'm comparing with how adults used to set up here. I didn't think putting out three buckets of water as setting up and getting the bottles. I don't see.	
Lead Teacher: What I do see is putting tables in a specific area, then the children don't want to leave the tables.	
Assistant: I don't care where the tables are I don't see the yard as pre-set up. It seems very free flowing to me when you think of it how you used to be.	
Researcher: You've placed a table here [referring to the inside table that replaced the home corner] because you hope children will come to it. The important thing is the reason why we do things [Avis].	There appear to be inconsistencies with what the Lead Teacher is saying, as the following day she spends all morning setting up outside.
Lead Teacher: It might be a practical thing like the water bucket is too heavy to lift.	
Researcher: So [to Lead Teacher] do you feel like it is a manipulative thing, to arrange the environment [Avis]?	
Lead Teacher: I just think we both come from different perspectives.	
Assistant: I don't see that as setting up the yard.	

In this example, it can be seen that the philosophy of the Lead Teacher shapes what may be possible within the kindergarten. The philosophy normalises a particular type of institutional interaction. Traditionally, early childhood teachers were expected to organise rich learning environments through providing materials, time and space for exploration. Philanthropic writings suggest that early childhood education was established to support children from poor families, where children were deemed to need safe spaces to explore while their families went to work (see Brennan, 1994). The norms that guided the institutional practices and the children's development were connected with keeping children safe and off the streets. The Lead Teacher provides time and space for children to be resourceful and innovative with the materials available. Minimal setting up by the staff is expected. The Assistant who lives in the community, and who does not have an early childhood degree, and therefore has not been inducted into the institutional norms, has an alternative perspective. The differences in views, highlight the institutional norms that the Lead Teacher is looking to maintain within the kindergarten she is responsible for managing. As researchers, it is important to look for these conflictual opportunities as they are rich with potential interpretations.

For instance, as researchers following a cultural–historical tradition, we believe that children's development takes place through their participation in societal institutions. Institutional practices found in preschools, as enacted through the activities (and hence perspectives) organised by the teacher, shape what may be possible for a child to experience or pay attention to. Understanding the perspective of the teacher is important in interactive research. Therefore it is important to include interview protocols on institutional practices. However, further interviews on the conflicts between the perspective allows for additional insights to be generated during the interpretation of the interview protocols. The conflict is highlighted further in the example of an interview protocol that follows.

Example of teacher assistant beliefs, practices and values

Context: The observer interviews the Assistant separately in order to document her beliefs about adult mediation for supporting science learning. The Assistant foregrounds the relations between the children's everyday concepts and the need for introducing scientific concepts in ways that support the children's motives and interest expressed through their play.

Interpretation

The Assistant is sensitive to the ideas, thinking, and experiences that the children have at home. She clearly values the children's perspective (see Transcript 5.4). However, she is also mindful of the institutional perspective of furthering children's learning. The conditions she creates for children's play take into account children's motives and goals. But she also provides other mediational tools, such as books, resources related to their play, and teacher talk, which helps the children to move beyond their everyday concepts. She creates a shared activity in which the children and she, as the Assistant, can be engaged. The conditions she creates foreground the child's project and the Assistant's project.

Transcript 5.4: Assistant's perspectives on societal institutions

Interview protocol	Researcher common sense interpretation
Researcher: What science and play do you see in the preschool [Avis]?	
Assistant: I believe it's happening all the time and I really believe the play that you've seen these last two weeks, like the play with potions and with all the funnels and the pipes, and what's happening with it, the drainage how it all moved to the sand pit, how it dispersed. I think it's happening all the time, it's happening again today, from a simple discussion really, someone was putting water into the sand and it changed and looked a little bit like quicksand and then we took the big dinosaur book out and they talk about fossils in the book and how this dinosaur stuck in the quicksand and how he became a fossil and that led to a lot of dinosaur play, in the sand pit with the burying and I know they've played dinosaurs all year really, one way or another, but this was a whole new idea of using the wet sand for quicksand.	The Assistant believes that there are many opportunities for concept formation in preschool play. The Assistant looks for ways of interlacing everyday concepts and scientific concepts – using books related to children's play is important.
Researcher: They were using the dinosaurs swimming and watching how they moved the other day. It's everywhere isn't it [Avis]?	

Interview protocol	Researcher common sense interpretation
Assistant: Yes, it's everywhere and I believe it's the role of the person in the preschool to just extend that with whatever they need at the time to extend the play, like more funnels and more pipes if needed at the time or books from the library if that turns out to be a sparking point – if we don't have something that's going to spark it off. I really believe that the children with the biggest database are the ones that have had a lot of conversation and I don't mean like an empty vessel that has to be filled with information. I don't like that thinking either, but I do believe that the adult has a role in extending it in whichever way they see fit to extend it, for example, with the perfume making today some bottles had come in yesterday with shaking lids and so they were shaking all their bottles and potions today [n.b. focus parents when interviewed, all talk about potion making in the preschool] to get more from the pot-pourri and by taking a lot of notice of what colours produce what smell and one of the children said it smelt like lemonade and that was Molly and she'd just put in lemon verbena dried leaves, so despite all the other smells that were in that jar she was able to say it smelt like lemonade and that was from the dried lemon verbena leaves that she'd added. *Researcher:* That's really deep thinking isn't it [Avis]?	The Assistant believes that a teacher should take an active role in children's play so that children notice the everyday science concepts and are primed to learning scientific concepts during play.

Interview protocol	Researcher common sense interpretation
Assistant: It was, yes, and I thought how astute because there were lots of other smells in the pot-pourri but the handful of lemon verbena made it really strongly lemon. And you know I know that's just one little example, but the whole process. Then E and B chose some ribbons to decorate their produce to take home so there was all the decorative effect and then the ribbons under the tree became a party, I don't know what the inside story was today, but a tray came out so maybe the party continued inside too, then they had music and musical statues. *Researcher:* The idea of listening, you're talking about extending and I'm wondering where you get that idea from? Do the children give it to you [Avis]?	The Assistant is aware of children's conceptual thinking.
Assistant: Yes. I can see the situation that we need to produce something extra, to make, to help the play along, they wanted to take their perfumes home so they really needed something with lids and you know then there was the idea because they'd seen in the potions and perfumes book, the bow on the neck of the bottle, so we had lots of ribbons, we've got resources mainly and there are lots of things from home that can be used to extend their play a little further. *Researcher:* ... and extend their thinking [Avis].	The Assistant is aware of the children's home play and interests and links her understandings of this to the teaching programme.
Assistant: ... extend their thinking absolutely. I think really the children who hypothesise the best are the ones who have had some input, it's not like, you will learn, this is what I'm teaching you, but doing something together, looking something up together, adding some information, that's a really important part of the process.	The Assistant expresses her belief that learning is maximised when everyday concepts and scientific concepts are interlaced; and that teachers have a role to play in doing this.

As researchers we need to also be mindful of the power relations that exist between staff, and therefore what can potentially be revealed during interviews of staff – collectively or individually. In the interview protocol (Transcript 5.3) of the Lead Teacher and the Assistant, the perspectives of the teachers are evident. However, the Lead Teacher is the qualified teacher with the positional authority and it is her voice that is dominant in the interview protocol in Transcript 5.3. When undertaking research using a wholeness approach, all the perspectives of the participants are necessary. Knowing that institutional cultures privilege the voice of the qualified teacher means finding opportunities for the voice of other participants to be heard. A separate interview with the Assistant was important for gaining information on the other ways that the conditions for learning were being organised (Transcript 5.4).

An interpretation of the different institutional perspectives is important for understanding the social situation of development for the child – particularly, what affordances are made available through the beliefs, values and perspectives of the teachers. In Table 5.1, an example is shown of how the different perspectives can be documented and used for the interpretations and for discussing the findings. The different columns illustrate the significance of the relations between the differing perspectives, generating an additional interview. As illustrated by Vygotsky (1997), in traditional research the field of vision of the researcher is often not considered during the process of interpretation:

> Usually the decisive moment of the experiment – the instruction – is left outside the field of vision of the researcher. It is not subjected to analysis and is reduced to a secondary, auxiliary process. The experiments themselves were usually considered after the elicited process involuntarily set in motion had stopped. The first trials were usually discarded, the processes were studied *post mortem*, while the active effect of the instruction was dropped behind, into the shadows.
>
> (Vygotsky, 1997, p. 36)

In this approach to undertaking research, the researchers' efforts and decisions are not discarded, but become an important dimension of the research protocol that develops as the research progresses over time.

Table 5.1 Summary of different perspectives

Lead Teacher's project (from video protocol transcript and context)	The Assistant's project (from video protocol transcript and context)	Researcher's perspectives
The Lead Teacher wants to have a 'free flow' programme where the environment is not set up. Mediation is planned through provided unstructured contexts and everyday materials.	The Assistant wants a programme where scientific knowledge is mediated through staff interactions with children as they engage with the set up environment.	*Children's development takes place through participating in societal institution* (see Chapter 2).
The Lead Teacher is not focused on concepts, but rather on processes.	The Assistant believes it is important for a teacher to have in mind the concepts she wishes to actively explore with children – to make conscious through play and with interactions with staff.	*Norms that guides the institutional practice and children's development are connected to conceptions of a good life and these conceptions can vary within the different types of institution* (see Chapter 2).

Interpretations

A wholeness approach to research frames the study design in such a way that the perspectives of all the participants are captured and analysed. Table 5.2 shows one way in which this can be achieved.

Table 5.2 Interpretation of different perspectives

Lead Teacher's perspective	Child's perspective	Researcher's perspective
The teacher wanted the children to focus on how substances such as vinegar, oil and water mix.	The children created an imaginary situation of 'cooking meat'. The sand was transformed into meat and the oil and water supported the cooking process.	The researcher is looking to document interactions which show the relations between everyday concepts and scientific concepts. The protocols show that the child and the teacher have different perspectives and limited opportunities for concept formation in science results.
From the adult's perspective, the interaction with a child is guided by norms and values which are explicated in the demands she raises in relation to the child (see Chapter 2).	*To understand what these demands of upbringing and education means for the child's development, it has to be viewed from the child's perspective, i.e. related to the child's intentions* (see Chapter 2).	*The interaction and conflicts between the child's goal-oriented activities and educators' demands point to what is happening developmentally for the child* (see Chapter 2).

Had the study design simply focused on the perspectives of the children, it would not have been possible to know that the framing of the play by the teacher was deliberately centred on giving the children the responsibility for knowing what to do with the materials. Similarly, focusing only on the Lead Teacher 's perspective would have meant that it would have been difficult to notice the children's motives in play. Collectively, the protocols and their summaries (Transcripts 5.1 to 5.5 and Tables 5.1 and 5.2) showed that the children created imaginary situations to make sense of the materials. Once these imaginary situations were created, it was difficult for the children to move back into the Lead Teacher's reality of studying the materials and their properties. Interpreting the different perspectives (see Table 5.2) allowed this important finding to be made.

This finding is confirmed not just through this particular example, but through drafting interpretation frameworks that transcend the immediate context. For instance in this particular case example, I specifically looked for video clips across the whole data set following the categories identified in Table 5.3.

Table 5.3 Categories used on the science project

Motives of children:
- everyday concepts or scientific concepts being played out by the children
- motives of children in relation to science during play.

Motives of staff:
- pedagogical practices which afforded the connections between everyday concepts and scientific concepts
- scientific concepts being introduced by the staff during play or formal group times.

Interactions between participants:
- pedagogical practices which afforded the connections between everyday concepts and scientific concepts
- scientific concepts being introduced by the staff during play or formal group times.

Competence of staff and children:
- teacher content knowledge of science
- children's scientific thinking during play.

Conflicts between different intentions and the activities:
- pedagogical practices which limited the connections between everyday concepts and scientific concepts.

Later the interpretations also focused on the conflictual practices, motives and values between staff within each kindergarten.

For each of these categories, video clips were grouped and interpretations were made. For instance, a collection of video clips was grouped under the heading 'interactions between participants', with the example of 'cooking meat' featuring. Alongside this particular category was also included the video clips entitled 'giving medicine to Humpty Dumpty', 'potions poison' and 'spray weeding'. This type of interpretation is at the institutional practice level, which transcends the single activity setting and combines several activity settings together.

In Chapter 4, Hedegaard outlined a system of line numbers that relate to the particular categories within her interpretations of Fredrik's everyday activity in the nursery school. The same system was adopted for the above case study, but rather than line numbers in relation to observational protocols, I used video clip titles which illustrated segments of play in relation to the particular category. It is through the saturation of data against particular categories within the interpretation framework that it is possible to identify important conclusions – such as, the children framing the science play experience in relation to an imaginary situation (e.g. cooking meat) which was different from that on which the teacher had focused in her interactions. This outcome pointed to significant insights into the nature of pedagogical practices which introduce, but do not cognitively frame, activities for children. Interpretations of this kind are clearly reflective of the activity, but in ways that move beyond the immediate situation and towards thinking about relations within general institutional practices. The researcher begins to distance herself from the immediate research context and treats the observational protocol as text to be analysed. In this kind of interpretation, the researcher builds a conceptual frame that seeks to explain the material gathered in relation to the research aim.

The researchers' perspective

Example from the Seaside Kindergarten

As was discussed above and in Chapters 2 to 4, the researcher is a part of the research context. In a dialectical research design, the researcher's project must also be noted. His or her activities are documented during the observation and interview protocols. The researcher holds a different perspective to the participants of the study and although the researcher is part of the study, he or she has a different role in the study to that of the participants. For example, in the case study discussed earlier, the researchers engaged with the staff in the kindergarten through introducing them to both the aim of the study and the theoretical orientation that had shaped the study design. Vygosky's (1987) theoretical writings on everyday and scientific concept formation was explicitly shared with staff across the three research sites.

The researchers' interactions were recorded while documenting the children and staff interactions. My goals for the study shaped the nature of the interactions, and documenting these interactions is important in an interactive method (see Transcript 5.5).

In sharing the goals and motives of the study, as well as sharing the theoretical perspective being used (i.e. cultural–historical theory generally, and specifically Vygotsky's work on concept formation), I was able to create the conditions for 'intervention in practices' (described in Chapters 1 to 4). Through considering concept formation, as the stitch within the fabric of a whole conceptual system, I was able to draw upon this metaphor for discussing the study goals and the research design with the staff.

As researchers drawing upon a cultural–historical perspective we need to decide upon the role we will adopt in the research site. Our role is not to 'play with the children' in order to gain insights or to believe that we are 'invisible' within the research context. Our perspectives significantly influence the directions of the protocols because we pay attention to those things that relate to our research questions and because we are a part of the research site inviting participants to make explicit their beliefs, values, motives and practices. What is important in cultural–historical research of the kind discussed in this book, is the acknowledgement of the researcher perspective. Table 5.2 (discussed earlier) and Transcript 5.5 provide two examples of how to document and factor in the role of the researcher.

Transcript 5.5: Defining yourself in the research situation

Video protocol (transcript and context)	Researchers' perspective – common sense interpretation
Researcher: Ultimately, we want to find out where the children's concepts move around; and how early childhood teams support this. What we are doing in some way is artificial but we don't have to be typical because we're trying to find out about children's thinking and then we can assume that children's ideas move about in this way so we can build some useful resources, booklets, strategies, and make up some papers and materials for teams to work with [Marilyn]. [Staff discuss examples of science conversations they have with children in the kindergarten.] *Researcher:* You know the lovely rocket example you just gave; maybe we can get an audiotape for you to help to capture those important conversations. And maybe the digital camera can be introduced one day and the children's view of things can be noted [some examples given] [Marilyn].	The research team shares with the staff of Seaside Kindergarten their research intentions. What is the connection between the theory and the methodology? *The research team is located in the research site as a participant* (see Chapter 2).

Video protocol (transcript and context)	Researchers' perspective – common sense interpretation
Researcher: We might take photos and get a story from those photos like that one [points of panels on wall]. We will make a little accompanying sheet to go home with the digital camera [Marilyn]. *Assistant:* I just hope we can help you. *Researcher:* I hope we can help you too [Marilyn]. *Teacher:* It will definitely be great for the children and for us, but can we help you? *Researcher:* We can't get everything 24/7 [24 hours per day, 7 days per week] to understand children properly [Marilyn].	
Researcher: You've placed a table here [referring to the inside table that replaced the home corner] because you hope children will come to it. The important thing is the reason why we do things [Marilyn].	The Researcher is interviewing two staff in the Seaside Kindergarten. There is a difference of opinion emerging about whether to set up children's play or not. The Researcher tries to keep the interview conversation going. *As researchers we are always a part of the interview subject's world, and cannot sit outside of the context we are researching (looking in or defining yourself in the research situation) (see Chapter 2).*

Conclusion

The research design reported in this chapter was framed from the perspective of understanding objects, events, institutions, and participants as connected within a social and conceptual system, not as divorced separate entities. Therefore, the study represents a dynamic 'process of development' and not a 'static entity'. This research condition allows the social situation to be analysed as a whole – where analysing the child's motives and the changing relations with others, are factored into the analysis (see Hedegaard, 2004, 2005).

Importantly, validity of this approach is gained through the act of analysing all the perspectives of the participants – their motives, projects and goals. The perspectives, when taken together, give meaning for actions within the social setting, resulting in a much clearer understanding of the video and interview protocols that are generated.

A study that seeks to undertake interviews and observations over time is dealing with an ever-changing movement of concepts, and this of itself, has been historically problematic for researchers, as noted by Vygotsky and Luria so long ago:

> As soon as we moved on to the study of activity from the viewpoint of the process to its 'Werden' (in a series of experiments drawn out in time), we immediately found ourselves faced with a cardinal fact: that, actually, we were not studying one and same activity each time in its new concrete expressions, but that, over a series of experiments, the object of research itself changed. Thus, in the process of development, we acquire forms of activity that were completely different in structure. This represented an unpleasant complication for all psychologists who at any cost endeavour to preserve the invariability of the examined activity; but for us it as (sic) once became central, and we concentrated all our attention on its study.
>
> (Vygotsky and Luria, 1994, p. 114)

A dialectical–interactive methodology, as described in the first four chapters of this book, and as illustrated in practice in this chapter, is a most productive approach for investigating the social situation of children's development in their everyday lives.

6 Interpreting research protocols – the child's perspective

Marilyn Fleer

Introduction

One of the defining features of research which has been framed from a cultural–historical perspective is the inclusion of the 'historical' dimensions of research. 'History' is not viewed as the study of events long since past, but rather, 'to study something historically means to study it in motion' (Vygotsky, 1997, p. 71). In order to study the everyday life of children as they engage in a range of activities across institutions, including preschool, we must also consider this dialectical historicity that is embedded within the contexts we seek to study.

In studying children's development, Vygotsky argued that:

> to encompass in research the process of development of some thing in all its phases and changes – from the moment of its appearance to its death – means to reveal its nature, to know its essence, for only in movement does the body exhibit that it is. Thus historical study of behavior is not supplementary or auxiliary to theoretical study, but is a basis of the latter.
>
> (Vygotsky 1997, p. 71)

Bakhurst (2007) has argued that 'the cornerstone of Vygotsky's "dialectical method" is the idea that everything in time must be understood in its development' (p. 53). Vygotsky stated that this view of studying development formed the 'basic requirement of the dialectical method' (p. 71).

The specific elements of a dialectical–interactive methodology were detailed in Chapters 2 to 4 and one case example of the importance of studying and interpreting the different perspectives of participants' activity was shown in Chapter 5. In this chapter, a further example is given, but in 'relation to the significance of documenting the historically embedded practices, beliefs and values of an educational institution in motion in order to understand the individual participants motives and goals during activities.

I begin this chapter with an example of a series of interactions between a group of children (aged 3.7 years to 3.9) and their teacher (City Early Learning Centre) to illustrate the difficulty of interpreting observations in isolation from teacher's goals, motives and practices across the institutional setting. Some of the features of this study design were shown in Chapter 5. This example shows the significance of Hedegaard's model of children's learning and development as outlined in Chapter 2. The second part of the chapter focuses on studying in motion the living history of values and goals that are enshrined in the institution. Further examples taken from the same research context are given in order to demonstrate how broadly conceived a dialectical–interactive method must become for reliable and useful interpretations to be made. In particular, interviews with teachers and observations of families are included so that the motives inherent within the traditional practices may be illuminated. The dialectical relations between historically located and future oriented goals and motives are examined in order to build a deeper understanding of a dialectical–interactive research methodology.

Activity and practice

In Chapters 2 to 4, Hedegaard illustrates the significance of framing research and interpretations in ways that take account of the interrelated concepts – 'practice' and 'activity'. Activity is referenced in relation to a particular person's perspective and practice is considered in relation to the institutional perspective. For example, in a study that sought to determine the relations between everyday concepts and scientific concepts across institutions, we videotaped both 'home practices' and 'preschool practices' when children were engaged in specific science learning activities in their City Early Learning Centre (the site for the research – see Chapter 5 for details). In order to understand how mature concepts were being developed for individual children, the perspective of the children was also required. As such, it was important to look at the 'science activities' in relation to the motives afforded for the children and what levels of cognition were being supported during the science activity. In beginning the interpretation (see Chapters 4 and 5), it was noted that, in all the activities in which the teacher and the children were interacting, there was a focus on the same content in every lesson over several months. The focus was for the children to study leaves. I initially thought this activity did not hold much motivation for the children, particularly over an extended period of time. Two transcripts are detailed below – 'introducing the leaves' to the children by the teacher; and 'drawing the leaves' as a follow-up lesson by the teacher. They are given to show the difficulty for researchers if they only look at one perspective in their research.

Observer: Avis

Introducing the leaves (extract of transcript)

Teacher: So first I'm going to show you something that I collected [gets some leaves that were on the shelf].

Jay: Leaves [children say this loudly]!

Not all the children focus their attention on the leaves and not all the children listen to each others' perspectives (two important goals the Classroom Teacher has in mind for the children).

Teacher: Jay, do you want to come around here a little bit so you're a little bit closer.

Monica: Matt – Matt can reach.

Jay: I can reach.

Matt: I can't reach.

Teacher: Before we touch them though – I want us to just use our eyes. Because I want to find out what you can see. What do you see? [Jay picks up a leaf and then Matt and Monica, also twirling leaf.]?

Jay: This one is a bit broke – broken [showing teacher] just a little bit.

Matt: That one ... that one – that one's a bit ?

Jay: And a big one! [showing Matt] Ooh [waving leaf].

Common sense interpretation

In the extended transcript (only introduced above), the teacher is keen for the children to carefully explore with their eyes the features of the leaves. She hopes that the children will articulate their observations to each other and that the children will listen to each others' observations. The children participate, but find it difficult to just use their eyes to investigate the leaves. They continue to try to explore the leaves with their hands, and explore the properties of the leaves by 'doing things to them', such as twirling, and dropping them and they are keen to feel the textures of the leaves by moving their hands over the leaves' surfaces. This is actively discouraged by the teacher.

In the next example, taken later on after the children had looked at the leaves and had talked about what they noticed, the children were asked to draw pictures of the leaves, with the teacher writing their comments next to their drawings. In the example below, Jay actively seeks not to engage in the experience, but the teacher continues to direct him so that he moves closer towards the goals she has in mind for the lesson.

Observer: Avis

Drawing the leaves

Matt: I think we have to do a drawing.

Teacher: You think you have to do a drawing? Okay. What do you think?

Jay: I want to do drawing.

Teacher: What do you think we might draw about?

Matt: I.

Jay: A werewolf! [Very excited.]

Teacher: A werewolf.

The other children discuss other aspects of the leaves they can draw, but Jay remains fixed on drawing a werewolf.

Jay: A werewolf.

Teacher: Yes you're going to draw the werewolf – but listen to me [teacher moves in closer to Jay] after the werewolf – can you draw about the leaves?

Jay: Now [nods].

This point of difference between the teacher's practice and the children's desired activity (see Table 6.1) highlighted for us a potential source of conflict that we were keen to further explore in our research. As discussed by Hedegaard in Chapter 2, the problems and conflicts in children's everyday activities provide insights into the motives and goals of children and teachers. Therefore an analysis of the transcript above helped me with the interpretations, as the perspectives of the participants become clearer in such interactions.

Table 6.1 A common sense interpretation of the children's activity and teacher's practice

The children's perspective	Teacher's perspective
The children wanted to touch the leaves and explore them with their hands.	The teacher wanted the children to look at the leaves and to talk about what they could see.
Jay wanted to draw a werewolf and was not interested in the leaves	The teacher wanted the children to draw the leaves and make statements about the special features of leaves.
The other children wanted to play rather than draw the leaves.	The teacher wanted to record the children's observations of the leaves next to their drawings.

I was unable to make sense of the activity [studying leaves] that was undertaken for such long periods of time each day or understand the particular practice that the teacher was framing for the children in these particular lessons. Through only making observations of the science experiences that the teacher planned, I was unable to make any sensible interpretations. I needed to broaden the study design and the research question.

The research question that drove the final stages of this particular study focused on 'determining what were the institutional beliefs, motives and values that I needed to know about in order to better understand the child's perspective and activity and the teacher's practice in the room'.

With this new focus for the research, I organised to videotape children's activities and the teaching practices throughout the day (rather than simply filming the teacher's lessons). I interviewed the teacher, the Centre Director and another specialist teacher (Pedagogista) who also contributed to the teaching practices. I thought this would ensure that we could have better insights into the children's activity in the classroom and the teachers' pedagogical practices as framed in relation to their motives, values and goals. Here I specifically attempted to document the children's activities during periods when the teacher had less control over what the children were doing. I was interested in observing the children during free play outside, where we noticed minimal adult intervention and more flexibility in relation to how learning was framed for the children. I thought this would allow for observations to be made that might give greater insights into the children's motives and intentions, as the children had greater control over what activities they might engage in and what sorts of projects might be realised at those times. Examples of the children's participation in their free play activities are illustrated in the next section. They provide an important contrast with the teaching practices (leaf exploration) given earlier in this section. I also wanted to know more about the children's motives, goals and values in relation to science through researching family practices. To do this, I invited the families to take photographs and make videotapes of important (to them) science practices at home, and to interview one family member about these photographs/videos.

Children's participation in other activities

In a dialectical–interactive approach we seek to observe the conditions surrounding the child as well as how the child participates in activities in order to conceptualise the study of the child's development as a whole. In researching the children's development in the City Early Learning Centre, I needed to understand how the children were participating in other activities where less teacher involvement was occurring. In interactive-based observation (see Table 3.1) it is important that diverse conditions for children's activity in local situations should be documented and analysed. In the example below, the children are outside in a small group near the side of the yard where the staff have limited involvement in the children's activities. Some children are nearby and are kicking a football. In this example, the children's actions and motives focus on a shared commentary of football, where Danny introduces and discusses electricity in relation to operating an imaginary microphone and speaker for 'calling the football game' that they imagine is being played. This example has been chosen because it illustrates nicely how the children create their own activities during free play in the centre. It also links with the forthcoming transcripts of the family practices, where Danny's interest in electricity is illustrated (see below – Interview with Danny's father).

> *Observer:* Gloria
>
> **Extract of transcript**
>
> *Danny:* Umpire.
>
> *Matt:* Umpire! [Walks away.]
>
> *Danny:* Okay you go umpire.
>
> *Matt:* [Gets football.] Ball up. Ball up. No ball up.
>
> *Jay:* No it's my ball.
>
> *Matt:* [Talking to Danny while boys talking above.] Mmm ... microphone? Mmmm ... microphone?
>
> Children continue to play football. They then sit near a tree and direct their attention to turning on an imaginary microphone in order to 'call the football game'.

Monica: [Comes up to where the children are.] No we already push the button. Press the button.

Danny: This is, this button and, here [touches base tree trunk like pressing a button].

Jay: We're incredible [moves closer to tree]. We talk into the microphone [taps tree]. Turn on – turn off the electricity.

Danny: I'll turn it on. [Uses finger to touch leaves.]

Jay: No turn off. [Danny touches leaf on tree.]

Danny: It's off. [Discussions continue.]

Danny is very interested in electricity and in football. Both of his interests are foregrounded in this play event. For Danny and the other children the motives for participating in the 'football commentary' were clearly different to those inherent in the activity of 'studying leaves'. In a dialectical–interactive methodology it is important to find not only examples that are similar, but also examples that are different – so that all the conditions for development can be considered as a whole when the interpretation and analysis are undertaken. These variations are important because they can point to quite different interpretations. Below is a transcript of an interview with Danny's father. This example, illustrates how Danny's interest in electricity, as realised through free play in the City Early Learning Centre, has been intentionally explored in the home.

Interviewer: Avis

Interview with Danny's father

Dad: Well here – Danny loves changing light bulbs. And we always discuss how when you've got an old light bulb one of the filaments is – is usually broken because that's burnt out. So here he is checking the filaments to see if …

Avis: That's – yes that's something you can easily see isn't it?

Dad: Yeah. I mean he won't understand how it works. I don't think I fully understand how it works but – he does understand that if you know the filaments are connected then this light will work and if they're not then it won't. So he was having a good look.

[*Dad* is looking at a photograph of Danny examining plugs and cables.] Yeah he does seem to understand about plugging things in and – how they know – how all that goes.

Avis: How many questions does he ask you – with things like that?

Dad: Oh he asks quite a few and he was very captivated – fascinated. We had, a power black out – And he talked about that a lot and about what happens with the electricity and where it goes and, you know, the tree fell on the power line and there was, yeah, he was – that kept coming up – over, you know – coming months.

When we examine Hedegaard's model (Chapter 2) we note that the institutional practices can include a diversity of practices such as, the school, the preschool and the family. In this research project, it is important to include observations of family practices, because we wanted to know about everyday practices in science. In the examples discussed in this chapter, it is possible to see that if the research seeks to study the relations between everyday concepts and scientific concepts, it is not possible to do this without also including the family practices in the study. In the example above, important everyday interactions at home about electricity were noted, which tended to match those exhibited in the centre during free play where the children were calling a football game. To this point, it is clear that connections between the centre and the home are seen, but they are informal and relate to the child's play activity and not the teaching practice. In a dialectical–interactive method, the question to be asked is how well can the researchers in their conceptualisations of the schooling practices begin to understand the different perspectives that emerge?

In Table 3.1, Hedegaard outlined how a dialectical–interactive methodology can also include interventions into everyday practice. Even after studying the children's home practices and examining the children's activities within the centre, it was still difficult for me to know why the teachers chose to study the leaves for such extended periods of time (within and across weeks). The free play observed provided examples of children's capacity to generate their own learning activities and these in turn provided powerful learning opportunities for teachers to utilise if they wish – a common approach in preschool education. Because I could still not understand the teachers' perspective on the pedagogy of 'studying leaves', I decided to show all the teachers in the City Early Learning Centre (Teacher, Pedagogista, Centre Director, Teacher B, Teacher C) the filmed interview clip of Danny's father and to discuss Vygotsky's theoretical work on everyday concepts and scientific concepts. In the transcript below, the complexities associated with studying children's development becomes visible.

The family values, goals and motives in relation to science in children's everyday lives are made explicit through this intervention. The staff discuss the challenge of the complicated everyday science that is occurring at home, and the science they set up in the centre. A range of perspectives about how to frame science learning are put forward by the staff in the centre.

Researcher: Marilyn

Staff perspectives on science learning (staff interview)

Teacher: I think you can change the children's experiences or – direct their experiences by having the stuff that you have around the playground, the stuff that you direct them to, even lots of the magnifying glasses, stuff in the playground; you know, you can give them lots of experiences … you don't have to call it science or whatever but practical stuff that they're actually doing – hammering nails, those sorts of things. They can easily be directed at school.

Pedagogista: But [teacher] what I was also saying is that science is happening – around us, even though we don't have magnifying glasses or hammers and nails. So it's happening every day.

Teacher: Exactly. And it doesn't have to be given a name.

Teacher B: No, but you have to have practical experiences. More so now because our intent one of our intents … is actually to delve deeper into – and to go deeper into children's thinking and out of that, comes a lot of understandings and, and views which, which might not have been. But Pat was saying in terms of – your intent and directing, you know, making it more visible and so, you know, to encourage that thinking and I know you're using the word direction but actually, you know, to focus on those questions that might bring out …

Teacher: Provocations.

Pedagogista: Yeah that's right. So it is definitely also in the way that we question or present provocations that keeps it broad as opposed to limited.

Teacher C: Sometimes it's hard to keep it real science because the science around is sometimes not – children friendly. If it's like the light bulbs so you do have to be very careful. Or the electricity– if it's the wires, glass so it is harder to bring the real science in that you – sorry – the science that you do call – we just say everything is science and it's also harder to explain the science that is behind the defining science if it's the leaves, falling down it's harder to get the – it's not as exciting as electricity or light bulbs because the falling leaves you see them … it's interesting and it's changing and they see it – but it's harder to do, we work a lot with leaves actually.

Teacher B: Cooking, yes.

Teacher C: All the scientific stuff that has to go into, a little bit of cooking.

Teacher B: And they do it in the sand pit with the water and the sand and they have.

Teacher C: They cook at home with their parents too, possibly – so that's a connection.

Teacher B: But when I think of what we could bring that is more like if it's the wheels or different things that one thing turns the other or some to understand these concepts – it is – a bit hard, a bit harder to find those resources that will get them thinking about the concepts and them trying to, to trigger them to try and understand and figure a way.

Teacher C: Or even things like the hoop – being rolled along here to find a way of stopping the hoop without using your hands or your body. That's the break, they have to find something to stop it.

When the transcript of the interview with Danny's father about his son's interest in electricity is considered in relation to the transcript of the staff discussing science learning within the context of this interview, it is possible to see that the staff and the family held different perspectives on the nature of the science content that could be explored by such young children. The staff believed that it was important for children to examine everyday science that could be safely introduced, while the family drew upon a real everyday occurrence of a blown light bulb and an electrical black out. That is, the teachers valued safe and uncomplicated science ideas (studying leaves), while the families focused on 'real science' experiences in everyday life (blown light bulb). These science events in everyday life represented complicated and real science learning for the children. They invited shared participation in problem solving and promoted curiosity in the children. The families valued these opportunities for the children's learning of 'real and challenging science'. These values, in relation to the content of science, shape the social conditions for children's development and determine the concepts that are examined by the children in the different settings. In this example, the school context framed learning for the investigation of leaves and at home children explored the real science of electricity in everyday life. Hedegaard (Chapter 2) argues that development is a process that integrates both a person's growing development of competencies with values. As such, a wholeness approach to research seeks to also document the value scale that both families and educators see as important. Both families and educators note what values and competencies are appropriated by children – informally but also formally through assessment. Hedegaard further argues that these value-laden competencies and motives are connected to what a society views as a 'good life'. Different institutions are likely to have various values and traditions and will seek to evaluate these differently, as noted when the family interview is considered alongside the staff interview. Where these values and traditions are complementary, there is no disjunction for children and their development is supported across institutions. However, for some children and families, the values and traditions are oppositional and this constitutes a conflict in what may be valued and measured across institutions. For example, Hedegaard (2005), in researching children from migrant families in Denmark, noted that what the Danish education institution believed to represent success in school and what the migrant children valued within their families and their home countries were different concepts. As such, the competencies the young migrant youth had acquired in their home countries were not valued in their new country and, as such, the youth were positioned in deficit. Researching the conditions of everyday life – whether conflictual or not – provides valuable information and gives insights into the cultural–historical traditions of institutions and the conditions they generate for children's learning.

A wholeness approach seeks to capture the perspectives of all the participants, and through this explore how institutions shape the social situation of development for children. In the case example used in this chapter, further interviewing was needed to fully understand the institutional perspective of the City Early Learning Centre. More was understood about the selection of science 'content' for scientific learning, but I still did not understand the motives of the teachers in relation to the pedagogical practices of repeated and detailed study of leaves for such young children. In the final interview, after 12 months of gathering video protocols and teacher and family interviews, the teachers were able to explicitly explore the values, goals and motives of the City Early Learning Centre.

Values, goals and motives of the City Early Learning Centre

In this section, the perspectives of the Pedagogista, the Centre Director, the teachers and the children are noted. A wholeness approach promotes the idea of the researchers and the participants of the research as communication partners. In this final session, I established this dialogue by stating: 'Today we thought that, as a way of making sure that we've understood exactly your beliefs, your practices, what you think is important and so on, we would talk about a series of six areas.' I framed the discussion so that the staff could focus their responses on the institutional characteristics of the City Early Learning Centre. In particular, I mentioned:

> One of the things that we noticed about your pedagogical practices and your philosophy and the theory – it's so rich, that you've used words like problem solving, collaboration, hypothesis, revisiting over time, thinking, etc., lots of really beautiful words – and so we really wanted to know if you could just give us a summary, individually and collectively, about your thinking, not necessarily about those words, although obviously you'll pick up on those, but around your pedagogical practices and your philosophical beliefs and then, then to talk, about where does that come from, what's guided you with your thinking in relation to some of those things, and are there things there that are specific to the City Early Learning Centre; you know, this is what the centre stands for and that parents and the community know it to be like this, or there are some aspects that are more individual and that you bring to this environment.

I was making clear that I wanted to know more about how the motives, goals and assumptions of the teachers shaped the social situation of development for the children in this particular institution. I wanted to know the traditions for learning – that were historically and culturally located within the institution – that shaped the current pedagogical practices of the teachers. Through this introduction, I was able to actively explore the cultural nature of pedagogy as located within the values, goal and motives of the institution. The focus of the research attention was on the dialectical relations between the Jewish practice of studying texts and pedagogical practice inspired by a philosophy of learning from the Italian region of Reggio Emilia. This philosophy for learning, as understood in the City Early Learning Centre, was focused on generating projects that were carefully documented by the teachers and used as a basis for further planning. Studying these documents is important in this institution because it follows some aspects of the practices within the Jewish tradition, as noted by the Pedagogista: 'If we talk about our culture as well, from a religious point of view, there's always been a lot of discussion, and a lot of … perhaps you've heard of the Talmud which is, you know, part of our, our heritage, where various aspects are written and there are sages and there are people that revisit certain situations and continue … it's not set in stone … whereas there might be some aspects it has always challenged and revisited, and so there might be scholars at this moment who are sitting and studying texts and looking at this in relation to what happens today.'

The teacher framed up her comments in relation to her teaching practice and with the documentation process (Reggio practice of detailing children's comments and practices in relation to a project): 'Well I guess from my perspective with the documentation – in some ways it's looking for a deeper understanding and a deeper meaning of what the children are doing, how they are perceiving something and when you've actually [focused on something], whether it's a photograph, a video or something written, or just, you know, something that you've observed.' The gradual shaping of the children's attention is evident when interpretations are made of the teacher–children interactions throughout the 12 months, as shown below:

Extract from video material

- We're going to do something a little bit different today (clip 2.2).
- Before we touch them though – I want us to just use our eyes. Because I want to find out what you can see. What do you see? (clip 2.3)
- Yours is down and Mathew's is down; let's see if Jacob can put his down in front of him. Can you put yours down too now? (Pause, looking at J.) Not yet. Because I've got something else for us to think about. And we can't really think when we're moving things around 'cause we get distracted (clip 2.7).

Through the intervention of showing video clips of the family practices, and reading through extracts of staff transcripts of interviews, the Centre Director and the Pedagogista discussed the close study of the children, as enactments of what is valued pedagogical practice and valued cultural practice within the Jewish community. It is only after this further intervention that I could begin to understand the perspectives of the institution, and hence make sense of the practice observed in the City Early Learning Centre. The observations made of 'studying the leaves' (and exemplified above in the extract from the video material) and discussed earlier in this chapter can now be understood as a pedagogy of 'close study'. It can now be understood as the teacher helping the children's close study of materials, exemplifying the valued pedagogy practice that the Jewish school enacts.

As a result of the additional interviews it was possible for me to begin to better understand the practices inherent in the institutions – practices that were historically located, but enacted in the present educational context. Below is an example of how I made the interpretations through contrasting the different perspectives of the children, the teachers and the families.

Interpretation example

The interpretation that was possible showed that:

Teacher's perspective. The teacher frames the learning experience so that the children closely study the leaves, in much the same way as the teachers and Centre Director study the works of scholars. The teacher actively invites the children to not only look with their eyes and to discuss what they notice, but to listen to each others' contributions. For example, when one of the children suggests that they draw, the teacher skilfully uses this opportunity to further the children's study of the leaves.

Although the teacher is respectful of the children's motives and goals, she nevertheless makes her intentions clear to the children. The depth of the intended study of the leaves, where the teachers discuss the importance of going 'deeper' and 'deeper' in their study, is very important in this centre. This approach to studying the materials is explained in terms of the cultural practices of studying the texts, and the value placed on education: 'I've noticed here, that it's a very, deep thing that the education of, you know, the children, is very important' (Teacher).

The Centre Director's perspective. The Director explains that due to both the persecution and the subsequent high mobility of the Jewish community, education is viewed as the one thing that 'can be taken with you and never lost'. 'And I think that that really extends from … from Jewish life over time … I mean, the one thing … I mean Jews … have been dispersed all over the world over and over again … the one thing they've ever been able to take with them is education.'

The societal values are imbued within the education system of the City Early Learning Centre. As Hedegaard (Chapter 2) states, these values, motives and goals represent the good life for the participants of this particular community. A good life is exemplified through the active celebration with children of what is valued; for example, the Centre Director explains:

'And so they've always, you know, that's been a very important part. We've got a festival coming up this week, and the festival really talks about how the Jews under the Romans were refused to … they were not allowed to study, and so they use to go into the … up into the mountains, into the caves with their bows and arrows pretending that they were going to hunt for animals but actually they would have their candles and they would be studying, so it's always been something and it's always been there. So it's lovely that you said that [teacher], 'cause that's how it is really.'

In this example we see that Historicity can be studied in motion within present-day institutional practices.

The wholeness approach goes beyond a rich or thick description of local events or as an audit trail from action to new knowledge across a large number of participants. Rather, a wholeness approach is focused on studying dynamic practice across social situations. The tables and transcripts have shown the significance of gaining perspectives from a broad range of participants for some connected understanding of the social situation of development for children to be understood in the City Early Learning Centre.

The focus of attention for researchers is on generating sufficient dialogue to understand differing perspectives and to gather broadly based protocols across different contexts (institutions) in order to have confidence in the conceptualisations made in relation to how the child's participation changes and how the child develops as a participant in a new activity. The finding that the recording and studying of children's activity as documentation is synonymous with the Jewish Talmudic exegetical commentary, is noted by the Centre Director:

> I remember when we were ... we were once looking at documentation, and we had a woman who was here from Israel and she ... her father's a Rabbi ... and she really studied the text and she said, it's exactly like looking at the text, you know, you would have the written piece in the middle and then, the next, the next round of people would've had their discussion that would follow all around it and then, the layers were just very rich and very deep and it ... and so it ... really, Helen's right, it fits so well into the work that we do here.

The study design was comfortable and familiar to the participants – I had introduced participants to research 'texts' and theoretical 'texts' for study. As a result, my goals, motives and values for research were consistent with the goals, values and motives of the teachers for furthering their own knowledge about their own practice. The wholeness approach allowed me not only to study the socially different settings for development within the City Early Learning Centre institution, but to note the similarities in perspective for researching pedagogical practices. Although, my analytical framework was more broadly based (as has been discussed here and in Chapters 2 to 4), there was sufficient shared intention in this study design to allow for greater validity to the interpretations made.

Conclusion

Through bringing together the differing perspectives of the researcher and the staff (in the context of the institutions), it is much easier to embrace the concept of the child not just as an individual, but as a member of a collective across settings. A wholeness approach positions researchers as organising protocols that go beyond the individual and into the settings in which the individual resides. The child's interactions, as noted through the investigations of children, occur within different social settings. In preschools, the educational programmes direct the children's attention and subsequent intentions towards the institutional motives, values and goals of the specific institution. Similarly, the family institution also directs children's intentions though the specific child-rearing practices and conditions towards the motives, values and goals of the family. The research methodology must capture the institutional motives, goals and values if the dynamic interactions of children within educational institutions and family institutions are to be understood. These must be understood as moving and dynamic. A wholeness approach seeks to capture all perspectives so that development can be conceptualised beyond something occurring within a child's head or body and move towards a dialectical relation between the child and his or her social situation across time and institutions.

7 Using digital video observations and computer technologies in a cultural–historical approach

Marilyn Fleer

Introduction

In the previous six chapters, the theory and practice of undertaking research from a cultural–historical perspective was presented. The activities of the researchers were exemplified through a series of examples. In this chapter, the relations between cultural–historical theory, methodology and methods will be detailed through a discussion of how digital video observations can be gathered, organised and analysed by the use of computer technology. The case examples given in Chapters 5 and 6 will be further elaborated in this chapter in order to discuss the theoretical and methodological ideas in relation to the method of gathering and interpreting digital video observations.

Research using digital video and computer technologies provides a useful framework for a dialectical–interactive research approach. Through video recordings of everyday practices and activities it is possible to document visually the practice traditions and the transitions and conflicts between institutions. These different perspectives can not only be easily recorded by a digital video camera, but the results can also be used as material (e.g. video clips) to share with participants, for gaining deeper insights, such as when discussing 'conflicts' or 'transitions'.

In Chapter 6, a series of interactions between a group of children and their teachers were given alongside the problem of how to understand the goals, motives and practices of the institutional setting. Because the aim of cultural–historical research is to study children in everyday settings in their social situation, it is important to examine the different perspectives of the participants being observed. Digital video observations make it possible to look at these different perspectives visually as video clips and to discuss these observations with participants either informally or more formally with interview questions. In Chapter 6, the teaching staff in the City Early Learning Centre were shown a video clip of the focus child's father being interviewed about family science practices. The researchers used the video clip to begin a dialogue with teachers about their teaching practices in relation to the motives and goals of the children as discussed by the father in the video clip and their values and traditions within the centre for fostering learning. This example will be discussed further in this chapter in relation to the digital video method used.

Documenting a child's perspective alongside the different institutional perspectives, such as family practices or preschool practices, can be facilitated through digital video recording. How researchers can capitalise upon this technology for not only recording observations but also for undertaking interpretations following a cultural–historical tradition is the focus of this chapter.

Generating digital video observations

In this section, I will discuss some practical and methodological considerations when using digital video technology for supporting a dialectical–interactive research approach for recording the social situation of children's development. I will draw upon the research project discussed in Chapters 5 and 6, which sought to examine the everyday science practices of children across institutions (e.g. home, school, preschool) in order to study the conditions for development from the perspectives of the child. This case example is given in order to exemplify the theoretical and methodological considerations for using digital video observations. In particular, this section will feature how the theoretical ideas of a cultural–historical tradition shape the way a video camera is used for making observations, why research teams must know about the research problem and the theoretical approach and how to use video clips as a valuable source of material for generating interviews.

Theoretically driven digital video recording

Where do you point the camera?

One of the main challenges facing researchers of any persuasion is the potential multiplicity of data sources and the sheer quantity of material that may be generated. Videotaping is no exception. Miles and Huberman (1994, pp. 55–56) suggest that 'All of this information piles up geometrically. Worse still, in the early stages of a study, most of it looks promising. If you don't know what matters more, everything matters.' Researchers following a cultural–historical tradition for studying children's development do not seek to capture everything they see through digital video technology. Rather, they aim to record the dynamic and evolving nature of the social situations in which children are located across institutions (family, community groups, and preschool) with a special focus on the child's perspective within those institutions. In contrast, sociological research approaches tend to focus on social contexts, documenting the social interactions of all the participants, while traditional psychological research generally examines the individual person. The theoretical and research tradition that a researcher holds matters when it comes to where the researcher points the digital video camera. If the researcher is interested in the social interactions of people, then the video camera will be positioned to capture how people are interacting within social situations – as would occur in sociological research. If the researcher is interested in 'the individual', then the video camera would zoom in on the individual and would pay less attention to the social interactions that the individual could potentially have. The camera operator might even stop videotaping if a social interaction occurs, as this could be considered as an 'interruption' and not of importance to the researcher. Conflicts between participants, including the researcher, would be excluded and not coded (i.e. deemed 'non-codable'). In contrast, a cultural–historical view of research would seek to document and examine these conflicts as important possibilities for development. The video camera would continue to record at these times and be positioned to gain maximum image and sound of the conflictual event.

A cultural–historical approach examines the person in relation to the conditions and possibilities for development found within the institutions in which a particular person participates, such as family, school, clubs, etc. In Chapter 2, a model (Figure 2.1) for children's learning and development through participation in institutional practice was shown. What is important here for cultural–historical research using digital video technology, is capturing the dynamics of a child's participation in several institutional settings and recording what possibilities this holds for the child's development. With this theoretical conception of children's development in mind (see Chapter 2 for further details), cultural–historical researchers using digital video technology seek to document the different institutional practices and the children's activities within those institutions. *As such, the researcher points the video camera at the children as they participate in everyday practices, including their relations with others.* The camera operator pays special attention to the children's activities within those institutional practices. In Chapter 1, an example of Louise's 'standing up and sitting down' game was given to illustrate how a 16-month-old child can be participating in the teaching practice of story reading at whole group time, while simultaneously generating a fun activity of her own. The motive for 'teasing the teacher' when she was no longer interested in the story was something the researchers were able to capture on video.

The video observations should also be able to show qualitative changes in a child's motives and competencies in relation to her social situation, particularly as she moves from one institution to another. Here the demands put on the child and the conflicts that may occur between the motives of the child and values and goals of the institution become an important source of observational material for documenting children's development. The study discussed in Chapters 5 and 6 sought to find out how children's concept formation in science takes place. I wanted to focus on children videotaped in each preschool engaged in the practices available, such as when the child was at play inside and outside the centre, while involved in group time, and during teacher-organised lessons. I was particularly interested in looking for opportunities in which the children's interests, goals and motives in relation to their activities and the science teaching practices could be videotaped.

The study also sought to find out children's everyday conceptions in science both at home and in the community, and to see how teachers used these understandings in their teaching programmes. Because the study focused on the child's activities in relation to the family and preschool practices, it was important to gain insights into the perspectives of the child, the teachers and the families across these institutions. The study used digital video cameras for capturing the science-related practices within both the families and the preschools, at the same time as recording the activities of the children in the preschool centre. To facilitate the electronic recording of family practices, I gave the families disposable cameras and a digital video camera and invited them to videotape or photograph the everyday practices at home that they thought supported science learning. The family material was used for interviewing the families, and as material for discussions with staff in relation to science-learning practices in both the home and in the preschools. This expansive approach to digital video generation, means that cultural–historical researchers can have digital video recordings across many different institutions and the material can be used in many different ways.

Working in research teams?

Video observations need not only be undertaken by the family, but can also be carried out by professionals employed to support the research process. For instance, Abbott and Langston (2005, 42) stated that 'the positive outcomes of having a professional film crew at our disposal should not be underestimated. Their presence meant, firstly, that we were free to truly observe, whereas had we undertaken our own filming we too could have been "stuck" behind the camera lens, blind to anything occurring beyond its narrow confines.' Having additional cameras in the research site in order to capture a number of children's perspectives is possible when more than one camera is used. Researchers can employ an assistant to accompany them on field trips, with the express view of following those children who move outside of the range of the main camera – such as when one of a number of children being observed moves into another room or goes outside. Abbott and Langston (2005) suggest that 'having a number of cameras gave a much broader scope to film multiple events, and offered other perspectives on the same event, which, in turn, provided a vast amount of data' (p. 42). A cultural–historical approach to research goes beyond simply offering 'other perspectives on the same event' because it seeks to explicitly capture the child's perspective in relation to the goals, motives and practices within and across institutions. Digital video cameras allow researchers to follow children, documenting their competencies, the demands placed upon them and those occasions when conflicts arise between the child and the caregivers or teachers.

Video recording the practices and activities in which children participate in their everyday lives might appear to be an easy option – because the researcher simply points the camera and shoots the child's activity in the everyday practice. However, there are many aspects of video technology that must be considered when making an informed choice about how to frame and organise the digital camera for recording observations. Abbott and Langston (2005, p. 41) also discuss this problem:

> We thought that the introduction of the camera crew would allow us to use our time to observe at a distance, discuss with the film director what we wanted to capture and talk to parents and staff about the children and their activities, giving us several perspectives on the same event. This did not happen. In reality, these factors amalgamated to conspire against us and we found ourselves trying to influence what was to be filmed via a film director with very different views about what the focus of the film should be. Our agreement to specify which aspects of practice and children's experiences in day care we hoped to find led our director to begin to plan ahead, requesting events like nappy [or diaper] changing to take place at a given time in a particular place, rather than waiting for its natural occurrence during the course of the day.

When Abbott and Langston (2005) were assigned a camera crew who had different goals and motives to those of the researchers, they found that they were having to conduct their research through this 'third party'. This can also be a problem for cultural–historical researchers who work with teams of researchers recording digital video observations. The principal researcher must work through 'a third party'. Although the problems mentioned by Abbott and Langston (2005) are important generally about following the natural course of the day of the participants, in a cultural–historical approach where researching the everyday lives of children is important, the research team must have the same theoretical lenses as the principal researcher. Their goals and motives must be aligned. In the study reported in Chapters 5 and 6, I discussed with the observer and with the teachers the theoretical approach and asked the observer to photograph and videotape the focus children in the centre when they were participating in science-related practices organised by the teacher or self-organised activities by the child(ren). Both the theoretical perspective of the researcher and the research question of the study, had to be discussed with the whole research team to ensure that the video cameras made observations following a cultural–historical tradition and were focused on events related to the research question. This is different to some psychological studies where the research assistant is blind to the research question and is given an interview script and a static research site to videotape, such as a table and three chairs where participants are directed to sit and with no knowledge of the problem area being investigated.

Capturing and maintaining complexity when generating digital video observations

Mapping

Penn (2005, p. 20) has argued then when 'an event is complex to understand then more time and more care are needed to investigate it thoroughly and unravel what is happening'. This is also true for cultural–historical research. The researcher enters the research site knowing that the dynamics of each institutional setting need to be mapped and understood if the conditions for development can be observed and interpreted. In particular, the researchers need to build a map of what they are noticing and how the differing perspectives are related to one another. The theory guides the researcher with this mapping process, because it acts as a frame for the 'descriptions of the practices and activities' being observed. The theory helps the researcher to work systematically in these very complex study designs.

Repeated viewing of video clips

Through the repeated viewing of the videotapes Graue and Walsh (1998, p. 149) have noted how microanalysis is possible:

Being able to view the interactions repeatedly and at times to review them frame by frame was invaluable for doing microanalysis of children's interactions. Unlike adults, whose language abilities are well developed, children's interactions are marked by nonverbal signs and body language. For example, spatial distance often is an important clue for understanding children's peer relationships. Having a video record also allowed me to ask the children to view their interactions and to comment on them.

Building on the arguments put forward by Graue and Walsh, a cultural–historical perspective would suggest that these repeated viewings of videotapes allows researchers to notice both the teaching practice and the child's activity. Video observations are particularly useful to cultural–historical researchers, who seek to examine the dialectical relations between participants, the social setting and the institutional practices and who need to revisit their material many times in order to make interpretations from a range of perspectives in order to understand the child's social situation for development.

In Chapter 5, an example of Molly 'cooking meat' within the practice tradition of science teaching in preschools was given to illustrate the child's motives and goals during play. Molly's activity is centred on something completely different to the intended teaching practice of science organised by the teacher. It was possible to notice this on repeated viewings and analysis of the video clips.

Using video clips of practices for interviewing participants

Graue and Walsh (1998, p. 150) state that the video camera 'has a limited view range. With peripheral vision, the human eye can see 180 degrees or more. The camcorder can see only a piece of that.' In cultural–historical research, this limitation is also noted. Miles and Huberman (1994, p. 56) provide some inspiration for dealing with this problem:

> The challenge is to be explicitly mindful of the purposes of your study and of the conceptual lens you are training on it – while allowing yourself to be open to and be re-educated by the things you didn't know about or expect to find.

In a cultural–historically framed study, the researcher pays very close attention to capturing the perspectives of the child, and because the researchers use digital video and computer technologies they can re-introduce observational material to children, staff and families in order to actively solicit the perspectives of all participants, including the child, so that the social conditions and demands placed upon the child can be gained. Researchers can specifically enter into a dialogue with participants in relation to the purpose of their study. As shown in Chapters 5 and 6, I wanted to know more about the children's everyday science concepts generated at home, teaching practices in science in the preschool and how children developed scientific concepts. Interviews with staff and families in relation to the video observations became important concrete material that would allow for further understandings of the problem area being explored. The staff were shown examples of the photographs (and interviews with both children and families) or video clips of observations made by the researcher and/or the observer, and these were used to invite the teachers to discuss their teaching practices in the preschools. The cultural–historical model outlined by Hedegaard in Chapter 3 was used to guide the research team on the types of question they should ask families and staff (further discussions for using cultural–historical approach to interviewing is detailed in Chapter 8). These interviews were either audiotaped or videotaped. In this way, digital video observations allow for additional material to be gathered in order to compensate for the limitations of only working within a 180-degree frame. In the next section, a range of examples are given which illustrate how the original digital video clips can be used expansively for interviews and follow-up observations.

Interpretations of digital video observations

The first part of this section presents a discussion of how the original digital video observations can be used iteratively for generating further digital materials, such as interviews. How to make interpretations of the digital video material introduced in Chapter 6 is outlined in the second part of the section.

Logging digital video tapes

To be able to use and revisit video observations effectively, it is important that researchers document or log their videotapes. In the science projects discussed in Chapters 5 and 6, I specifically downloaded all the tapes on to an external hard drive and labelled each file (as one tape) with the same name as the videotape – to ensure that I could easily work across both platforms as required (for example, if an electronic file became corrupted, I could download the tape again). The folders were then described in a logbook, so that I could easily move back and forth between files in relation to the content and what I was interested in examining. An example from the science research project at the City Early Learning Centre follows. Here we see that the family has identified a range of science practices that they believe are important for science learning, such as 'cooking' or 'discussing a power black out'. They are simply listed as names against the video clip.

Video clips – links to science project at the City Early Learning Centre

Site:	City Early Learning Centre and Danny's home
Context:	Family videotape: 'Danny'
Interview transcript:	Interview of Danny's family (document name)
Video log:	
Clip 01:	Dies and celery experiment
Clip 02:	Cooking – steam
Clip 03:	Voice – feeling vibrations
Clip 04:	Guitar – feeling vibrations
Clip 05:	Making kites
Clip 06:	Discussing power 'black out'

Logging can also occur electronically. The screen dump (Figure 7.1) shows how the researcher can open both the video digital file and a word document for logging. This figure also shows what the electronic interface is like for the researcher using digital video methods.

Figure 7.1 Screen dump of a video observation within an Imac project (Imovie).

Because these files are electronic, I could use the standard video software program that came with my computer (Imovie). I could easily move the video material forwards and backwards in relation to time segments that I had logged. Or I could jump quickly from one science family practice to another – such as looking at the video clip of 'making kites' and then looking at the video clip on 'power black out'. This is much faster than using a video camera and tapes because they need to be previewed in real time. The electronic files can be viewed easily and quickly – and a quick scan is possible within a few minutes. The logging of the electronic folders of the video clips is important because with this approach there is no need to make written observations.

Conceptual framework for making interpretations

Importantly, Flick (2002, p. 30) has stated that:

> If qualitative research relies on understanding social realities through the interpretation of texts, two questions become especially relevant: what happens in the translation of reality into text, and what happens in the retranslation of texts into reality or in inferring from texts to realities?

Flick has provided some inspiration for dealing with this problem.

It is possible to see that researchers following a cultural–historical tradition dialectically build video images of 'reality' and from those video images generate interpretations about the motives, goals and values of the participants within the practice traditions of different institutions. These interpretations must speak back to reality, but give new insights about both practice and activity. Figure 7.2 shows the relations between practices, activities, video recordings and interpretations.

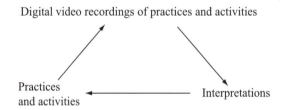

Figure 7.2 The relations between practices and activities, video recordings and interpretations.

Many researchers new to digital video analysis underestimate the complexity of managing and reducing the material they have generated. As suggested by Miles and Huberman (1994) and further elaborated in Chapter 4, summaries and interpretations are based upon the research questions and the conceptual framework being used by the researchers. In a cultural–

historical tradition, the relations between perspectives needs to be fore-grounded and the organising and labelling of the video observations allow one to follow the interplay between practice and activity and between the participants motives and values in their activities and transitions between practices and between activities.

For the science research project, I began my interpretations by record-ing the activities of the participants as video clips. I then transcribed video observations that were of interest in relation to the research question. Working electronically meant that I could generate an overview of the material and keep it intact.

A significant advantage of video observations is that researchers can rearrange their observations and interpretations as themes evolve. For exam-ple, when the content theme of 'electricity' for Danny and some of the other children in the science project at the City Early Learning Centre emerged, as something that was highly valued by the child (see Chapter 6), the research-ers could return to the video observations and closely examine how, when, and over what period of time 'electricity' was featured within the science teaching practices in the preschool and pedagogy in the home. For example, in the science project we knew from the family interview that 'electricity was important for Danny'. When we coded all science play, and science lessons, we also looked specifically at the 'content' of the *lessons* and *play activities* for 'electricity' examples. One example is given in the category of the institu-tional performance and this is linked to the transcript shown in Chapter 6. To complement the digital video observations, I also transcribed the content of each of the named video clips that were of interest and which had been coded (see Table 5.3 for full details of categories used).

Categories

Motives:

- Everyday concepts or scientific concepts being played out by the children.
  (*Clip: Footy calling and playing with electrical switch and microphone.*)
  Children are playing football outside in the City Early Learning Centre playground. They then sit near a tree and direct their attention to turning on an imaginary microphone in order to 'call the football game'.
- Motives of children in relation to science during play.

Motives of the staff:

- Pedagogical practices that afforded the connections between every-day concepts and scientific concepts.

- Scientific concepts being introduced by the staff during play or formal group times.

Coding example: Helen

I think it's interesting listening to the parents' reflections and for us the connection between play and science. And I know that [staff member] brought this up about, do the children know what science is; do they know the word science and the definition of science? And it's interesting that when the father was asked about play, not about science, and the relationship between what happens in the kinder-garten and what happens at home and he said I don't really know. He was not necessarily thinking about the learning of play but rather thinking about play as a social relations, and so I think there's still an area where the link between play and science, but other experiences, not necessarily taking science in isolation of other experiences, that we know have happened through play.

This process of coding and linking transcriptions to the coding sheet continued until all the video clips had been examined for this 'content theme of electricity'. Taken together, the video clips and the transcription provided the researcher with an overview for each observation that was coded. In order to gain further insights into the importance of this particular area of content, the video clip of the interview with the father was shown to the staff in the school. The staff were able to comment on this, and their comments were coded.

Conflicts and transitions

In this science project I was interested in the different practice traditions and the conditions these create for children's development. Conflicts and transitions were important for the researchers to notice as they often point to developmental opportunities. As Hedegaard has argued in Chapter 2, conflicts can be found in a child's social situation as a result of the different values that are connected to practice in different institutions (e.g. family, school), which in turn can generate *crises*. For example, in Chapter 6, we can see, conflicts between a child's motives and the dominating motives in an institution. For the science research project, conflicts were understood from several perspectives in relation to the science practice – from a societal, institutional and child perspective. The methodological implications as discussed by Hedegaard in Chapters 2 to 4 include:

- The children's social situation and the child's motives and relations to other people.

- Including activities in which the child participates and the demands and oppositions they meet in relation to these activities.
- Whether or not the activities in one setting could be recognised in another setting.

In order to answer these types of questions, researchers following a cultural–historical tradition need to note in their interpretations the activity of the children and the practices of the institutions. For example, in the log and summary detailed previously, both the practices and the activities can be noted and coded. When we begin to code activities across settings, we can determine if an activity or practice in one setting can be recognised in another setting (Table 7.1).

Table 7.1 Coding different perspectives

The children's perspective (Activity)	Family perspective (Practice)	Teacher's perspective (Practice)
Calling the footy and playing with electrical switch and microphone during free play time in the preschool.	Talking about electricity in the context of a power 'black out'.	Science lessons should focus on studying leaves because studying electricity is difficult in preschool.

Conclusion

Penn (2005, 20) has suggested that 'We cannot invent "facts" but we can certainly report them wrongly, or interpret them wrongly.' What is important for cultural–historical research is the close link between theory, methodology and method. Research that is dynamic and seeks to examine the perspectives of the participants as they enter into everyday practice across institutions, requires a method that will allow researchers to capture the wholeness of the children's social situation and where the relations between practice and activity can be foregrounded. Digital video observations and their associated computer technologies, allow researchers to not only focus on both the child and the complexity associated with the different perspectives across institutions, but also to make interpretations in an iterative way – as was highlighted in this chapter through the case example of 'Danny's interest in electricity'. The theoretical approach discussed in Chapter 2 to 4 helps to frame researcher practice in ways that focus their attention on both conflicts and transitions as opportunities for children's development. Specifically making interpretations of these either as categories or as themes, means that researchers gain insights into the conditions that potentially support opportunities for children's development (see Chapter 2). Researchers interested in the daily life of children in everyday practices need a theory, a methodology and a method that will allow for a wholeness perspective to emerge. Digital video observations and computer technology methods can be used for realising this interactive approach to research.

8 Conceptualising the environment of the child in a cultural–historical approach

Jytte Bang

Observational protocols offer concrete descriptions of children's specific patterns of participation in specific institutional settings. A researcher who studies children's play in preschool activities may spend a lot of time observing and collecting data. But what can a researcher learn about child *development* when the data collected reveal activities and activity patterns within time- and space-limited situations (like among a specific group of children in a specific kindergarten over a few weeks)? The researcher may build her study on the assumption that preschoolers develop through their shared play activities. She may imagine that the group of children are playing with dolls in a quiet corner in the kindergarten and having experiences and feelings that are important in relation to how they develop. But can development be studied *directly* by examining the data collected in an activity setting or should the (any) researcher accept that there is a gap between micro- and ontogenesis and that development, therefore, can be studied only in retrospect? In this chapter, it will be argued that potentials for developmental novelty are embedded in the activity setting and that those potentials might be studied directly when interpreting the data. Studying potentials for development in an activity setting means studying forwards rather than in retrospect. This implies that what the researcher studies is in progress. This approach is greatly unsettling for researchers but this perspective may throw light on how it is to be a child participating in the process of *becoming*. The particular activities are historically and culturally embedded. They are part of an ongoing flow of life that transcends particular pockets of time and space. Experienced meaningfulness is what connects the immediate activity with the flow of life for the child; it provides the 'who am I?' and 'who am I becoming?' questions with certain contours and possible pathways. The researcher needs to make observations of the child in different activity settings over a span of time. In the study, the researcher should also be aware of conflicts and crises of developmental importance to the child (see Chapter 2 in this book).

The aim of this chapter is to present an interpretive method by which the researcher might get a closer look at emerging novelties in an activity setting. Specifically, we should examine how the researcher proceeds from the transcriptions of protocols based on observational studies to analysis and interpretation of the developmental novelty of a child.

In this chapter, the relation between potentials for development embedded in the activity setting and the developmental movements going on over a longer span of time is thought of as the 'relation between *small* and *great* novelty'. The local and specific patterns of activities may add to the overall development of the child and make possible certain (rather than other) directions. We have great novelty when particular developmental pathways seem to occur; and when general capabilities emerge which allow the child to expand her activities, interact in new ways and/or with new people; and when the child begins to experience herself and her life in new ways.

Great novelty, hence, is novelty on an ontogenetic level. Small novelty, by the same token, refers to the ongoing flow of everyday activities in the activity settings into which the child takes part. The child contributes to the ongoing flow of everyday activities. In this process, she appropriates and adds to cultural practice. The child may find new ways of viewing things or of appropriating new environmental properties and things (artefacts). She may find her way in surroundings which are not so well known. She may develop new actions, relate to new people or to well-known people in new ways. She may experience herself as a participant in new ways, etc. The list of small novelty, of course, is endless and it assumes that great novelty rests on the developing patterns of small novelty which the child displays in her activities across different settings in her ongoing life.

An environmental affordance perspective

One of the basic assumptions in this book is that the researcher should always be aware of acknowledging the child as a whole person. A wholeness perspective on child development implies a wholeness perspective on the activity setting studied. Participation within a practice means that a child is being active and adds to certain environmental and social conditions which are historically shaped and continue in ongoing practice. As a consequence, viewing an activity setting from a wholeness perspective means that the concept of *environment* and what we mean by that is being put into focus.

School, for instance, is a societal institution with a specific history and this history *surrounds* the child in the form of things (artefacts) with specific properties; so do the classmates and the teachers, etc., present in school. I shall argue that it makes sense to also say that the child is part of her own environment; she experiences herself as being 'someone' – a participant among other significant participants. The notion of environment presented here views environment as the dynamic unit of *things, social others* and *self*.

I shall draw upon James Gibson's (1966) concept of *affordance* in order to better show how specific environments may stimulate a child and be the basis for potential novelties. The concept of 'affordance' stresses an awareness of the functional significant properties of the environment in relation to an individual (Heft, 1988). The environmental affordance perspective suggested in the present article also finds inspiration in the integration of Gibson's work with that of Roger Barker and Herbert Wright (1966, 1971) as suggested by Heft (1988). In all, an environmental affordance perspective adds to the cultural–historical perspective outlined in the book in that (a) the physical properties and their organization and (b) the affordances of individuals is being highlighted and included into the interpretation of the activity setting.

In this chapter, the unit of analysis shall be constituted through the interpretive method of things, social others, and self. I shall present the method by analysing Louise, a 10-year-old girl, participating in a maths lesson.

Louise in the maths lesson

I shall now present an analysis which shows how developmental potentialities of child–environment reciprocity might be studied. I shall do so by analysing an example from a study where children are observed and followed across different institutional activities in their everyday life. The analysis of child–environment reciprocity is based on an observation of a girl – Louise – who participates in a math lesson in a Danish elementary school. Louise is a 10-year-old girl and a fourth grader who lives with her family close to Copenhagen.

The observed activities are presented in the left column of the scheme. In the right column are listed the researcher's immediately experienced units of intentions in the data which mark the first of the interpretive steps. I will name it the *intention unit*. The intention unit is the perceived (assumed) intention of the individual (whether reflective or not) embedded in the activity. From a dialectical–interactive perspective presented in Chapter 3, the researcher is no neutral 'fly on the wall'. The researcher's intentions and motivations are part of the research process. Of course, this also holds true for the interpretive steps including the perceived intention units. Being present as an observer means perceiving the intentions of others and not just their behaviour. Even though the subjectivity of the researcher offers space for pointing out a variety of intention units, it also provides a solid base for perceiving the wholeness of the activities rather than just fragmented or formalised elements. The suggested intention units listed in relation to the present observation are not exhaustive, of course. I have listed only some of those units that seem to present Louise as an agent in the specific activity setting. However, whatever is going on in the classroom has an impact on the developmental potentialities embedded in the setting.

I shall interpret the activity setting by help of the concept of affordance with respect to 'things' (the physical environmental properties), 'social others' (the social environmental properties), and 'self' (the child being her own environmental properties). The presentation is an example of how the researcher might make the step from the observational protocol to interpretation of data while keeping in focus the wholeness of the child (Louise) as a person actively engaging in a setting (the math lesson) by relating to culturally reified artefacts (books, etc.), to social others (classmates; teacher), and to herself. There are four steps in the interpretation: During the three steps, I shall examine the affordance of things, social others, and self. On the fourth step, I shall integrate those three perspectives into an integrated wholeness perspective on the interpretive move from small to great novelty.

The maths lesson

Louise is one of several students doing maths with her teacher. The observer writes down Louise's activities as part of the wholeness of the situation. In this way, the protocol expresses the observer's attempt to follow Louise's perspective while following the class activities as a whole. In the beginning of the lesson, the teacher is communicating with some boys about their behaviour. After a little while the work begins. The teacher wants to test how well the students can do their multiplication tables. This will fully occupy the teacher's time because the individual students will come to his desk. Therefore he organises the class to work independently with their maths calculations when not being tested. In the observation, the focus is on what Louise is doing it this situation; she tends to spend a lot of time communicating with classmates while also keeping up with her individual work.

Transcription of the maths lesson	Common sense interpretation with the focus on intention units
1 Louise sits very still and does not say much.	Louise collaborates smoothly in relation to expectations set up.
2 They are asked to pick up their books which everyone does. Louise picks up her book as well as her folder. She starts writing a little in the folder.	
3 Louise goes on making her calculations as one of a very few students in the class while the teacher counts the students. She talks quietly with the classmate next to her as they focus on the arithmetic problems.	Louise talks and focuses.
4 Louise talks with the classmate next to her as she points at something in the book.	
5 The teacher wants everyone in the class to work individually with some tasks about coordinate systems and then he asks each of them to come to his desk and show him one by one that they do master the tables. Today it is the girls' turn to come up to him. Louise is the first one to be called forth by the teacher and she is going to do the 5, 6, and 7 multiplication tables which she does most satisfactory. The teacher is very pleased; he tells her to return to her seat and asks Karina to come up. Louise goes to her seat and energetically resumes her work.	She collaborates and manages multiple agendas simultaneously. She presents herself to the teacher as a good student and seems to gain new energy.

Transcription of the maths lesson	Common sense interpretation with the focus on intention units
6 Again the classmate next to Louise asks about something and Louise responds as she continues to focus on the book. She sits and concentrates on her books. Louise goes to the bin next to me and empties her pencil sharpener. I (the observer) ask her if it went well with the tables and she says that it did.	She helps while focusing on her own work.
7 Nick, who sits opposite to Louise, asks her about an arithmetic problem and she explains how she figured it out. He accepts this and starts doing it himself. After a little while he asks who I (the observer) am. Louise answers that this is Kasper, who is a researcher. I smile at both of them.	She helps and collaborates and receives help.
8 Apparently, Louise is unable to solve an arithmetic problem. Nick, who sits next to her, and Louise talk about it. Louise gets a little annoyed because she is unable to solve the problem immediately. They do not ask for help, though, but try to solve it themselves.	She wants to solve the problem, hence experiences and (e)valuates the frustrating conditions of learning.

Transcription of the maths lesson	**Common sense interpretation with the focus on intention units**
9 Louise looks briefly at the teacher who is about to hear how well Sandra, the girl next to her, is doing the multiplication tables. She is engaged in hearing how Sandra is managing the tables. Rita, who sits on the other side of the table, comes down to Louise and Sandra. They start talking about how the previously mentioned problem should be solved and Rita shows them how to do it. She goes back to her seat when they have finished looking at/solving the problem.	She is engaged in with others' performances. She collaborates and receives help.
10 Still Nick did not solve the problem and Louise gets his book so that she can solve it. She starts writing in Nick's book.	
11 The boy next to Nick asks Nick for help. Louise looks in his folder from the other side of the table and notices that he did make an error. Sandra and Louise are talking with each other in ways as if they want to keep it a secret what the boy next to Nick did wrong. The boy next to Nick gets a little annoyed but Nick helps him.	Louise and Sandra seems to keep the boy out.
12 Louise turns over the pages in the book and notices with great satisfaction that she only needs to do two pages more. She continues working with the math problems.	She continues to work as she experiences her own progression.

Transcription of the maths lesson	Common sense interpretation with the focus on intention units
13 Rita comes down to Louise again and they talk about a problem in the book. Sandra has her doubts about some problem and goes to ask the teacher for help. Rita helps Louise to draw some coordinates in the book. Louise says to Rita that it is still incorrect and she stands up with her books and goes to the teacher to ask for help. On her way she meets Louise and they are whispering together. Louise goes and stands in a line to talk to the teacher. When it is her turn, she asks him how to solve the problem. The teacher remarks humorously that she has scribbled in her book but she defends herself and says that she did not do it. The teacher tells her that she needs to find a connection between the other coordinate systems and the present problem. Louise goes down to her seat again.	She asks for help.
14 She sits down and right after she calls for Rita. She is about to lose her motivation but as she collaborates with Rita, she continues with her work.	Louise collaborates to keep up her motivation.

Interpretation of the maths situation – things, others and self

I shall now take the first three steps presented earlier in the chapter, which means that I shall focus on how to apply the environmental affordance perspective on things, social others, and self when turning the attention to Louise's participation in the activity setting of the math lesson.

Things

In the data from the maths lesson, things like books, folders, multiplication tables, chairs, tables, etc. are available to the children.[1] Everything mentioned are artefacts that afford certain activities of the children, like initiating action, picking up information, experiencing emotions, reflecting on values, etc. Heft (1988) argues that things in the surroundings of a child should be viewed from a functional perspective, that is from the perspective of which activities may be helped, initiated by the particular environmental properties. In my view, one might very well turn this view into a developmental point. Climbing a tree or a fence, for instance, may be an aim to the child who likes to play; but also it is a means for the child to learn in general about environmental properties, about climbing and about herself (climbing). Similarly, an artefact like a book is an aim to a child who enjoys the playfulness of reading; but also it is a means for learning to read. In fact, one can sort through each aspect of dealing with different artefacts. The particular thing in a particular setting reveals general cultural environmental properties and those general properties may help to initiate action. Reading, for instance, appears for most children in its general-ised form after a period of time of practising reading. The child comes to know about books (in general), reading (in general), herself (as a reader – in general). These *generals* already are potentially embedded in *particular* activities. The affordances listed on the right part of the scheme below are the affordance of things in Louise's particular activity setting. The things may help to initiate and sustain particular activities into which general developmental potentialities embedded.

Different objects in the classroom have different properties; therefore they may afford different activities which are all part of a culturally developed pattern of activities. The objects in the classroom contribute to the overall idea of what it means to 'go to school'. They are artefacts invented by humans, thus mediating culturally reified meaning (Leontjew, 1977) and they help organise and regulate the activities of the setting. They enable the child to participate in particular activities; at the same time they serve to frame the actions of the child. An incomplete list of things which belong to the maths lesson includes: books, folders, multiplication table, teacher's desk, tables, chairs. They are culturally invented artefacts supporting the classroom activities that are valued in the school.

From this affordance-based interpretation of available things in the classroom it follows that things in no way should be thought of as neutral environmental elements. Certain environmental things and properties in school afford and support specific activities and have a general functional significance to the classroom practices maintained by the participants. The functional significance of things are meaningful as part of the ongoing practice. They gain their functional significance as a means to maintain and organise that practice.

Children do not always experience the value of those artefacts in ways hoped for by the teacher. Some children even reject what things afford if the functional value they have to the child is a negative one; such as, if the child feels that she is forced into participating in activities that are experienced as meaningless or emotionally painful to her.

Things	*Afford*
Books	Looking into;
	Turning over the leaves;
	Reading;
	Searching information;
Folders	Writing into;
	Solving maths problems;
	Working individually;
Multiplication table	Rote learning;
	Mastering;
	Performing;
	Evaluating;
Teacher's desk	Seeking help;
	Being watched;
	Performing;
	Being evaluated;
	Being corrected;
Tables	Sitting at;
	Putting something onto;
	Working at;
	Leaving;
	Returning to;
Chairs	Sitting on;
	Hanging on;
	Turning around;
	Getting up from;
	Leaving;
	Returning to

How does Louise relate to the affordances of things in the maths lesson and how might that reveal small novelties? I shall answer those questions by working through the transcription above.

Chair and table: To Louise, the chair and table seem to afford having a *base* – these two things together mark 'her' space in the classroom; it is a place to leave and return to (1; 5: 13–14). As the teacher is having an exchange in the beginning of the lesson, she remains quiet at her seat, and as the class starts working the table affords *sustaining* her folder and her book (2–3; 11). The teacher encourages and supports the base affordance as he tells

Louise to return to her seat after having asked her to come to his desk (5). Being seated at the table also affords *communicating* with students nearby, in this case mostly about the calculations (4; 6; 11; 13–14). Also, it happens that other students leave their 'base' to go to talk with Louise about a calculus problem (9, 13).

Books and folders: Louise seems to be quite familiar with the affordances of books and folders. They seem to afford *being put on the table to do calculations* (2; 4; 6–14). Books also afford *being using as a source of information and action* in the conversation with classmates and *reading in* as she studies the content of the book (10).

Teacher's desk and multiplication tables: The teacher's desk is a place connected with the teacher's position in the class. It is a place that affords *come to and to leave again* and is used to organise specific events like testing the children individually; it is the teacher's domain, hence also affords *communicating directly with the teacher about a particular matter, being asked to do something, being evaluated*, etc. Louise is aware of the affordances of the desk as she goes up to do the multiplication tables and then leaves for her seat again (5), and as she goes to stand in a line to ask the teacher a question (13). The multiplication table activities are in focus in the maths lesson. Showing the teacher that one can perform well is an important activity of the day; it organises when to perform for the teacher and what to do when not performing. Louise seems to have practised well because she does the multiplication tables well (5). Because of the organisation of the test situation, the multiplication tables seem to afford *rote learning, mastering, performing*, etc.

The researcher's study of small novelty should focus on the relation between the affordance aspects of an activity setting and the agency of a specific child. The study should be carried out by analysing the relations between the intention units and the affordance aspects of the activity setting. In this case it should be carried out by analysing Louise's intentions and engagements in relation to the affordance aspects of the maths lesson.

Social others

While interacting with peers (like classmates) or adults (like teachers) the child also comes to know about the general positions and ways of doing things in ongoing practice. Being a student, for instance, the child must come to know about the commonly expected relations between her and others in school. Classroom activities are expected to be taken seriously and she probably would get into trouble if she does not know or respect the social set up sufficiently well (students do get into trouble, especially if 'maladaptive' behaviour continues beyond the early classes).

In her interactions with the teacher, the child comes to know about a variety of general expectations, activities and values; she comes to know about the teacher as an *agent* and as an individual who inhabits the general cultural/institutional *position* of teaching children in a class room; hence, the teacher's presence represents the functional value of experiencing the valued order set by others in the school. Also, the child comes to know about herself as an agent and as someone inhabiting the position of being a school student among other students. By interacting with classmates she comes to know about peers as individual agents and as someone who inhabits the position of being a classmate; because of this position, she also comes to know what counts as important in the classroom compared to what counts as important in recess, in after-school activities, on the playground, etc.

Analysing an activity setting thus offers opportunities to follow how a child manages to be herself as an agent who (in the institution) is also a *student* among other students contributing to the ongoing practice of school. There may be conflicts in the child or between the child and others; the child may like some activities more than others; she may like some peers and adults more than others; she may sometimes collaborate and enjoy, collaborate with resistance, resist openly, give up collaboration or remain quiet and invisible. Thus, the analysis offers an opportunity to study the possible general positions embedded in the variety of particular ones among participants; of course, this analysis may include tensions, resistance, coping with the inevitable, etc. and how relating to different general positions may contribute to developmental paths. It is far from being obvious that a child appropriates the expected patterns of interaction and of activity smoothly or homogeneously/unidirectionally. A detailed analysis may reveal the variety, richness, and contradictions of potentialities in (and across) activity settings.

Since individuals are intentional agents, the affordance perspective needs to include the intentional aspect of interpersonal relations in the classroom. A *double-perspective* is needed because other individuals who surround the child interact proactively with the child. The double-perspective suggests that an agent (like a teacher or a classmate) affords certain actions. This may have to do with the shared history of particular interpersonal relations between the child and that other agent, as well as with the general positions possible in an institutional practice. *The double-perspective on individuals grasps the simultaneity of the teacher being a representative of the specific cultural practice, on the one hand, and a socially interacting human being (agent), on the other.* The child who interacts with the teacher comes to know about both sides in the same process and through participation she develops a subjective position that mirrors specific experiences during the history of interaction. Similarly, classmates are often expected to be proactive *as* classmates contributing to the activity setting and, simultaneously, to be agents who interact subjectively with the child. Now, because of the double-perspective on the individual's participation in shared school activities, an affordance analysis *must* highlight interactions among agents. In social interaction, others do have affordances because they interact in socialised and culturally developed ways and not only as single de-contextualised individuals. Being an intentional agent, the teacher affords *interacting with* and *relating to*; the affordances of an intentional agent are different from the object affordances surrounding the children because the intentional agent is responsive and proactive. But the teacher is not just an intentional agent, he inhabits an *artefact-like* cultural position which affords activities specific to the activity setting.

While interacting with others, the child attends those affordances. In the process, the child *must* include her own agency and agent position while paying attention to the teacher (or others). The child must, for instance, include her own agency of *receiving instruction* (the agent aspect of what the teacher affords) when the teacher *instructs* (the cultural position aspect of what the teacher affords). In other words, when it comes to social situations, the concept of affordance must be an interactive one.

Below is a list of what is afforded by social others in the maths lesson. The list suggests a variety of details concerning agent positions to which Louise can relate; hence, it intends to stimulate the researcher's analysis of how small novelty may emerge out of social situations.

Social others	*Afford*
Teacher	Being listened to/listening to;
	Instructing/receiving instruction;
	Performance/performing;
	Evaluating/receiving evaluation;
	Helping/receiving help;
	Organising/receiving organisation;
Classmate	Individual work/working individually;
	Talking/talking with;
	Helping/receiving help;
	Inspiring/ receiving inspiration from;
	Comparing/comparing with

The teacher: Because of the teacher's cultural position as a teacher in school, he possesses a variety of functional values to the child who, like Louise, is engaged in school activities. The list above suggests some of those available affordances in the maths lesson. From the personal stance of the Louise, he affords *being listened to/listening to* and *organisation/receiving organisation* each time he interact with the class – no matter if he criticises students, is framing the general expectations and organisation of the class (2; 3; 5; 9; 13); when he instructs the students to get started with their *individual work* (5), when he listens to Louise performing the multiplication tables (5), and when he helps her with her calculation (13). The teacher affords *instructing/receiving instruction* in the same situations, at least those situations where the students work. He affords *performance/performing* and *evaluating/receiving evaluation* especially in the situation where the students are performing the multiplication tables (5). He affords *helping/receiving help* when Louise and other students are running into difficulties (13). In general, the teacher seems to be an agent from whom much is expected; organising and instructing effort, in addition to controlling and helping.

The classmate: Louise is mostly interacting verbally with her classmates. They afford *talking/talking with* in all cases of interaction (3–4; 6–11; 13–14)) and when they share calculation matters and problems (numbers as above) they may afford *helping/receiving help*, sometimes *inspiring/receiving inspiration*, and maybe also occasionally *comparing/comparing with*. Quite often Louise seems to be the classmate who affords helping/receiving help, etc., to others.

Self

As Louise receives instruction, is being evaluated, helped, corrected, etc., she experiences her own participation in these processes and she also experiences herself as someone who experiences this. Her experiences of self are phenomenological in this double sense; in general, this double aspect of phenomenological self-experience assumedly is a key to understanding how a child actively contributes to her own development. The child experiences herself as a person being actively involved in activities valued by significant others in an ongoing practice and, simultaneously, she experiences herself as experiencing all this. In this sense, the child is not only the centre of agency, she also experiences her agency (first-person perspective) from the side of the possible and available cultural positions (third-person perspective) in the interaction with social others. In this sense, the child also inhabits an agent position in relation to herself. Being an experiencing agent, her subjectivity includes her social position – her being a social other to herself. Baldwin (1899/1973) puts the dialectics of self and other nicely when he says that 'ego' and 'alter' are born together. Following this notion of 'self', the child's thought of herself is filled up with her thoughts of others and her thought of others are filled up with herself – it underpins the social nature of self.

While participating in social practices, the child gradually develops ideas and understandings of participation and of being a participant. She learns about her social position in relation to others, about her performances, values, etc. It all merges into more or less generalised experiences of whom she is and who she is becoming. The child not only affords a variety of activities in others; she also may afford activities in herself. She may experience herself as a source of inspiration to herself, hence while experiencing herself participating her *motives* for further activities and explorations may emerge, become strengthened or undergo changes. One should expect those motives to be of a complex nature and to maybe go in a variety of different and even contradictory directions. The affordance perspective on self hence throw light on emerging end developing motives for actions, feelings and values in a child.

The motivational development in the child should be researched alongside her capabilities to manage different activities; like being capable of playing soccer and experiencing the capability as something that affords playing again to practise skills and have a joyful time (or being bored, etc.). Hence, there may be a self-stimulating aspect of participating in social practices similar to what Baldwin (1899/1973) calls the *'try-try-again'* tendency (which might be developed into a complex notion like try-try-not-again, try-try-again-with-resistance, etc. which breaks with conformity of imitation). The principle of try-try-again expresses that learning and changes are dialectically embedded into persistent imitation. In societal institutions for children, activities are socially organised and give rise to different experiences with the self-stimulating aspects of participation. Different activity settings have different repeated patterns which, to some extent, constitute the valued practices of an institution. The child will have to explore what it means to be a participant in relation to those practices.

When Louise is getting herself engaged in activities like listening to her teacher's instruction, she experiences herself as 'receiving instruction' and she also – and simultaneously – experiences herself as someone who is 'able to receive instruction' and maybe even 'wants (values) to receive instruction'. In each aspect of the process, she experiences herself as an agent and as someone who invests her agency into positions and processes available in the social situation. It is an experience of quasi-otherness as the first-person perspective merges with the third-person perspective.

In those social situations, small novelty of capabilities like being able to receive instruction and to find inspiration (motivation) in that may emerge as a budding greater developmental possibility. Those small novelties often live a relatively unnoticed life in the activity settings; hence, the researcher has to study them carefully in her attempt to study great novelty in the life of a child. In a larger time scale, those small novelties may give rise to greater novelties that have an impact on the future activities of the child. Greater novelties may see the light if the shifting and complex stream of experiences lead to observable confirmations of who the child experiences herself to be and who she is becoming; or it may lead to shifts in interests, motives, values, etc. Such developmental possibilities in ontogenesis emerge on the basis of the child's exploration and appropriation of culturally available positions and artifacts in her environment. No matter how the child explores the available positions and artefact of an activity setting, she will also experience what her life is about, potential conflicts, challenges, changes, etc.

The list below attempts to illustrate how Louise is part of her own environment. On the left side is listed her first-person experiences of participating in activities. On the right side is listed the quasi-otherness position which allows her to experience capabilities as something that may (or may not) afford further activities; hence is a resource for the move from small to great novelty in her life.

Self-experience (first-person perspective on activities)	*Affordance: Motives* (quasi-otherness)
Receiving instruction	Instruct-able; Listen-to-able;
Continuing work	Focusing-able; Ignore-able; Being-independent-able; Experiencing-progress-able; Control-able;
Working individually	Individualise-able; Focusing-able; Control-able;
Talking while focusing	Multi-task-able; Pro-social-able; Focusing-able; Ignore-able; Listen-to-able;
Helping classmates	Control-able; Help-able;
Listening to a friend	Friend-able; Support-able; Emphatic-able; Compare-able; Support-able; Listen-to-able;
Seeking help when experiencing troubles	Frustrate-able; Seeking-help-able; Learn-able; Problem-solving-able; Listen-to-able; Getting-annoyed-able;
Performing standard tables	Smart-able; Control-able; Being-praised-able

It appears from the list that each activity includes a variety of experienced capabilities that may afford certain activities of Louise; further, similar experienced capabilities seem to appear across different activities. The identification of the estimated frequency of certain potentially experienced capabilities assumedly reveals how valued those aspects of the activities are in certain institutional settings even though, of course, they may vary greatly. Some experienced capabilities only appear once; others appear several times in that they are distributed across the activities. Even though there is no simple connection between frequency and institutional value, the researcher nevertheless might use frequency as one of the guidelines in her interpretations of where to look for developmental potentialities.

It appears that Louise may experience several capabilities having affordance qualities (motivational value) while participating in shared activities with social others in the classroom. Let me work through the potentially experienced capabilities that are made available in the activity setting and may afford further exploration and development.

The affordance *listen-to-able* seems to be very common and distributed. It is embedded in several first-person perspectives on activities like receiving instruction (2; 5; 13), talking while focusing (3), helping classmates (6–7), and seeking help when experiencing trouble (9; 12). The frequency of having a social exchange is very high and in each case it includes listening to others. As Louise communicates with her classmates and responds adequately to their needs, She may experience aspects of the self-social other relationship, such as being *empathic-able, support-able* and *compare-able* (6; 7; 9; 10; 14). The frequency of the affordances *focusing-able* and *ignore-able* is also quite high. Louise seems to probably experiences this capability while working individually and continuing her work (2–3; 5; 13). Also, the experience seems available as she is able to both talk with classmates and continue working on her own (3; 6). *Multi-task-able* is a frequent capability as well as it appears to be a part of much of Louise's exchange with her classmates (3; 6; 9; 11–13). In addition to the most frequent ones, the list includes a variety of other embedded capabilities that may afford further activities of Louise. Those are being *instruct-able* (2; 5; 13), being *independent-able* and being *individualise-able* which especially is related to her initiating, continuing and resuming work (2; 5; 12) as well as to performing the calculation tables (5), and helping classmates (see above), *control-able* as she is able to stay in control with her activities while focusing on the maths problems and performing the calculation tables (2–14). As she experiences her own success (5; 7; 10–12), she may also experience being *smart-able*. In addition, she may experience *being-praised-able* as the teacher expresses satisfaction with her performance (5). Being *help-able, friend-able,* and *support-able* all are potential capabilities embedded in helping classmates (see above), but she does not only help, she also needs help herself, and so *seeking-help-able*, being *frustrate-able*, *learn-able* and being *problem-solving-able* are all aspects of that part of experiencing participation (8–9; 13).

Small and great novelty

Let us now analyse how the environmental affordance perspective unfolded above helps to reveal potential great novelty for Louise in the maths lesson – who is Louise *becoming* on the basis of her local participation? What is mostly striking in the analysis is that 'novelty' in this case seemingly and to a great extent should be interpreted as 'continuation' of what she is able to do and how the capabilities may inspire her in the future. Much of what Louise does, how she interacts and the ways she makes use of things in her surroundings, indicates that she is already quite familiar with what it means to go to school. In this observation, she does not seem to break any rules or turn her back to the activities, for instance. Apparently, she does not violate the affordances of things; she utilises their affordances in accordance with what they are culturally made for. Hypothetically, other students might not accept this; they might violate or add creatively to the affordances of things (standing on the table, making flyers out of the paper in the folder, hitting each other with the book, etc.). Louise does not do this. She accepts the base character of her table-and-chair arrangement, hence also the way the space of the classroom is organised for improving the goals and activities set by the teacher. She does not break with the affordances of social others; she seems to accept the position of the teacher and does not put herself in opposition to him, at least when judged from her explicit actions and attitudes. She accepts much of the rules of the 'going to school' game; she apparently has done her homework with the calculation tables, otherwise she would not be able to do so well in the verbal test. She also manages to keep working in a focused and independent way even though several of her classmates want her attention and many activities are happening at the same time. She is turning the expectations of the teacher and the school in general into personal expectations; she wants to do well and seems to get into trouble with herself if she finds it difficult to manage the calculations. In addition to accepting the affordances of the teacher embedded in his cultural position, she also accepts her classmates as being people with a legitimate right to occupy her time with calculus-relevant interventions. The acceptance of classmates is an important value in the Danish school system; collaboration among classmates is much expected and so being collaborative is a must if the students want to succeed in the eyes of the teacher. In fact, *not* being collaborative is one of the most potentially excluding factors for a student in a Danish school. Louise does not fail here; she lives up to being collaborative in the ongoing flow of the lesson. There seems to be only one exception in the data material; during one of the helping episodes (11), Louise and Sandra are talking with each other in ways that indicate that they want to keep it a secret what the boy next to Nick did wrong; the boy gets a little annoyed. In this episode, Louise is first having a helping attitude towards the boy, but also, she seems to want an intimate exchange with Sandra which excludes the boy. In other words, there seems to be a conflict in her motivation and in the way she acts. One cannot know from only one observation why that is so or if there is a history among the students behind her actions. But the researcher might want to study the material and the background further for the conflict situation. It might be a critical point and a potential for small (and great) novelty in Louise's life. Because of her general acceptance of the physical and social order, she seems to include this acceptance into the way she experiences her participation and herself as a participant. All of the capabilities listed on the affordance side of the scheme elaborated earlier, are some that belong to being 'a good student making good progress' in school. Louise seems to make herself available for a broad variety of affordances concerning herself; this might be interpreted so that she is not experiencing much conflict between how she participates and how she experiences being a participant. The general expectations lying in her physical and social sur-roundings are not only accepted, they are turned into expectations to herself. An example of how she manages turning the cultural and social expectations into her own is in the situation right in the end of the lesson where she begins to lose her motivation (probably feeling tired). In this situation she starts collaborating with Rita; specifically, she keeps herself up by being actively involved with a classmate and so she manages to continue working till the end of the lesson. In general, this seemingly experienced conflict in Louise is resolved by including the stimulating nature of things and others in her surrounding – she utilises excellently those affordances and succeeds in regulating her level of activity and maintaining (and maybe even expanding) her capabilities of keeping up with the expectations embedded in the activity setting.

Learning from Louise

What can we learn by applying the environment/affordance perspective on the activity setting in which Louise takes part? We do learn something about Louise as a participant and as a person being engaged with activities common in her culture. Louise does not seem to seek out conflicts much in relation to social others. Neither does she seem to experience conflicts much in herself concerning her participation; she does not make a big deal out of herself and does not do much to get attention from others. Children like

Louise often are those overlooked in the school system because they appear as being 'unproblematic' and 'well adapted'. The researcher should be aware not to end in such a position when overlooking children; that definitely would violate her attempts to study things from the child's perspective and she might end having only a very general and unchallenged view on cultural practices. The researcher should be aware to use an optic sensitive to each particular child. In Louise's case, continuation of adapting to increasing expectations and demands occur to be an essential point following the analysis. *This is small novelty as well.* In a longitudinal study, one might expect to find that Louise becomes a person to whom education plays an important role in her life; also, one might expect Louise to become a person who is very able to regulate herself as a participant, controlling herself in relation to social others, adapting well to different settings, etc.

Also, the analysis reveals that the relative lack of conflict matter might be something to research in deeper detail. Does this hold true only for this particular activity setting? Does it hold true in general in relation to school activities? Is the same pattern to be found when Louise is at home, in after-school activities, etc.? Those are research questions that may help the researcher direct her attention when studying child development. Perhaps the child can become *too well adapted to too many cultural and social expectations*? The analysis may reveal this as a particular developmental resource for a child that tends to lay out certain possible pathways for her. Perhaps the child needs help *to not* adapt so well? Perhaps the child becomes restricted in her participation if the pattern of adaptation is distributed all over her life? Perhaps the relative lack of conflicts constitutes an issue in the life of the child? Only a close analysis of the wholeness of the activity setting and across activity settings can help the researcher to focus on such details and questions. Also, it stresses the importance of following the child's perspective as a participant in social practices, as presented earlier in the book.

Conclusion

The analysis presented above is intended to illustrate an example of how studying small novelty in activity settings might help the researcher to study great novelty in child development. The analysis has revealed the richness of developmental potentialities embedded even in a very brief observation with a child taking part in ordinary school activities. Also, it has put a focus on the importance of following the child's perspective as a participant in shared activities. The steps suggested is to analyse the affordance of *things*, *social others* and *self* in an attempt to develop a very detailed but also a very integrated perspective on the child's participation as the basis for studying development on an ontogenetic level.

The child in school, for instance, does not just come to know about school matters. The list of what she comes to know about should be extended to ways of doing school and to how she experiences being a part of that, especially considered in relation to whom she experiences herself to be at the given moment and who she might become in the future. This development is greatly unsettled, but not completely unpredictable; the study of what kind of *generals* may be embedded in any *particulars* is a way to come closer to the developing child as a citizen in a particular society and a particular community in a particular historical period of time. Each child participates in particular activity settings which, in a variety of ways, support small and great novelty. The affordances embedded in Louise's maths lesson are potentialities that belong to her surroundings and to the wholeness of the situation in which she takes part. But they are also potentially developing capabilities in Louise.

Note

1   We may add an unlimited amount to the list: the architecture of the school, the outdoor facilities, which rooms for which classes, the cantina, refrigerators, location and standard of the room for the teachers, organisation of schedules, time available for what, posters, photos, etc.

9 Interviewing using a cultural–historical approach

Pernille Hviid

Introduction

This chapter will discuss the research method of *interviewing* children, from a cultural–historical perspective. As a practice of getting information, interviewing has been applied since ancient times. Thucydides interviewed the warriors of the Peloponnesian wars in order to write the war story and Socrates used dialogue to develop his philosophical knowledge (Kvale, 1997). In *research*, the use of interview as a valid method for getting data has fluctuated with dominant epistemological paradigms. In times of positivistic dominance, psychology relied little on interviews and mostly used this method as a way of creating 'more reliable' instruments, such as tests. Today, under the influence of the socio-constructivist paradigm, the interview has received status as a legitimate and useful research method within both education and psychology at large, supposedly supported by a societal age where the intimate, biographical self has come into focus (Kvale, 2006).

Interviewing children is a special case, since the tendency of conceiving children as less mature and less knowledgeable than adults has dominated social sciences. Within this perspective children have mostly been interviewed in order to investigate how differently from adults children think or how much less they know or can remember (Tiller, 1988).

Then how can an interview with children be conceived and practised within the cultural–historical perspective outlined in this book? What implications does a perspective of a child, conceived as a developing participant and an active co-constructor of her own sociocultural conditions, have on the method of interviewing?

As shown throughout the chapters in this volume, research practice must be understood as a dialectical practice involving both researchers and researched. The dialectical nature of interview, in its implication of *dialogue* between persons, highlights the necessity of viewing the interview as more than questions and answers, but rather as shared knowledge construction and deconstruction while dialoguing. This process thus not only affects the researcher in her work, but, in a way that is perhaps more visible than in any other research method, also affects the researched children. Given this, this chapter will pay special attention to the possible implications of participating in research processes for children and thereby highlight attention to ethics that must guide the overall research practice.

In the first section, some general remarks on interviewing as a research method will be presented and discussed in relation to the general theoretical framework of children's development. The second section will focus on possible implications of research intervention in children's everyday lives. This 'meeting' can be viewed on different levels, from the impact on the child in the concrete interaction to the potential community and societal changes for children. The section will highlight ethical questions relating to research with children. In the third section, I focus on the arena of research that the children enter. As research participants they introduce knowledge, expectations and interests that are more concordant with their everyday life structures than with structures and principles of science (see Hedegaard, this volume; Schutz, 2005). The insertion of new material and practices by children can likewise be discussed in terms of levels of scientific activity: from knowledge acquisition in concrete empirical research, to production of new research methods.

Data from two investigations will serve as illustrations. Firstly, 'Child's life in school and after-school' (Hviid, 2002),which included approximately 100 6- to 9-year-olds and was conducted through observation and interview. The aim was to understand how these two institutional arrangements were experienced by children and what kinds of developmental opportunities they gave rise to. In the second investigation on 'Children's experience of their own developmental processes' (Hviid, 2008) a more tightly constrained examination of children's experiences of their own developmental processes was carried out. The children were asked to map out their contextual lives on big sheets of paper, thereby giving context a representational form, to guide the interview on their experiences of 'growing up'/'becoming big'. This investigation included five 12-year-old children, each of them participating in 3–4 interviews of approximately 1.5 hours.

The research interview

An interview consists of dialogues between two or more persons focused on a specific set of topics that are most often chosen by the interviewer. The research interview differs from an ordinary dialogue in some critical ways. According to Plato a dialogue is:

[A] process, where two people understand each other. It is a characteristic of a genuine dialogue the each of the participants are open
towards each other, accepts his points of view as worthy attention
and develops empathy in a such degree, that he understands; not a
particular person, but what he says. It is the rightness or falseness in
his opinion that must be understood so they can agree on the
subject.

(Plato, cited in Kvale, 1997, p. 32)

Although the interview maintains the idea of mutual understanding as in a
genuine dialogue, the overall aim is to understand aspects of the life world of
the interviewed person and her relation to these aspects. Thus, the interviewer's personal point of view and her life-world is irrelevant to the interview.
The interviewer aims to understand the life-world as it is *described* in facts to
her as well as the *meaning* this life-world has to the interviewee. The meaning
of a particular dimension of a life-world is not ready at hand for the
interviewer, and thus a conversation with many entrances to the specific
topic is needed. Both with respect to adults (Kvale, 1997) and to children
(Tiller, 1988) the use of pre-made categories (such as gender, values and
types) is problematic, since they pre-close too fast or too vague meaning
making, due to the level of children's concept formation. Rather, an appeal
to production of detailed and nuanced descriptions is advised. Here, it may
very well turn out that the information on a particular subject has internal
contradictions. This can be due to poor interview performance by the
interviewer, lack of stable meaning on the part of the interviewee or —
perhaps most often — an adequate reflection of variations, and presumably
contradictory aspects and tensions in the life-world of the interviewee (Kvale,
1997) which might lead to *polyphonic* utterances (Hydén, 2000). The interviewer must stay as open and receptive as possible to the content and from
time to time reveal her understanding of what has been said in order to
reconfirm or correct her understanding.

Since it is the researcher who is in need of the interview, she is
supposed to express (and feel) gratitude for the information given and to aim
at making the situation pleasant and stimulating. The respondent is guaran-
teed certain rights. Ethical standards generally demand that participation in
research must not damage the interviewee during or after the interview. Data
must be handled professionally and confidentially during and after the
research process and the interviewee has at any time the right to terminate
the interview, and to withdraw personal material.

Piaget's clinical method

In developmental science, Jean Piaget stands out as the grand old man with
respect to his research interviews with children, most often (and critically)

quoted in relation to his research on children's conservation. In *The Child's Conception of the World* (1929), Piaget introduces the clinical method as a tool for investigating children's cognitive development. Although the case here is not abstract de-personalised and de-contextualised cognitive development as such, but rather the child's development as a person through her or his participation in everyday life, Piaget's reflections are rare and to some extent useful in the following discussion. The clinical method is an experimental method, since the researcher aims at investigating a problem based on a hypothesis and tested during the interview. The novice in interviewing is threatened by double difficulties, Piaget writes: 'to accept every answer the child makes as pure gold or on the other hand to class all as dross' (Piaget, 1929, p. 9). Piaget find it alarming to think of the 'exaggerations that would result from questioning children on a number of subjects and regarding the answers thus obtained as being all of equal value, and as revealing equally the child's mentality' (Piaget, 1929, p. 25). Thus, Piaget sets out to make distinctions between different types of answers and their relative information on the child's thought processes and thereby their scientific value in general. He presents the following five categories of answer:

- *Random answers*, given from a disinterested child. There is no system in the random answers; they are unstable, contradictory and meagre.
- *Romancing answers*, given from a playing, maybe teasing child. The child makes up answers for his own private fun, but maybe also in order to tease the experimenter. Romancing answers are seldom repeated by the child on the same question, or produced by other children. To Piaget, a romancing answer also can be a transitional answer towards a new understanding and thus be a pre-form of a liberated answer.
- *Liberated convictions* are answers containing novelties in the child's understanding. They are created through the child's participation in the interview, yet still considered to be an original reflection of the child's own thought processes since 'neither the reasoning it performs in order to answer the question nor the sum totally of the previous knowledge on which it draws during its reflection are directly influenced by the experimenter' (Piaget, 1929, p. 11). Liberated answers are neither spontaneous nor suggested, but a result of reflection containing a *tendency* of the thought processes of the child.
- *Suggested convictions* are aimed at satisfying the interviewer. These transient answers will erode on counter-questioning, since they are primarily given to fall in line with the perceived wish of the interviewer. They have little scientific value as reflections of the child's cognitive processes.

- *Spontaneous convictions* are already consolidated and produced understandings of the child. They are visible in their quick release, confronted with relatively vague questions from the interviewer, and are resistant to suggestions.

These distinctions are both illuminating and frustrating to a dialectically oriented developmentalist. They are very informative in the sense that they offer information on how the child is responding; out of boredom, in playful teasing, on an established opinion, while ideas pop up, or out of a desire to please the interviewer. All these situations are realistic scenarios. But at the same time, the presentation of these categories is frustrating, since they rest solely on the responses given by the child and thus cut the dialogue into two halves. The questions posed or the styles of questioning are absent in construction of the categories. The reader is denied a reinterpretation of the dialogue as a whole; of *what the child heard and answered*, in order to follow the dialogical logic *'that the child always answers correctly to the question heard'* (Hundeide, 2004, p. 166). I suggest that this paradox can be understood as a result of the use of an individualistic developmental framework, approached through a dialogical method. In a dialectically oriented theoretical framework of human development, as with the one here presented, the reactions Piaget describes mostly raise new questions as to what the children were asked when they responded, and what they heard being asked.

Children's development as the object of research

[T]o encompass in research the process of a given things development, in all its phases and changes – from birth to death – means to discover its nature, its essence, for 'it is only in movement that the body shows what it is.'

(Vygotsky, 1978, p. 65)

In order to discuss interview research in a cultural–historical developmental framework, some short re-introduction of the phenomenon of *development* seems appropriate. Development has been introduced as an interdependent phenomenon including and fusing maturational, experiential and cultural contributions (Hedegaard, this volume; Magnusson and Cairns, 2001). As the focus in particular is on the development of children as persons, some levels of structures are more relevant than others.

In personality development, the child's activity constitutes a vehicle for development. Human activity is understood as goal seeking as well as creative, goal generating (Valsiner, 1997). Creative teleogenesis refers to the way people produce new ends to solve problems or produce solutions in complex surroundings. On this level of development, interdependence takes place as creating and going beyond living conditions, through activity that is part of the living conditions they participate in creating. As the basic unit for the study of children's personal development, Vygotsky proposed the child in 'the social situation' (Vygotsky, 1998, p. 198). The social situation is not an environment in its totality, but the child's understanding, meaning making of and engaging in specific aspects of the environment:

> [T]he most essential turnaround that must be made in the study of the environment is the transition from absolute to relative indicators (...): most of all we must study what it means for the child, what the child's relation to the separate aspects of the environment is.
>
> (Vygotsky, 1998, p. 293)

Corresponding with the social situation, the child's experience was chosen as a unit for investigating children's personal development:

> All experience is always experience of something. (...) But every experience is my experience (...) in experience, environment is given in its relation to me, how I experience this environment; on the other hand, features of the development of my personality have an effect.
>
> (Vygotsky, 1998, pp. 294–295)

Vygotsky argued that children's experience of their social situations change with the child's development. New needs and new motives develop, old ones transform or disappear. In these processes of transformation, Vygotsky underlined the child's active participation in restructuring his relationship with the environment, creating new life-conditions:

> [W]e have studied inadequately the internal relation of the child to those around him, and we have not considered him as an active participant in the social situation.
>
> (Vygotsky, 1998, p. 292)

The key feature in these concepts is their ability to contain the interdependence between the child as an active person and an environment as an inevitable condition for the child's development. The modern concept of 'the child's perspective' is already build into Vygotsky's basic formulation of his developmental theory, since Vygotsky is making the child the person that interlinks contexts and social situations.

Vygotsky's concept of 'interest' aimed at uniting the child's aspirations and tendencies (Vygotsky, 1998, p. 4) with aspects of the environment in a longer term temporal fashion. Interests develop through the child's selective participation in her given environment and suggest direction to the child's activity over longer periods of time. Notwithstanding, I would like to suggest an even 'smaller' unit with respect to duration, a concept that can capture and unite the child's involved participation in the 'actual social situation'. I suggest the concept of 'engagement'. In existential philosophy, the concept of engagement was introduced aiming to reinstall personality development in the concrete world. When engaged, human beings get involved in the situation, thereby changing it, and thus creating a future for themselves as persons (Lübcke, 1999). In a developmental perspective, engagements can be seen as situated zones of potential development. It unites potential interests of the child with certain aspects of the environment. Like interests, engagements are generated by the child *in* the situation she experiences. Certain characteristics of the situation stimulate or invite her engagements. Vygotsky writes: '[T]hings and events we meet manifest for us a more or less determined will, they stimulate us to certain actions: Beautiful weather or a lovely landscape move us to take a walk' (Vygotsky, 1998, p. 10).

In engaged situations, humans experience a sense of losing themselves or being absorbed in a situation. Here, the child is 'more' than herself – she is herself and the situation (or object) of her engagement. This partial fusion between child and surroundings optimises the rise of novelty; in a microgenetic sense (Hviid, 2002). Overall, engagement might appear to be an emotionally positive condition; but engagement can be seen in delightful floating on the stream of absorption as well as in banging into a problem with great force and anger.

Vygotsky's describes how development proceeds in different paces at different times. Sometimes in smooth, flowing movements with small, 'microscopic changes of the child's personality', at other times development proceeds abruptly, chaotically and perhaps obviously subversively, in relation to earlier ways of thinking, acting, and feeling:

> Development takes on a stormy, impetuous and sometimes catastrophic character that resembles a revolutionary course of events in both range of the changes that are occurring and in the sense of the alterations that are made.
>
> (Vygotsky, 1998, p. 194)

Personal development is thus a system that from time to time undergoes radical structural transformation, whereby something already there, disappears at sight. The child 'loses interests that only yesterday guided all his activity and took a greater part of his time and attention' (Vygotsky, 1998, p. 194).

Like other central concepts in cultural–historical theory, 'developmental crises' are not to be understood as internal to the child, but rather as changes in the child's experience of the social situation. In crises, the child's engagements and interests change very radically. She reorients and repositions herself in the social situation. Levels of conflicts may escalate and new spaces for participation are visited.

For this reason, attention to children's steady and changing engagements in the world are of basic interest in developmental psychology, including alterations between seemingly smooth ongoing everyday life, conflictual interactions and reorientations in the child's relationship with surroundings, because that points to strong interconnections between psychological and environmental fields and is thus considered to be in the foreground of the child's potential development. In this respect, the development of engagements, interests and conflicts *within* the practice of research are not essentially different from those developed in ordinary everyday life. In the following, I will discuss children's potential development through their participating in research.

A researcher enters children's lives – the social situation of research

The basic motivation for research is obviously the researcher's research questions. But interview research has often been considered to benefit the respondents as well, since an *interview* aims precisely at sharing views between speaker and listener (Kvale, 1997). Interviews have been considered to be emancipating, progressive and giving voice to the common people (Kvale, 2006). Still, this interactive and engaged participation does not make the child into a 'researcher'. The child is not knowledgeable with respect to a scientifically constrained system to guide her activity and therefore she will, in the subsequent text, be named as a 'research participant'.

The interview process will be discussed with respect to both matter and form.

The question of matter – do we dialogue on something interesting?

An opportunity to exchange views and opinions is generally considered as having a positive effect on a person's (and a child's) well-being, provided that the subjects discussed can be seen as interesting. If that is the case, we must assume that a successful interview can enrich that child's way of meaning making or dealing with aspects of her life. Piaget noticed the importance of relevance in his clinical interview. He writes that 'observations must be the starting point of all research dealing with the child's thinking'. and 'the questions we shall ask them in the matter and in the form (are to be investigated) by the spontaneous questions actually asked by children of the same age or younger' (Piaget, 1929, pp. 4–5).

Our cultural–historical approach would agree with this. A search for subjects of engagement to the child would take place, because these could point towards potential zones of development in the child's life, which is the core issue of the research. By the very relating to these fields of engagements it is anticipated that they develop and change. In Vygotsky's (1987b) work on the zone of proximal development (ZPD), he assumed that the child's development was mediated through interaction with competent peers or adults. Therefore, novel forms of understandings and actions could rise from the child–researcher interaction. In this sense the notion of the ZPD is very similar to Piaget's (much narrower) notion of 'liberated convictions' with respect to a co-constructed platform for novelties. Issues of relevance and importance are thus not 'only' sought for, in order to please the children, but also to give potential to developmental processes, which are the core interest for the developmental researcher.

In the last interview session in investigating children's experiences of their own developmental processes (Hviid, 2008), the children were asked to reflect on how research participation had made an impact on their lives. Two children's experiences are reported briefly below:

> *Michael:* It was fun, because you come to notice things you don't think of. I never think about my life that way, but when you sit and draw it, it comes little by little.
>
> *Interviewer:* Did anything surprise you?
>
> *Michael:* Yes, I was surprised how long my life has been even though I have only lived for 12 years. And how planned my life is, I have almost planned all my life, a century ahead. I know already what is going to happen. Many people take one day at a time.
>
> *Interviewer:* When you take a look at the life-map, then how well does it cover your life?
>
> *Michael:* It is my life … it is like that – (smiles) – my life.

Michael seems satisfied with the map as a representation of his life. The new experience he gets from research participation is that his life has been long, and this might be taken as some kind of evidence for an experienced richness of the investigation. The degree of planning seems new to Michael, perhaps also partly enforced by the 'mapping'.

Eve, also 12 years old, looks at her map when asked:

> *Interviewer:* Have you come to think about anything new, by being here?
>
> *Eve:* Yes and no. It is like (points on the map) I have had all this inside my head, right? And I have thought a lot about it. And yet, it is a new angle. I think it is a good idea to draw it. Thereby you get an overview.

> *Interviewer:* Have you ever made such a map before in your life?
>
> *Eve:* (laughs) Never! I have it all inside my head, like here (points at the map). It is strange, it is this drawing exactly, that is stuck in my head, in fact.
>
> *Interviewer:* Do you remember if it was there, before you drew your life-map?
>
> *Eve:* Yes.
>
> *Interviewer:* ... (Pause) ... Was it?
>
> *Eve:* Now ... now it has stuck into my head.

The talk of the potential impact of the research on Eve's life is much fuzzier than in the talk with Michael. Eve knew and didn't know at the same time. Logically, she is right about this. Still she saw her life from a 'new angle', and the figure was there already, yet wasn't there. Some kind of fusion has been going on, and Eve judges the result as harmonious. But still the representation also had some minor 'crackles':

> *Eve:* There are of course details, things like ... small details, that could have been put on [the map] ... but in some way don't really belong here. And some things that I might not have wanted to share with you, but that is things that somehow don't say much about my development.

Generally, the children evaluated their participation in research as productive and enriching their lives by acquisition of new angles and overviews. Their comments thus demonstrate the potentially bidirectional relevance of the interview, although the motives engaging in the shared activity differs from those of the researcher. Knowing which kind of relevance the process had to the involved children provides information on how they understood the task and gives the researcher a possibility for re-evaluating their answers, in the light of what she knows, about the children heard being asked. In a cultural–historical approach, this could strengthen or weaken the internal validity of the research.

What is the dialogue about? Problems in research interviews with children

Critical ideas on the method of interview have been voiced recently and the myth of its inherently 'good', 'warm' and 'progressive' quality has been debated. Feminist researchers have discussed the 'faking friendship' (Kvale, 2006, p. 3) and Fog (2004) describes the interviewer as a 'Trojan horse' who through different techniques and warmth gets behind the barriers of guarded subjective sensitive information. Interviews with children are no exception when it comes to mismatch in the contract of *what we are talking about.* Hundeide points, more consistently that any other researcher (Hundeide, 1989; Aaronsson and Hundeide, 2002; Hundeide, 2004), to the reversal of roles in interviews with children, caused by the blurred intentions of research. From a series of interview studies, Aaronsson and Hundeide (2002) conclude that researchers often have different perspectives on the research contract than children do. The authors argue that researchers often act according to a monological perspective, whereas the child acts according to a dialogical, relational perspective. In that case, the answers of the child possess a striving towards establishment and re-establishment of an understanding relation with respect to the researcher's points of view, while the researcher is focused on the quality of the child's answer considered in isolation. One could argue that Piaget's clinical method falls into this category.

According to the authors, this mismatch of meta-contracts will tempt children to follow the researcher in her questions and suggestions more willingly than adults ordinarily do, including making completely absurd answers to absurd questions (Hundeide, 2004). In a social–contextual developmental perspective, children depend more heavily than adults on social contracts because the process of individuation, in principal, is social. More specifically, it could be argued, that children's appropriation of language and concept formation happens through the active use of language, and therefore we must expect children to make use of concepts and understandings before they know their full contents. Seen this way 'suggestibility' comes closer to basic ideas of 'imitation', as a vehicle of development, as proposed by Vygotsky and 'appropriation' as lending and tasting utterances in order to make them one's own, as Bakhtin suggested. Still, Piaget (1929) noticed that 'suggested convictions' had the least relevance to research. Suggestibility in terms of manipulation can pose a threat to the child's personal integrity. But to distinguish manipulation from mutual social responsive communication one needs to analyse the communicative *interaction* as a whole process and not only the answers of the child.

How to dialogue – learning the interview script

There seems to be evidence that children, by participating in research, get acquainted with methods and forms of interaction of which they previously had only a more distant knowledge (Aldersson, 2000; Hviid, 2002). Aldersson (2000) reports young children participating in different levels of making research and conducting excellent surveys, questionnaires, focus group interviews, etc. Thus there are reasons to believe that children not only get to know their own life by participating in research, but also learn to make use of new technologies, and through the affordances that these new technologies bring, they can see things and their own life from 'a new angle', as Eve puts it. Still, it is worth mentioning that interviews as verbal interactions are only one form of communication among others.

Piaget (1929) discussed the value of different forms of participation and appreciated, in particular the 'spontaneous' and the 'liberated' responses, whereas the 'romancing answers' – the playful, maybe teasing responses – had little interest. Yet, children strive towards development through play. Vygotsky (1982) saw play as a generator and a transitory stage between everyday and scientific thinking. The connections between 'as-if' and 'what-if' potentialities give rise to novelty (Bateson, 1976; Nelson and Seidman, 1984). Accordingly, playful responses are developmentally interesting and can be found to be the most appealing forms of participation to children. In a cultural–historical approach, the 'best way' to communicate is through the modality that gives the richest opportunity to express one's points of view, be they dances, theatre, drawings, etc.; and contrary to Piaget, I would argue that multi-modal communication on a specific topic could suggest a convincing density of the answer given. In the last section of the chapter, I will return to the dialogicity of production of research forms.

To sum up, *the social situation of research* can be an opportunity for children to discuss subjects of importance and it can be an opportunity to learn something about research practice and even to appropriate this 'new angle' or voice on particular life circumstances and their own being. In this sense, participating in research can be seen as a special developmental opportunity. On the other hand, participation in research can also constrain children to activities they find irrelevant and boring in subject matter, confusing in goals and strategies or difficult to respond to within a restricted repertoire of modalities of communication.

Research stretching into the children's community

In recent decades a growing number of research projects and welfare/health and child policy projects have been carried out with active participation from children. This relatively new cooperative tradition breaks with a prevailing interest in understanding the child as 'a threat, a victim or an object of socialisation' (Thorne quoted in Tiller, 1988, p. 43). Rather, the projects mirror the child as an active, competent human being and as a valuable specialist on her own life conditions (Christensen and James, 2000). Furthermore, the authors of such agendas often refer to the human rights of the child (Roberts, 2000; Taylor, 2000). There seems to be an overall optimism in the new methodology and a strong belief on the rightness of this approach (Alderson, 2000; Christensen and James, 2000).

Numerous accounts of the effects of children's participation on a local community level have been reported, where children get their 'message through', as in Oscar Lewis's (1964) book *The Children in Sanchez*, which brought attention to their conditions as an exploited Mexican group. In other projects, children participate actively in the improvement of their situation, as in building a fence for protection from wild animals, digging a well, refining playgrounds or the school environment, etc. (Aldersson, 2000). This goal seeking and creating demonstrates from a developmental perspective the very potential of human activity. Yet participating in such agendas will properly confront children with conflictual 'real' life circumstances of people opposing or neglecting their needs and thus alert the researcher to question the potential danger to the children. Attention should be brought to what could or might happen. Even in a well-planned project everything is not foreseeable; but researchers are obliged to think of the 'worst case scenario' in intervention and omit certain types of activity that might even have the smallest risk of damaging the research participants. That might mean waving goodbye to an opportunity to get wonderful data and wonderful changes and there is *nothing* to be done about that.

Children entering the arena of research

When children participate in research they do so partly constrained by their own biography, their existing understanding of research and their potential interests. In the following, I will take a closer look at the developmental impact that the vital, meaning-making and goal-generating activities done by children can have on research.

The overall concern of a developmental researcher is 'historical becoming'; processes of transformation and movements of some kind. In a cultural–historical orientation the focus of the research – interaction with children is to get knowledge of how they participate in their own development by participatory activity in the social situations in and by which they live, how they create meaning and new meanings, how they seek and generate goals and develop interests and experience conflicts or crises if and when there are serious mismatches between them and their surroundings.

When children enter this 'arena of research', the researcher has – intertwined with the specific research question in mind – an excellent opportunity for a close-up study of how children participate in new arenas of research. She can monitor developing understandings on what is going on, how children over time deal differently with the phenomenon in focus, how they discuss it, cooperate with it, deal with its obstacles, agree or disagree with it, choose insertion of technologies to make it work, get assistance and guide the researcher on behalf of their understanding of the subject. This newly established layer of 'children dealing with arenas in a social–cultural world' opens right in front of the researcher's eyes, because she created the possibility herself.

In the following (Hviid, 2008), Jonathan addresses this personal inter-ference of the researcher in his production of data on his own developmental experiences. From Jonathan's point of view, his contribution was less than optimal, because of the research:

> *Jonathan:* You could have spent 20 minutes telling about yourself. Where you live, if you have a boyfriend and what your hobbies are. It is actually easier to answer your questions, when you know the person a little. Then you can give deeper answers. You could then ask more private questions and get more deepened re-sponses than you might need.

> *Interviewer:* I understand what you say, but why?

> *Jonathan:* Because, I feel I can trust the person the more I know who the person is. Then I know how you are. Then I can decide to put a limit to what I tell you or just be open. But I know this is an educational matter to you. So I will help you.

A more genuine dialogue seems to evoke the confidence Jonathan needs to dialogue in an open and secure fashion. His own rationality, to 'help the researcher', guided his participation. The interviewer replies that she has been trained differently. In research and in therapy, the psychologist is trained to listen, but not to interfere with her own life experiences:

> *Jonathan:* We are in a different situation now. In fact, it is not you helping me, it is me helping you.

> *Interviewer:* Yes (laughs). That is an important difference.

> *Jonathan:* It is your decision, but I advise you to do so. That would be another style of psychologists. That would only be good.

Jonathan questions the rightness of the therapist–client analogy in research and he has a point. From thereon, the interviewer tries to explore the dialogical interdependence in an interview, on an equal basis, together with Jonathan. Jonathan is certain that he would have responded differently had he been interviewed differently or by a different interviewer:

> *Jonathan:* Because people have different attitudes towards different things, different questions and different points of view, they would ask questions in different ways and I would answer them

in different ways. When you ask questions as you do now, I answer as I do now, but if you asked different questions in different ways, I would reply in ways that would fit those questions.

It is difficult not to get the feeling of Bakhtin reincarnated in this young thinker. Bakhtin wrote about the utterance as 'a product of the mutual relationship between the speaker and the listener', as made in 'anticipation of the perspective of the other' and as a 'bridge between me an the other' (quoted in Hundeide, 2004, p. 197) The issue of the interdependency between the researcher's attitudes and her questions and the respondent's interpretation of the social situation at hand, including his interpretation of the researcher herself, raises a traditionally delicate question and a problem of validity in empirical research. Within a developmental perspective, these interdependent changes are understood as a process of becoming; a historical generation of the child's relation to the phenomenon at hand in interaction with the researcher. Jonathan is content with his product given the research conditions:

> *Jonathan:* I think I have done a good job. It (the map) mirrors much of me, but there are still a lot of things through which you don't know me. I could have engaged myself a hundred times as much in this matter.

Since intersubjectivity is basic to interview research, Jonathan's invitation to a more evenly shared contribution raises questions of how far the researcher will and can stretch to develop methods in cooperation with the children.

Co-construction of genetic methods

> [T]he task is not to seek to be master or controller of our surround-ings, by imposing upon them prior plans of our own, but simply to seek to be sure and confident participant in them, to feel 'at home' with them to such an extent that, at every moment, we know how to act in ways responsive to the 'calls' they exert upon us, or the 'invitations' they offer us.
>
> (Shotter, 2000, p. 243)

To study something historically, in a Vygotskian sense, does not mean to study the past events of a phenomenon. Rather it means to 'see the present historically'. Vygotsky (1978) argues for a methodology that encompasses the nature of a given phenomenon's development. In our case, the phenomenon is children's development as persons. Therefore, the research methods must be able to encompass children's engagements and activity, their conflicts and crises as they are key components to personality development, not only in the interpretation of data, but also in their research participation. Being responsive to the children's wish to change the arena of research and aiming at coordination with their engagements can create zones of potential development in the intervention itself. It is assumed that research on the child's zone of potential development (Vygotsky, 1998) might give rise to a 'zone of potential research', with respect to methods.

Research that illustrates children's contribution to the zone of potential research was created in an ongoing dialogue between the researcher and the children in school and after-school care (Hviid, 2002). Since the principal of this school rejected the researcher's wish to produce life form interviews (Andenæs, 1991, 1997) in the empty after-school during school hours the researcher faced problems. The researcher discussed the problem with the children who suggested a 'hidden researcher' as a solution to the problem. To 'hide' would of course solve the problem of the attention the researcher created among 100 children, but obviously (to the researcher) new problems would have appeared, within both practical and ethical domains of the research. But maybe the idea of 'hiding' could be twisted a little and work after all?

During the ensuing days, 12, 8- and 9-year-old children were taught to use small portable tape-recorders and instructed to move around in the after-school context, localising and reporting on their involvements from these places. For ethical reasons, they were reminded that the tape would be listened to by the researcher. The children mostly chose to participate in pairs. Equipped with tape-recorders, the 'reporters' (as they were named) were confronted with the task of guiding the researcher's attention by accentuating, describing and discussing important dimensions of their everyday life. The activity was an interview where the questions were almost fully constrained by the respondents.

In analysing the data, three different but interwoven engagements were observable. First of all, the children seemed occupied by getting along as pairs while solving the task. The data showed many incidences of decision making and negotiations with respect to what to focus on and how to describe the place or activity. Second, they related to the issue of research – i.e. the different qualities of the after-school from their point of view – the data sought. But here I will only focus on the third type of engagement; the engagement in research participation. Did the participation mirror research engagements or was the activity in just a friendly talk among peers? Did the absence of the researcher blur the activity, thereby causing ethical problems? At one of the recordings two boys discussed as follows:

Christian: I think you can hear the wind and it is raining a little, but of course you can't feel that.

John: If they could feel how cold it is, I am sure that they wouldn't like it.

Christian: No, and especially not when they are not wearing a jacket.

John: No, because you are not by chance wearing a jacket indoors.

The boys addressed a listener: the researcher. In their reporting activity, they made judgements of what was research relevant and what was not, thereby co-constraining the zone of research. After a break, John said: 'Pernille, we are now turning the tape-recorder on again; it was just something private.' At other times, they showed great sensitivity to the fact that the listener could not see what they saw. So they described what they saw in detail and discussed eagerly together if the talk was understandable to the researcher as a blind participator. The general conclusion was that the reporting children did negotiate with their friends, did relate to the subject of research and did have the research in mind while reporting. During the research process, several asked if the research job was 'vacant' when they became adults. I take this as a sign of engagement in research participation. This particular 'reporter' method came into being because of blocked research activities combined with an attempt to be responsive to the children's 'invitations' or to their 'calls', as Shotter puts it (2000, p. 243.).

An obvious drawback with trying to coordinate with children's engage-ments in research, searching for appropriate child-relevant strategies of data production, is that it can fail. Seeing history in the present also means anticipating potential futures from the present. But to incorporate these potential futures into a method level, trying to combine children's creative and playful 'what-if' solutions to everyday problems with the stringent requirements of research methods might, in the worst case, result in a fuzzy pool of activity, recognisable as neither play nor research.

Conclusion

In this chapter, it has been argued that within a cultural–historical perspec-tive and its conceptualisation of development, children inevitably are partici-pants in research; and when being so, this will in turn affect their develop-ment. I have argued that developmental processes are in principal social and that a developmental interview must be conceived as an *interactional* process where understandings, meanings and practices develop over time. Within this perspective, interviews are not only research tools, but they can also enhance children's developmental possibilities, in line with the modern 'turn' in social sciences outlined earlier in the chapter. This notwithstanding, children's participation in research can also pose them problems in the concrete research setting as well as in their life in the local community.

In order to meet these developmental potentials, some degree of responsiveness is required, implying some degree of co-construction of the constraints that underlie the research activity.

Interviews depend not only on interpretation of what is observed by the researcher, but actively seek negotiation of meaning with the subjects in question. Thus, intersubjectivity and interactivity are basic to interview research. Achieving intersubjectivity between researcher and interviewee is not a scientific result in itself: It requires a theoretically informed perspective on what the intersubjectivity is about.

In agreeing to interact with respect to the *form* of the interview, the researcher is necessarily confronted with the dialectics between her theoretically constrained setting and the children's interpretations and meaning making concerning what activity they are participating in. Upon considering on the *content* of the interview, the inductive, generative process of carrying out interviews and analysing interview data consists of a dialectical relation between the intersubjectivity achieved during interviews and the researcher's theoretical perspective.

10 Framing a questionnaire using a cultural–historical approach

Jytte Bang and Mariane Hedegaard

As stated in the introduction to this book, a cultural–historical approach implies studying children's development by following their everyday activities in their local settings. The institutional and societal conditions are considered as resources for the child's development in a variety of ways. Therefore, it is important to explore how a child relates and contributes to those conditions. This also implies that we must study how a child relates to herself and how she feels about being a participant in specific activities embedded in specific institutional practices. A variety of methods can be used to gain information about the child as a participant in different activities. Observing the child through videotaping (see Chapter 5 and 6), for instance, is one source of information, and interviewing the child is another (see Chapter 7). When interviewing and observing a child (or a group of children) one can acquire knowledge about the child's thoughts and feelings and learn what is important to this specific child, what kind of problems, commitments, etc., the child is occupied with.

In addition to observing and interviewing, using a questionnaire is another source for gaining information about the lives of children. A questionnaire is useful for researchers who want to study practices in which practitioners work with *planned activities* as well as *planned goals* for groups of children; further, it is also useful for practitioners who need a tool by which they are able to evaluate the practice in order to improve developmental conditions for children. In other words, a questionnaire can be used meaningfully in those cases where many children are involved in institutional activities; however, it need not be restricted to societal institutions where many children are located (like school or kindergarten); the family is also a societal institution and a questionnaire can be used to study and compare children's developmental conditions in or across families. Whenever a researcher or a practitioner wants to develop a questionnaire, she should consider the local and national values that are relevant to the study. By focusing her attention on that, the researcher will have a better chance of understanding the actions and feelings of a child or a group of children. It will help her to gain a wholeness perspective on the children when she includes the historical and societal values embedded into the local and national practices. Of course, those values may transcend national borders, but potentially this only widens the perspective.

It is often assumed that a questionnaire is useful only as a means for acquiring quantitative data about anonymous groups of people in order to differentiate activities, values, etc.; but answers given in a questionnaire are also meaningful as a qualitative source of information about a single child's developmental conditions in relation to other children. A questionnaire can be used to let several children reveal their own thoughts and feelings about specific issues in concrete practices; hence a questionnaire created for developmental purposes within institutional practices takes full advantage of qualitative data in a quantitative way and vice versa.

'Strong' and 'weak' poles in institutional practices

The societal institutions not only vary in respect to what kind of activities they offer; they also vary in the degree of goal-directedness. These variations have an impact on how children's self-evaluation may influence the practice and the goals of an institution. Not all activities within an institutional practice are directly related to narrow goal-directed practice; free play is an example of children's self-organised activities that transcend specific goal-directed practices. When, for instance, a child participates in free play with other children in kindergarten she does not participate in any goal defined beyond the play itself (Leontiev, 1977). However, even though the play is free (viewed from an institutional point of view), it is motivated (viewed from the child's point of view). In any case, self-organised free play is part of the opportunities suggested by institutions for children to be engaged with. Some institutions, such as school, do not value free self-initiated play very highly. In school, explicit goals are often greatly valued and this has a great impact on the structure and organisation of activities in everyday life. In these different settings, self-evaluation takes on different values, as in the more implicit goal-oriented activity of free play.

In other words, self-evaluation can be considered as having a 'weaker' and a 'stronger' pole depending on how close to the specified goals of an institution the self-evaluation is being displayed. If a questionnaire is being used in institutions with strongly formulated goals and values, the question-naire may be constructed to gain an insight into how a child thinks about herself and her participation in relation to those goals and values. This study may find itself at the 'weak' pole as long as the perspective of the child as a respected person is being put into the front. The danger, of course, is when the child's perspective is being diminished. This may be the case if the motive for developing the questionnaire is to control children's actions and perspectives on themselves, which brings the questionnaire closer to the 'strong' pole. The closer to the 'stronger' pole, the more the developmental perspective of the questionnaire seems to become restricted. A highly restricted use of the questionnaire in the end only studies how a child lives up to specific and well-defined goals set by an institution. In this case, it becomes a serious ethical issue for the researcher whether she really is including the child's perspective in her study or whether it is a case of forcing the child to live up to predefined standards of participation. While the former is the aim of the cultural–historical research outlined in this book, the latter is the aim of those who do not worry about setting forth processes that aim to make individuals internalise power relations (Rose, 1999). When planning to construct a questionnaire that uses self-evaluation, the researcher should be aware of the 'strong–weak' pole problematic and commit herself to act ethically and sensitively in relation to this.

Values and goals related to different perspectives

By taking the different perspectives of a practice into consideration (the societal, the institutional and the child's perspective), it becomes possible to examine how the competencies and motives of the child develop and how these competencies and motives are connected with what is regarded as 'a good life'. Conceptions of a good life vary depending on the practice tradition of different institutions and the concrete persons participating in this practice.

A researcher who wants to use a questionnaire as a method has first to invent the questionnaire. Questionnaires grow out of historically developed practices, as described above. Attention should be paid to which kinds of questions are proper in relation to the aspects mentioned above: how *an individual child participates in valued activities*; the relation between *the individual child and other children* as well as the relation between *the individual child and significant others;* and *how the child thinks and feels about his or her own participation.*

In the following sections, we will exemplify how a questionnaire that includes self-evaluation can be designed. The aim has been to design a questionnaire that could be used by teachers to evaluate how subject matter teaching in school creates conditions for children's personal development. We will approach the task from the three suggested perspectives: the societal, the tradition of the specific institution and the children's perspective.

The societal perspective

As stated above, it is important initially in the design process to reflect upon the characteristics of the institution the research is addressing, including its societal and local history. In the case example of the questionnaire presented here, it was carried out in relation to students in the Danish elementary school (9–10-year-old children).

Even though (roughly speaking) the overall goals and values of school may appear similar all over the world, this is not the case when one takes a closer look at national school systems. National school systems are historically developed and have grown to become a part of the school policy of the country; the school policy resonates the diversity of cultural, political, and economical developments in a country. In the Danish school, social continuity is highly valued throughout a child's school years and the elementary school has for many years been based on traditional social democratic values of 'equality through education' as well as of educating to democracy. In the published goals for the Danish elementary school, the Ministry of Education explicitly stresses values, like preparing the students for future participation in a society with freedom and democracy. The school should be a place that promotes the freedom of spirit, equality and democracy. Also, the school should develop a desire for learning and for knowing, being sensitive to one's own and other cultures, etc. (EMU/*Danmarks undervisningsportal*). As a budding citizen, the personal development of the child as a member of her class in school is considered important and pro-social behaviour and supportive attitudes towards other students are valued in all kinds of activity. It is a spoken value that everyone should feel comfortable going to school. The continuity of the class structure offers an opportunity to make the social and individual development of the children an integrated part of learning; the practice concept of learning is a wide one.[1]

In the Danish school system, the institutional practice and discourse, however, is *not* homogeneous. On the one hand, some values speak for a pedagogical tool that can be used to evaluate how the personal development of the child is taking shape over time. On the other hand, courses and goals in recent years are becoming standardised at a national level with testing being suggested as a valued activity to control and evaluate learning outcomes (see Figure 10.1).

This creates a dilemma within which we had to work. On the one hand, we had the traditional values that stressed the importance of personal development and development through shared activities; on the other hand, we had the growing ideological influence that suggested testing as a means for evaluating quality and progress. What we *did* want to design was a tool to be used by practitioners who wanted to explore and improve their local practice. In this respect it was important that the questionnaire gave the

Figure 10.1 Children working in a Danish 3rd grade.

children opportunities to express themselves in relation to activities and social relations, because that would be a 'real life' criterion for developmental possibilities. What we did *not* want to design was a test for evaluating children's personal development independent of school practice and the child's own self-evaluation. *Neither* did we want to develop a questionnaire only with the aim of controlling how children live up to testable standard expectations of the school. The aim is to develop materials that can be used for 'dialogue, mutual understanding' and for 'shared future planning'; those are values that we as researches resonate with and find are worth maintaining as societal values; 'valuations' and 'selection' is part of contextual research practice.

The institutional perspective

As a societal institution, school should not only teach the children, but also evaluate the learning outcome. In recent years, Danish schools are putting more emphasis on encouraging and evaluating the personal development of the child. The discourse focuses on an individual in an internationalised world where it is important to stay open to future possibilities and developments. Therefore, the personal development of the child increasingly becomes a part of being educated. Learning and development merge as processes and the school is in need of pedagogical tools for evaluating the personal development of the child.

The child's perspective

According to Vygotsky (1998), evaluating a child's development means evaluating its movements and potentialities within the zone of proximal development. Evaluating a child's development means taking a look into the possible future of the child, rather than into its past. When taking a look into the potential future of the child it becomes possible for practitioners to explore the motivations and emotionality of the child, the possible paths the child can follow and how to contribute in responsible and supportive ways to the general development of the child.

Following Vygotsky's ideas, we advocate a 'weak' model of self-evaluation in a 'strong' system because we want to evaluate the child's perspective on goal-directed activities without turning it into an instrument against the child herself. This point is important from a cultural–historical perspective, because it is 'the potentialities for development in the community of practice' which we think the questionnaire should be aimed at, rather than the evaluation of the child on the basis of fixed, rigid, and alienated predetermined goals.

Unfortunately, this point is crucial to mention because much effort can be put (and is put) into systems of evaluation and control. We are critical about systems that attempt to evaluate and control children in schools through national testing, and through the use of logbooks and diaries. The test regime is being displayed all over the world. Vygotsky (1987a) has already criticised the limitations of testing children's development on the basis of predetermined goals. This kind of testing only (at best) gives an idea of how the child has developed up to the time of testing. It has no anticipative value in relation to the future developments of the child. This insight led him to formulate his idea of the 'zone of proximal development'. In her critical discussion of the use of tests in American schools, Linda McNeil (1988) focuses on how teaching in classes turns into teaching for the test which means that open exploration of some subject matter becomes diminished or even irrelevant. Teaching and learning become instrumentalised and progress is turned into 'scoring well in tests'. The other attempt at first glimpse seems like one that includes a child's perspective on learning. We are thinking here of the introduction of 'diaries' and 'log books' into classroom practices, which have also developed as a common practice in some national school systems. Diaries and log books are used to help children to gain a meta-cognitive awareness of their own participation and continued progression through the learning process. However, if such peda-gogical tools are being used to discipline the child, self-evaluation has turned into an internalisation of unquestioned power relations in the classroom. Obviously, this has not much to do with taking the child's perspective; hence, it is far from qualifying as a child's perspective.

Construction of a questionnaire based on a cultural–historical theory

Using a questionnaire in institutional practices to evaluate children's social situation of development means asking each child in a structured way about issues assumed to be relevant to many children who – on an institutional level – share similar developmental conditions. A questionnaire makes it possible to study specific children as members of a group who share developmental conditions in institutions like kindergarten, school, family, after-school activities, sports, etc.

A questionnaire that addresses the child's social situation of develop-ment – which means taking the perspective on the child's participation in practices – should reflect (a) *how an individual child participates in institution-ally valued activities*; (b) *the relations between the child and other children*; (c) *the relations between the child and significant others* (pedagogues, teachers, parents, etc.)*;* and (d) *how the child thinks and feels about her own participation.*

The first three aspects address how a child participates in activities with other children and adults. The fourth aspect offers the child an opportunity to reflect upon herself as a participant. We will refer to these views on self as a participant in activities as *self-evaluation*. It is essential to note that the self-evaluating aspect is more than self-reflection. It is self-reflection in relation to activities in which the child participates together with others in her everyday life. It is meaningful as a way for the child to think about herself in relation to others and in relation to shared meaningful and valued activities.

In general, self-evaluation as a method is often used by groups (such as research groups) to reflect on how work is progressing and to identify problems relevant in this process; in this respect, self-evaluation has an internal function in a group but it is also expected to imply changes needed for further progression. When self-evaluation is being used to research a child's development, some adjustments are needed. A child's development, for once, cannot be studied as progression along a predetermined line or with reference to clearly defined goals; children's development is dynamic in nature and to a large extent indeterministic (Valsiner, 1987). Children are different and develop differently. Self-evaluation as an aspect of the question-naire should reflect this dynamic of determinism–indeterminism of chil-dren's development.

First source of inspiration: the national goals and curriculum outlines

The Danish Ministry of Education has formulated a guide called *The Common Goals*. The guide specifies the general aims and specific goals at different grade levels both for children's development of personality and for their appropriation of subject matter competence within different subject areas. *The Common Goals* constitute the countrywide foundation for all subject areas, which means that each teacher should teach with reference to those national goals.

Goals for children's personal development

The goals in the guide express the value of viewing 'learning and personal development as an integrated and inseparable unit' in the Danish school system. These values rest, as previously mentioned, on historically developed values in school and society. Those values are specified in three integrated domains:

- Many ways of learning
- Desire to learn
- Learning together with others.

Many ways of learning expresses the idea that learning is a multi-dimensional process that should include several different activities. It is assumed that each child has her specific knowledge basis when attending school. This should be taken into consideration and respected when planning how to organize the learning process.

Desire to learn stresses how it is important for a child to experience positive emotions in the learning process as well as the excitement to know more and master more – the development of curiosity, interests, and the joyfulness of activity is regarded important.

Learning together with others points out that learning should not be considered an isolated individual activity; rather, learning means sharing, exchange of ideas, listening to each other, helping each other, and contributing to the class (and school) community. Those are essential values in a democratic society.

Second source of inspiration: observing classes with a focus on teaching practice and values

The second source of inspiration in our formulation of questionnaires for children's personal development within the area of Danish and maths was observing the activities going on in classrooms within Danish and maths lessons. Both authors have many years' experience observing in school classes (Hedegaard, 1988, 2002; Bang, 1996). In this concrete project, we followed four 3rd grade classes in both Danish and maths lessons for 1 day each – two classes in a suburban school, two in a central city school.

We wanted to acquire a general impression of the school activities and practices within the classroom in order to build a contextual understanding for the materials we were aiming to develop. Our aim was to construct material that was neither too general nor too specific; the questions should resonate with classroom practices and values in Danish schools and it should make reference to the subject areas of Danish and maths. Observing the classroom activities helped us to reflect upon whether our questionnaire seemed to be in accordance with the everyday activities in school. To illustrate how we worked with the information, a sequence from a Danish lesson and one from a maths lesson is presented. In the left column is the transcription of the observation made in the classroom. In the right column are the initial interpretations made by the observer once the observation has been transformed into a *text*. Those initial interpretations serve to order the material as well as to advise the researcher's awareness of possible interesting aspect of the activities to go on with in a further interpretation and discussion with the other observer.

Danish subject teaching in 3rd grade

Copenhagen North School, Class A, Teacher A, Tuesday 8–9 am, observer JB

1 *Teacher A* announces that the children themselves are going to start writing a story.	The lesson is part of a continuous activity concerning story telling and the use of fantasy in relation to reality. Today the children will be the writers.
2 In the beginning of the class, they read aloud a story from the textbook about a character 'Fabian' who experiences incredible things.	

3	*Teacher A* has a conversation with the class about what are the unlikely events. The children find that cutting out one's eye and putting it in the back of the head is unlikely to happen; so is a horse eating with silverware or keeping oneself awake for 20 years. This conversation about Fabian's experiences apparently is meant to inspire the children into telling their own fantasy stories containing unlikely elements. They are going to pretend that they are Fabian and write a story by themselves of what he experiences.	Teacher–class conversation focusing on storytelling elements. Pretend-to-be (I-perspective) focused.
4	*Teacher A* asks if the children already have some good ideas to present to the class. Almost all of the children have ideas and they share them one after the other as teacher A writes down the ideas on the blackboard.	Teacher A invites children to share ideas.
5	*Nina:* A horse who likes to dance break dance.	
6	*Teacher A:* Okay, but please remember that it is you who are going to tell the story – what do we call such a type of storyteller?	Almost all children collaborate and have ideas.
7	(No responses from the class.)	
8	*Teacher A:* An 'I-storyteller' (goes a little deeper into it).	Meta-focus on genre
9	*Anton:* I would like to write about a rock star that drops his underwear on the stage.	
10	*Mathias:* I want to write about Fabian who finds a treasure map and then finds a thing; he pushes the buttons and it shows up to be a time machine and he arrives in the 30th century.	Suggestion with a plot.
11	*Teacher A:* That is a good suggestion; you do have a good fantasy, Mathias.	
12	*Karoline:* I would write a story where Fabian gets bitten by a monster and comes up to God and Jesus.	

13 *Mette:* What about a house that can sing?	The next few suggestions seem to be spontaneous and inspired by each other – image-like without a plot.
14 *Karoline:* What about a horse who goes shopping?	
15 *Lasse:* Or what about a monkey who wears a woman's dress?	
16 *Mette:* A cap that can talk!	
17 The class continues like this for a while and in the end the teacher has written all of the suggestions on the blackboard.	
18 *Teacher A* reads the suggestions aloud and it is time to begin writing.	
19 *Anton:* I don't understand what we are going to write.	Teacher A is taking all suggestions seriously; they are all shared.
20 *Teacher A:* We are going to write what Fabian would like to tell …	Shift of activity – individual writing.
21 *Anton:* But we have only 15 minutes left for today …	Child seems uncertain about the activity and how it is framed.
22 *Teacher A:* Well, we shouldn't expect to finish our stories today, we can continue when we meet again.	The teacher helps to frame the activity.
23 The children leave their seats to form groups. Some of them stay in the classroom; others find some tables in the space outside the classroom. *The observer* asks *Elias* what he would like to write about.	Children select each other by choice.
24 *Nina* also wants to know that.	
25 *Elias* says that he will not tell her (Nina) unless she also tells him what she is going to write about.	
26 *Nina* says that she wants to write about a horse that likes to dance break dance.	Interaction between children to get started; speaking/acting to frame the writing process; negotiating conditions of the exchange.
27 *Nina* and *Elias* start talking about whether a horse really can do that.	

28 *Nina* lies down on the floor to show Elias what a horse might not be able to do; then she leaves Elias to sit with two other girls.	
29 *Elias* says nothing.	
30 The three girls start talking aloud about the unlikely elements in their stories.	Interaction with focus on the core of the activity – the unlikely elements and how to work with them in personal ways; communicating as part of the individual work.

Interpretation of Teacher A's goal and values

From a research perspective the observations presented gives an impression of Teacher A's goals and values in relation to *The Common Goals* from the Danish Ministry of Education.

Sharing focused attention on subject matter of the day (1–22). The activities of the day are a part of an ongoing, continued activity which connects one lesson with the next one. In the beginning of this specific lesson, teacher A has conversations with the class and it is expected that every child should be actively listening to what the teacher has to say. Time is spent on focusing the children's attention on the specific task and issues of the day and each child is expected to co-focus along with the teacher. In this case, Teacher A is trying very hard to focus the attention of the children on specific elements like storytelling, pretend-to-be (I-perspective), and unlikely elements in the stories. These are practical examples of goals described for Danish as a subject area and they illustrate how goals are finding their way into practice.

The group as a platform for individual work (23–30). Teacher A expects the children to contribute individually by giving ideas prior to writing their own stories and all ideas are accepted and unquestioned. The child may-and-should contribute to the community of practice as well as to her own work process. Individuality, hence, is a may-and-should activity embedded in the shared participation. It is also present later in the lesson when the children are going to work by themselves. Working by oneself still means being with others and sharing with others; the classroom is not a silent place where each child is only occupied with his or her own individual tasks to the exclusion of others; it is a social place where the sharing of ideas, framing of the actual task, and general social exchange is taking place. Very often, as shown above in the observation, the children sit at a table with other children and a multilayered communication is taking place.

Summing up values. From a research perspective, some of the essential values in this historically developed classroom practice include: collaboration; giving and receiving help, inspiration, and instruction from the teacher and from classmates; being focused on the subject area and the task put by the teacher; respecting the teacher's authority given by the historically accepted possibilities and constraints of the institution; respecting each other's contributions; expecting individual contribution to be a *may-and-should*; and being able to master individual work in a shared participation with others.

Maths subject teaching in 3rd grade in a suburban school

Copenhagen North School, Class B, Teacher B, Tuesday, 10–11 am, observer JB

1 The class is gathered on the floor and receives instruction from *Teacher B*. Today they are all going to do measurements. The children are going to form three groups, each group working on a specified task.	Shared focus on the task of the day – *measurements*. Group formation.
2 In one group are two girls and two boys. They want to measure the size of a football.	One boy is more active and communicating. No units, no thoughts about 'size'.
3 *Ole:* I did measure it and it is 20.	
4 *Teacher B* asks him to put it away.	
5 *Ole* (to Karoline): You look like someone who I saw yesterday on television …it was an odd girl, one could see her underwear.	Personal communication about something else.
6 They all have each a piece of paper and have a conversation about how to partition it. Pencils fly across the table.	Shared relevant activity.
7 *Ole* (to Karoline): I want to write the result. You have Pipi Longstocking tails.	Personal communication about something else.
8 *Teacher B:* You all need to continue working – what are you doing?	Teacher B starts structuring and focusing the group work by asking questions; Children answer the questions and act accordingly.
9 *Ole:* Making a multiplication table.	
10 *Teacher B:* What are you going to use for that?	
11 *Ole:* Pencils.	
12 *Teacher B:* Where are they?	

13   *Ole:* Over there!

14   *Teacher B:* Go pick them up (she helps the group find a sharp pencil and instruct them how to solve the task. The group remains quieter and everyone tries to make a table).

15   *Teacher B*: Did you measure a book?

16   *Ole:* No, a ball.

17   *Teacher B:* Then you write 'ball' (on the paper) and what did you find the measurement of the ball to be?

A book probably is the standard, but the ball is accepted.

18   *Ole:* 20... no 22.

19   *Teacher B:* That was not what you said before.

Teacher B asks for precision.

20   *Ole:* (makes another measure) 20 (cm, JB)

Teacher B wants each child to do the measurements by themselves.

21   *Teacher B:* Well, and now you may put it away again (the ball).

22   *Teacher B*: Walid, did you measure the ball yourself? Are you sure that it is 20, 2?

Teacher B does not trust Walid's answer.

23   *Walid*: I did measure it.

24   *Teacher B:* Did you do it yourself?

25   *Walid:* No.

26   *Teacher B*: Then I think that you should do it

Teacher B wants Walid to do the measuring.

27   *Walid* goes to get the ball and makes a measure of it.

28   *Walid* tries unsuccessfully to bend the ruler around the ball.

29   *Teacher B:* Maybe Ole can advise you how to do it.

Teacher B suggests collaboration and is successful.

30   *Ole* laughs a little but then he shows to Walid how he can make the ruler stand on the table besides the ball.

31   *Walid:* 20...?

32   *Teacher B:* Okay, now write that down ... how long did you expect the ball to be?

33   *Walid:* 22!

34 *Teacher B:* 22, you can write it there (in the table)… Walid, what can you do now to show what the result was and what was your guess?	Teacher B tries to make Walid focus upon the difference between a guess and a measure.
35 *Walid* says nothing.	
36 *Teacher B* suggests that he can write the numbers with different colors and tells Walid: You got a ball to put back into the closet.	Teacher B suggests a method for the registration of differences.
37 *Walid* puts the ball back.	
38 *Teacher B*: What would you do next?	Teacher B appeals to Walid's initiative, unsuccessfully.
39 *Walid:* I don't know.	
40 *Teacher B:* You should write the numbers down; you can do that.	
41 *Teacher B* leaves the group to go help another one.	The children now work on their own again.
42 The two girls Karoline and Maja collaborate.	The two girls who were only watching are now getting active.
43 *Maja:* What are we going to write?	
44 *Karoline* (to Ole): You have to do the measure yourself!	Rejects Ole.
45 *Maja* tries to get the book which lies next to Karoline.	
46 *Karoline*: No, I am going to use that now (she begins to measure it)…22 (puts the book in the middle of the table).	Rejects Maja's initiative. Maja seems to accept the dominance.
47 *Maja* takes the book and begins to measure it.	
48 *Karoline* takes the football and makes a measurement of it with the help of two rulers, then she puts it away	
49 *Maja:* What is it that we are doing, why don't you tell me what you are writing?	Uncertain, appeals for help (a little blaming).
50 *Karoline* still mostly focused on Ole; she does not really collaborate with Maja.	Karoline ignores her.
51 *Maja* does not do much, plays a little with the pencil.	
52 *Maja:* What am I going to do?	Maja tries again.

53	*Karoline* makes a 'how stupid are you?' attitude with her hands.	Karoline rejects her, makes her look stupid.
54	*Karoline*: You are supposed to measure it!	
55	*Maja* twists her hair, seems to give up.	Maja resigns.

Interpretation of Teacher B's goals and values

Sharing focused attention on subject matter of the day (1). In the beginning of the lesson Teacher B is having a conversation with the class about the activities of the day. They are all going to do measurements in different groups and Teacher B is instructing what to do.

The group as a platform for individual work (2–7). The children form small groups and are expected to do the measurements individually but as a shared activity. The present observation is focused mostly upon the group work because observing this part of the lesson takes the most time. Even though every child is expected to contribute to the group process (as parallel measurement activities) the contributions are not distributed homogeneously. One boy, Ole, in one of the observed groups, seems to talk more and to do more measurements than the girls in the group. He communicates with the other three participants by shifting between personal communication (especially in relation to one of the girls – Karoline) and communication about the measurement. The measurements are done by the help of a ruler; however he does not operate with any measurement units, nor does he reflect upon the concept of size.

The intervention of teacher B (8–38). Teacher B apparently notices the inhomogeneous contributions and appears to help to structure the group activities according to the expectations initially set up. Teacher B structures and focuses the group work through asking questions; and the children accept Teacher B's intervention by just answering the questions and by doing what they are told to do. Each item that the children select to be measured is accepted by Teacher B, but precision in measurements is asked for by the teacher. The demand of individual–shared activity is communicated to the children through Teacher B focusing on Walid's work. This interaction with Walid becomes a kind of practical demonstration of what is expected of the children in this lesson.

When Teacher B leaves the group (39–53), the remainder of the group (Karoline and Maja) becomes more active, both verbally as well as in doing the measurements. However, they do not collaborate well, nor does Karoline offer much help to Maja who eventually resigns.

Summing up values. In relation to maths, it seems that some of the essential values are similar to those in Danish, however the subject areas differ. Similar values seem to be: collaboration; receiving help and instruction from teacher; giving and receiving help; being focused on the subject area and the task put forth by the teacher; respecting the teacher's authority and right to make an intervention; being able to follow instructions and to work progressively; respect each other as an individual in a shared activity; expecting individual contribution to be a may-and-should activity; being able to master individual work in a shared participation with others.

Implementing values from maths and Danish subject teaching into a questionnaire

The sequences of the observations have made it clear how the values of the Danish School presented earlier (values that have grown along with the cultural–historical traditions of practice and activities) appear in the lessons. For instance, one may mention the following values: children are expected to be active and co-construct the learning situations; learning may be an individual process but the single child generally participates in shared activities; the teacher is a practitioner who has to balance between setting up the activity, structuring the process, and offering the children opportunities to express themselves together with others. Problems in handling a particular practice becomes perceivable to the researcher as she makes her observations.

From these classroom observations in this specific cultural–historical context, we learned that *not being able to participate individually or to contribute to a shared activity, not being respected and listened to, not being able to give and to receive help, not being able to receive instruction or to trust the teacher, not being able to trust others, not knowing what the tasks are about and not knowing what to do with it, not mastering the learned-about preconditions or skills necessary in relation to a specific task* (*like reading or counting*), *etc.* are all examples of specific issues that may grow to be a potentially larger developmental issues for a child. Hence, from an analysis based on a cultural–historical perspective it is very important that the pedagogical tool invented reflect such potential developmental issues so that the professionals who care for the child and its development will be able to manage those issues and to invent their own practice in order to advance the child.

Nevertheless, it is possible to identify certain traits, goals, expectations and values that are the culturally shaped developmental conditions for those children. In a tool made for evaluating the children's personal development by help of self-report, those developmental conditions should be reflected. Identifying those conditions helps to identify what a child might consider as being difficult and so it becomes possible to identify developmental issues for a child within the activities in which she is supposed to participate each day.

These considerations should be regarded as a preliminary guideline for the further development of a pedagogical tool. The questionnaire, for instance, should be able to grasp those values because they are the foundations upon which the school rests and are the bases for children's development through participation in school activities. As pointed out in Chapter 2, what is considered good development and a good childhood cannot be evaluated without taking into consideration (a) the developmental conditions and value systems in which children grow up and (b) the opportunities that children have to contribute to and participate in activities set up within those conditions.

In the theoretical section we stressed that children's self-evaluation, even in institutions with strong goals and values such as school, should open up and give room for children's self-evaluation oriented towards their own goals (have a weak pole for self-evaluation). When we focus on the three areas of *The Common Goals* for children's personal development: 'many ways of learning', 'desire to learn' and 'learning together' in relation to the two subject areas the questions for self-evaluation have to be formulated in relation to children's everyday life. One way to do this is to question how the school education was transferred into everyday activities and vice versa. For instance, when the children worked with reading and writing Danish and with mathematical tasks, what engaged them and how were their relationships with children both in class and outside class? In constructing the questionnaire, it is important to develop questions that reflect the subject area without being a subject matter questionnaire, and to focus on the diversity of learning, engagement and social relations. The questions should also be formulated so that they are not only meaningful to the children, but they are also able to read them. This is especially important for the early grades. The questions should be very simple statements so that the children understand them and at the same time the questions should relate to what is important for the children.

Construction of a questionnaire

From the two sources of inspiration: the national goals and curriculum outlines and observation of teaching practices and values within the subject matter of maths and Danish we constructed a set of questionnaires for self-evaluation within Danish and maths teaching for children in 3rd/4th and 6th/7th, grades, respectively. This included booklets with questions, theoretical considerations and instructions to administer in the use of the questionnaires for teachers and information material for parents.

These two age levels were chosen because we wanted to invent a pedagogical tool that matches the culturally specific transitions periods in the Danish school system. The 3rd and 4th grades mark the transition from being a newcomer to becoming a mid-school child; the 6th and 7th grades mark the transition from being a mid-school child to starting to be an adolescent preparing for further education.

In the following, we will only exemplify the questionnaire at the first level: i.e. children's self-evaluation in 3rd or 4th grades.

In the first three years in school, the focus on Danish and maths is:

- *Danish:* (a) the spoken language, (b) the written language (to read), (c) the written language (to write), and (d) language, literature, and communication.
- *Maths:* (a) numbers and algebra, (b) geometry, (c) applied maths, and d) communication and problem solving.

The richness and relatively high level of detail of *The Common Goals* made it urgent for us to extract those aspects that seemed to cover essential concepts and skills to be learned (within each subject area the general values are specified into a detailed set of goals at 1st grade, 2nd grade, 3rd grade, etc.). We also found inspiration from a selection of concrete school material. Based on those sources of information we worked out a questionnaire for children's self-report within, respectively, the subjects of Danish and maths in relation to the three aspects of learning activity: many ways of learning, desire to learn, and learning together with others (see Tables 10.1 and 10.2).

Table 10.1 Example from the questionnaire of Danish in 3rd to 4th grade related to the Ministry of Education's Common Goals (Hedegaard, Bang and Egelund, 2007). The left columns show the researcher's theoretical consideration

Many ways of learning				
		In class	At home	At after-school care or other places
How an individual child participates in institutional valued activities	I read mostly books			
	I read mostly comics			
	I read mostly magazines			

Desire to learn			
	To play	To read	To go out and do things
How an individual child participates in institutional valued activities	What I like doing best		
		When I play	When I write	When I do projects
How the child thinks and feels about his own participation	I like to come up with ideas		

Learning together with others			
	Ask the teacher	Ask a friend	Nothing
The relation between the child and other persons in school	When you are writing at school and cannot spell a word, what do you do?		

Learning together with others			
	Other children	Your teacher	Nobody
The relation between the child and other persons in school	When you are doing Danish who helps you, when you feel sad?		

Table 10.2. Example from the questionnaire of mathematics in 3rd to 4th grade related to the Ministry of Education's Common Goals (Hedegaard, Bang and Egelund, 2007). The left columns show the researcher's theoretical consideration

Many ways of learning				
		Mostly in class	*Mostly at home*	*Mostly at after-school care or other places*
How an individual child participates in institutional valued activities	Do you play games where you count and ad up?			
	Do you sometimes measure something and work out its size?			

Desire to learn				
		Often	*In between*	*Seldom*
How an individual child participates in institutional valued activities	Do you enjoy doing maths?			
	Do you enjoy doing maths homework?			

Learning together with others				
		Often	*Sometimes*	*Seldom*
The relation between the child and other children	I like to do maths projects with others			
	I like to sit by myself when I do maths			

Learning together with others				
		Often	*Sometimes*	*Seldom*

How the child thinks and feels about her own participation	When the teacher asks a question in a maths lesson, do you give your opinion?			
The relation between the child and significant others	When you have maths lessons, do you feel sad?			

Testing the questionnaires in the classes

Once we had created an outline for the material, the next step was to test it in practice. We needed to see if the questions appeared to be meaningful to the children; if they understood the questions; if they were able to understand the procedure and to fill out the questionnaire; if we operated with proper and meaningful categories of answers; if the material could be 'scored' for the purpose of acquiring an overall (as well as a specific) impression of the child's development as a basis for a dialogue with the child.

The questionnaires were tested in the same classes as those in which we made our observations. By carefully noticing and writing down the concerns and the questions from the children, we were able to see weaknesses in the questionnaire and revise them. Typically, the weaknesses concerned:

- *words that the children did not understand, categories that seem easy to differentiate for the researcher but not for the children* (such as a differentiation between 'close friend' and 'classmate' which puzzled many children because these categories seemed the same);
- *too much ambiguity concerning the filling out of answers* (the general limitations of filling out questionnaires especially is a challenge when the target group is younger children); and
- *questions that do not make much sense to the children for several reasons* (such as if activities mentioned in the question are too far away from what a child would like to do, so that the child cannot identify herself with the activity).

Scoring the questionnaires

Having tested the questionnaire in the classes, we scored the material to discover not only the variations of answers among the children in each class but also, the variations across the classes. This informed us of the possible patterns in a class and/or for each child. Our scoring principle was simple. First, we wanted to get an impression of tendencies and variations in answers for the class as a whole. We counted how the children's answers were distributed across the possible categories. This would give us an impression of homogeneity (or in-homogeneity) that might reveal some shared experiences of what it was like to be a child participating in this particular class. Second, we worked through each child's answers in the two questionnaires (Danish and maths) together with the teachers of the classes to see if the children's answers, as well as the questions, appeared to be meaningful to them. On the basis of the teachers' comments we revised some of the questions. Also, the teachers were surprised by some of the answers given by particular children and we utilised this situation as an opportunity to learn more about whether the teachers' surprise was due to a lack of knowledge about the children or due to a lack of comprehension of the questionnaire. We spent about one and a half hours talking with the teachers about the answers of each class. This provided us with useful information which enabled us to finish the questionnaires.

Conclusion

In the presentation above, we have tried to make the point clear that, in drawing upon a cultural–historical approach for the development of a questionnaire, this requires active researcher engagement with teachers and cannot be carried out at the researcher's desk. It must be stressed that a significant amount of pre-study is needed for developing tools that seek to study children's lives. In our recent work, we needed to study values and published goals at both a societal and an institutional level. Further, we needed to study how those values and goals were worked with and implemented into particular practices both by studying books used in classes and by being present in the classes ourselves. We became participant observers in a number of classes for a period of time. We collaborated with children and teachers to be able to revise and improve our work-in-progress. Further, we needed the teachers' help in that process because teachers would be responsible for carrying out teaching and setting up conditions for the children's development. Also, the teachers were those who knew the particular children. All this helped us to develop the questionnaire on a more solid foundation relative to ongoing practice.

Note

1   In Denmark, students are not put into courses at different levels. Rather, the teacher should try to teach the child in a class by giving

her material within a common subject area which meets the 'level' of the child. This is called the 'differentiation of teaching'.

11 The educational experiment

Mariane Hedegaard

Within the cultural–historical tradition there is a history of using natural experiments as an intervention into everyday practice. Research by Vygotsky and Luria (i.e. Luria and Yoduvich, 1959; Luria, 1976) represents the beginning of the research tradition. Also Western research inspired by Vygotsky, such as Scribner and Cole (Cole and Scribner, 1974; Scribner and Cole, 1981), has used the natural experiment for researching children's literacy competence. Their research in Liberia related to different natural variations in education practices as a result of changes in cultural traditions.

A cultural–historical methodology reflects the conceptions of dialectical thinking and knowledge that are realised by research into social practice. In this chapter, I seek to capture the natural experiment or intervention into a practice (i.e. when practice changes the phenomenon studied) from a cultural–historical perspective. An example of this type of research can be found in the work of Luria and Yudovitch where they researched two identical twins who:

> ... suffered from a peculiar defect which created conditions for retardation of speech development; added to this was the twin situation which did not create an objective necessity for developing language and so constituted a factor which fixed the retardation.
>
> (1959, p. 120)

In this study, two twins around 5 years of age developed a way of interacting where speech and action could not be separated. They could understand each other, but it was difficult for the caregiving persons in the institution to understand them. Furthermore, they could not use language divorced from action and were therefore unable to plan activities or organise complex play. As a first step of intervention, the twins were separated and the second step was to give one twin special language training lessons. These interventions influenced the language and planning activity of both twins, especially the one who received extra language training and a significant increase in intellectual competencies was noted.

Scientific knowledge formation from a cultural–historical perspective

In Chapter 3, I argued that within the cultural–historical approach observation, interview and the experiment all have to be seen as dialectical–interactive methods that are based on intervention into practice. But the experiment as a dialectic–interactive method has to be seen as more grounded in a theoretical analyses of relations and therefore is more systematic as a planed intervention than occurs for interviews and the observation methods.

Theoretical–dialectical thinking presupposes an image of the undeveloped homogeneous whole which reflects the theory of the subject area as well as the problem area being studied. Therefore, the scientific process can be seen as having two main phases: the first pertains to the undivided image of the problem area and the second constitutes the analyses of the relations in the specific objects in the wholeness of the problem area.

These two phases do not directly need to follow each other in the same research project. The point is that within a new problem area concepts are more vague and fragile. If the problem area has been established and conceptual relations have been formulated or modelled, these theoretical concepts can then be challenged through experimental research.

In the first phase, the research is closely connected with the life situation of the subjects, the researcher's model of how to invent and what to ask is very vague. The researcher (more or less intuitively) records her impression of the changes and contradictions in the process; through participant observation or through interviews she becomes part of the context, collecting protocol material. Through interpretation of these protocol records some conceptions about the object of research can be formed and the researcher can systematise the knowledge and formulate models of relations.

In the second phase, the researcher builds on already formulated conceptual relations within a problem area that were outcomes of the studies that took place in the first phase and thereby it becomes possible to formulate more integrated models of conceptual relations. The researcher in the second phase uses the conceptual relations and the conceptual models formulated through the research in the first phase. Here she explores if the conceptual models are useful by either focusing on natural experimental variations or by creating experimental intervention into everyday practice. This allows for an evolving theoretical understanding and for the creation of new and better practice conditions for children's development. The methodological aspects of the second phase are characterised by the researcher's intentional transformation of practices in the problem area to bring out the central relations. This experimentation is the topic of this chapter and will be illustrated by the educational experiment. The educational experiment has a history as noted in the studies by Vygotsky and Luria of the natural experiment and in Bronfenbrenner's formulation of the ecological experiment.

The ecological experiment

Bronfenbrenner's (1977) formulation of the ecological experiment is in line with the agenda of Luria's and Vygotsky's work of researching change in institutional practice, as illustrated earlier in the identical twins example of Luria and Yoduvitch.

Bronfenbrenner advocates, from an ecological point of view, the experimental method where several systems (such as different societies, institutions or settings) are studied at the same time:

> An *ecological experiment* is an effort to investigate the progressive accommodation between the growing human organism and its environment through a systematic contrast between two or more environmental systems or the structural components, with a careful attempt to control other sources of influence either by random assignment (contrived experiment) or by matching (natural experiment).
>
> (1977, p. 517)

Although there are close similarities between Bronfenbrenner's ecological approach and the cultural–historical approach that we advocate in this book, there are also some differences. The first is connected to Bronfenbrenner's model of ecological systems. He writes: '*The ecological environment is conceived topological as a nested arrangement of structures, each contained within the next*' (1977, p. 514). The model presented in Chapter 2 (see Figure 2.1) does not depict conditions for children's development as nested but rather outlines how a child is always dialectically related to several forms of institutional practice – where a child through its own activities contributes to the practice and thereby to its own developmental conditions. Bronfenbrenner, in later work (1995), conceptualised the relation between person, process, context and time; an important improvement of transcending his earlier model of inscribing the child within a nested system. Still Bronfenbrenner's conceptualisation of development, is a 'bird's eye' view where the different perspectives of person and practices do not necessarily interplay as described in Chapter 2. In our approach, children's development has to be seen as a dialectical relation between a person's activities and institutional practices. A person's development of motives and cognition are dialectically related to his or her creation of activities in practices with different demands. Children's activities and institutional practices are conditions for each others change and development and these conditions have to be seen as related to the traditions and values in the institutions.

The second point where Bronfenbrenner's approach differs to our approach is where he points to himself. He writes that cultural–historical researchers have taken a step further than the ecological experiment allows. The research in the cultural–historical tradition is not oriented to 'how the child came to be what he is, but how he can become what he is not yet' (Bronfenbrenner, 1977, p. 528).

The ideas in Vygotsky's, Luria's, Elkonin's and Leontiev's research were not only to study consciousness of the mind but also to show how, through education, one can contribute to children's intellectual and personality development. The child learns through being together with more competent people and through their guidance the child's competence is considered (as formulated in Vygotsky's concept of the zone of proximal development; see Chapter 3). Bronfenbrenner is very positive about this aspect and argues for an ecological experiment:

> Research on the ecology of human development should include experiment involving innovative structuring of prevailing ecological systems in ways that depart from existing institutional ideologies and structures by redefining goals, roles and activities and providing interconnections between systems previously isolated from each other.
>
> (1977, p. 528)

Bronfenbrenner suggests that examples of this kind of transforming experiment are rare but can be found. He points to the research of Klaus et al. (1972) for the importance of the first post-partum days for maternal attachment. This kind of research has had tremendous influence on changing hospital practice in the 1970s in relation to childbirth in Scandinavia, where the newborn baby stays with the mother after the baby is delivered. 'Transformative experiments' in attachment research have been influential in changing societal practice (see Schaffer's 1998 review and critique of early research within this area).

With Davydov (1990), the transformative experiments as intervention into practice took another step forward. Davydov pointed to the difference forms of scientific knowledge, and advocated theoretical–dialectical knowledge, as a foundation for educational practice. With Davydov's concept of theoretical–dialectical knowledge, the foundation for the educational research experiment was laid for creating the transformative educational experiment.

The educational experiment

The educational experiment contains elements of the paradigms of both the traditional experiment and of action research, but there are significant differences between the methodology of the educational experiment and that of the traditional experiment.

In the paradigm of the traditional experiment, the effect of an independent variable on a dependent variable is investigated by changing the independent variable in a predetermined way. On the basis of a theory about the connection between the two variables, hypotheses are formulated from the results of the changes introduced. But the paradigm of the traditional experiment, in which all conditions are controlled and only one factor varies, cannot be used when trying to understand the development of a child within the complexities of a normal life pattern. The parallel between the educational experiment and the traditional experiment is that both involve a systematic intervention of the studied area, which is based upon theory and a systematic registration of how planned changes or interventions will influence a specified system.

The parallel of the educational experiment to action research is to be found in the fact that the researcher must cooperate with educators to carry out the pedagogical intervention in people's lives (Lewin, 1946; Edwards, 2005). The researcher can then observe whether such an intervention results in changes in the complexities of the child's normal life activities by monitoring and studying these activities over a protracted period. In this way, it is possible to undertake research into the importance of different conditions for the child's development. The difference between action research and the educational experiment is that the intervention is planned in relation to a theoretical system and not simply from agendas of practice.

With Davydov's conceptualisation of theoretical–dialectical knowledge 'the educational teaching experiment' became central to cultural–historical research. The educational teaching experiment applied in school contexts examines planned teaching in school practice and analyses how the intervention influences children's learning process and subsequent personality development. In this type of research, it is very important to have clear models of how teaching content should contribute to children's learning and motive development. From a societal perspective the educational experiment also has to relate to the important values that children should gain from their activity in school. Values related to societal aims of teaching are also important theoretical considerations. Fragile and intuitive conceptual relations have no room in this phase. The educational experiment is a multifaceted planned preparation of teaching which has, as its goal, the creation of optimal conditions for the learning and development of the participating children.

The origin of the educational experiment

The educational experiment was inspired by Davydov's ideas of theoretical–dialectical knowledge. Over the years this tradition has had several names – 'teaching on a theoretical basis' (Markova, 1978–79, 1982; Davydov, 1990, 1982), 'ascending from the abstract to the concrete in teaching' (Lompscher, 1985, 1999), 'developmental teaching' (Davydov, 1988a, 1988b, 1988c, 1999), 'the double move in teaching' (Hedegaard, 2002), and 'radical local teaching and learning' (Hedegaard and Chaiklin, 2005). All aspects of these names denominate a part of the teaching approach. The focus is on children's learning and development in relation to subject matter teaching which is based on the principles evolved from Davydov's theory of theoretical–dialectical knowledge (see Chapter 3).

When we look at how the research that has been initiated in Russia and former East Germany as based on Davydov's theory of 'theoretical–dialectical knowledge' and 'developmental teaching' (Lompscher, 1984, 2001; Zuckerman, 1999), it has been ideas from the natural science research paradigm that have dominated – for instance, comparing learning effect in the experimental class with a control class using empirical measurement techniques.

The differences between research in natural science and in social science methodology formulated in the Russian and East German research have not been sufficiently explicated. It is difficult to see how Davydov's theory of knowledge has changed the way the experiment is analysed and scientific knowledge can be accomplished in social science. The focus has been on the documentation of students' scores in examinations and comparison of the effects between an experimental and a control class instead of focusing on the variations in dialectical relations. To follow Davydov's ideas one should follow the transformation in the relation between central concepts in a core model of children's learning and development. In the following section, I will demonstrate how a methodology based on the theory of theoretical-dialectical knowledge actually can be outlined in relation to the theory and model of children's learning and development as presented in Chapter 3.

What should be analysed is the relation between the theoretical principles behind the experiment, the teacher's concrete implementation of teaching practice, the children's activities and how these contribute to the children's motive development, and the appropriation of knowledge and thinking strategies. I have tried to explicate these considerations in my research about the 'double move in teaching' (Hedegaard, 1988, 1990, 2002; Hedegaard, Frost and Larsen, 2004; Hedegaard and Chaiklin, 2005) and will draw on an example from this research to illustrate my conception of an educational experiment from a cultural–historical perspective.

The principles of the double move in teaching as a foundation for the educational experiment

The methodology of the educational experiment in the projects that I draw on is conceptualised as planned intervention. It uses the double move between planned activities and students' actual activities. Formulation and revision of the general plans are seen as a dialectical process that are done jointly by the teacher and researcher and the implemention is undertaken by the teacher through class activities. The experiments conducted within this approach have to be planned on the basis of theoretical considerations of learning, teaching and development in relation to the content of the subject matter area. Together these theoretical considerations shape the plans for both the concrete method and content introduced through teaching. The effect of the teaching following the idea of the 'double move' should be reflected in the learning activity in the following relations, and the educational experiment should reveal:

- How group activity, cooperation and division of work influence children's problem solving and development of motives.
- How using models in teaching help students to formulate their own models which create connections between theoretical concepts and specific events.
- How subject matter methods and teaching strategies lead to personal thinking strategies and changes in children's conceptual models.
- How using procedures influences children's active explorations and their development of motives.

The methodological aspect of the experimental research is connected closely to the theoretical consideration about learning activity and teaching didactics. For our present purpose, I simply want to demonstrate the complexity of the design for the educational activities and how the experimental intervention, as a form of teaching activity, can influence children's learning activity and development. The first relation is based on the presumption that children participate together in learning activity. The second and third take a departure from the conceptions about theoretical–dialectical knowledge and thinking and the fourth is related to the developmental consideration that children's engagement and motive development is central in all learning activity.

The teaching activity must consider children's engagement with each other and the demands of solving tasks together; it should also ensure that the tasks draw on the children's everyday knowledge and interest, and promote shared engagement. The teaching activities should seek to combine these elements with the educational goals and subject matter knowledge in ways that transform and combine children's everyday knowledge and goals, with their motives and interest, into new motives.

Learning is a process that takes place in relation to prior knowledge and how this is transformed into everyday knowledge, as well as how children's motives develop in relation to the goal of teaching, has to be framed as the fifth relation when researching through experimental intervention:

- How stages in teaching relate to phases in students learning: goal phase, model phase, evaluation phase.

This means that the model should be seen as a spiral model in relation to the introduction of new problem areas within subject matter teaching.

An educational experiment within history teaching

The design of educational teaching in 4th grade

The teaching approach will be exemplified by extracts from a 3-year teaching experiment in an elementary school in Denmark from 3rd to 5th grade in biology and history focusing on the themes: evolution of animals, the origin of man and the historical change of society (Hedegaard, 2002). The examples in this chapter will focus on the activity of a single teaching session in 4th grade from the 2nd year of the educational experiment. The example comes from the 12th teaching session (12th week of teaching in 4th grade). Each session covers three school periods (of 50 minutes). There were 37 session in the school year. The teaching in this session was related to the thematic teaching of the historical change of society. In 4th grade the teaching focus is on the following two research questions:

- Why do people live differently today in different places in the world?
- Why did people live differently during different historical periods in Denmark?

The modelling of central concepts into core models was used as a tool to help children to relate theoretically to the historical reality (see Figure 11.1).

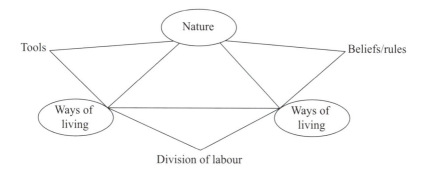

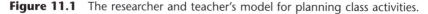

Figure 11.1 The researcher and teacher's model for planning class activities.

Research methodology

In the actual research the educational experiment proceeded through planning meetings between the teachers, the leading researcher and the research assistants. The aim of the teaching was outlined. Each week the teaching and research staff met and discussed a plan for the next teaching session. The observation of the teaching was discussed in relation to the specific teaching plan and a new teaching plan was formulated for the next session.

The students' learning activity was observed through participant observation. The observations were conducted by two observers who focused on both teaching and specific students' activities.

After the school year had finished the observations were interpreted and the material collected from the students and used to evaluate the end result as a qualitative change in students' learning in the form of goal formation, their use of research strategies, their model building and group activities and their ability to reflect on both their own competences and the content of what they had learned in relation to future plans (see Table 11.1. for the categories of interpretation).

Table 11.1 Categories for interpretation of teaching and learning activity

Teaching activity

1. How does the instruction run?
2. What themes are used?
3. What concepts are used in the teaching?
4. What types of conflict does the teacher introduce to be researched?
5. How does the teacher create motivation?

Learning activity

1. *What is the nature of the social interaction of the observed child with the teacher and other children?*
   - Is this social interaction centred on the subject being taught or is it more in the form of a digression from the teaching?
   - Does the child help other children and does s/he seek help from other children?

2. *What motivates and interests the child?*
   - What motives dominate the child's activities?
   - How does the child react to the assignments and requirements of the teaching?
   - Is the child, or does the child become, motivated to participate in the learning activities?
   - What factors provoke an interest in class activities?
     - (a) Are they requirements and assignments set by the teacher?
     - (b) Are they requirements and involvement evinced by the other pupils?

3. *How does the child's thought processes develop?*
   - How does the child structure his/her thinking in relation to the three main activities in the teaching?
     - (a) Problem formulation and model formulation?
     - (b) Use of procedures and models?
     - (c) Evaluation and changing of the model and of own capacities?

4. *What characterises the child's concepts about the topics introduced in the teaching?*
   - What characterises the child's perception of time and of periods of history?
   - Can the child work with models that connect nature, conditions of life and society for certain periods of history?
   - Do these models eventually embrace an element of change?
   - Does the child learn to explain the changes that occur in ways of life and in society from one period of history to the next?
   - What types of problem characterise the child's conceptual understanding?

Realisation of the principles in the double move approach

The theoretical principles for the educational experiment have to be concretised to follow how the transformation of experimental planning influences children's learning and development. In the following, I outline this for the five theoretical principles presented earlier in this chapter. These principles are also reflected in the categories of interpretation (see Table 11.1) that are used to evaluate the teaching and learning activity.

- *Using group activity, cooperation and division of work to advocate children's problem solving and their development of motive.* One of the methods used was to establish a common bond between the children and their activities, so that no child focused her attention solely on the teacher and sat and waited for the teacher's assistance, even if something were difficult. In addition, no child needed to wait for the teaching to comment. Developing the children's ability to work in small groups was therefore given a high priority, both because of the motivational factor, but also because of its importance for the children's cognitive development.

  The importance of group work for cognitive development lies in, among other factors, the division of work among the children when they are researching and carrying out assignments in class. Group work makes it possible to break down the components of any one assignment by giving each child in the group a sub-assignment which forms a part of a larger entity to be solved by the whole group.

  The group work led to a greater involvement in class discussions, because no group said the same thing when reporting what they had done or how much progress had been made. Another advantage was that children in the groups learned how to help each other, both to follow what was going on and also in order to draw together the various elements of their project work.

- *In using models in teaching and avocation, students formulate their own models and create connections between theoretical concepts and specific events.* In the building of conceptual models, teachers can create a wholeness orientation rather than focus on a single learned element of a subject area. We worked with this aspect in the experimental teaching through creating an entirety so that the central concepts of the history subject could be seen as a core model for the history subject (see Figure 11.2). The task for the children then became to relate the different matters they work with in the class activities to the model. The children gradually became able to use this core model to analyse specific matters, i.e. to understand the connection between tool use and ways of living and later between division of work and the structure of society.

- *In using subject matter methods advocating personal thinking strategies – and change in children's conceptual models.* In the teaching experiment, the traditional methods of teaching was changed qualitatively from memorising historical matters to the exploration of problems in cooperation with other children. Such a change in teaching methods implied that the teacher had to explicate the teaching methods more directly through tasks and in the structure of the class activities.

  The teaching was built around two types of method: a general research procedure where model formulation was a central element, and specific historical methods, involving the interpretation of findings and the use of analogy. These specific methods built upon a Scandinavian social tradition in the history subject (Dansk Social-historie, 1979–80; Kjelstadli, 1992). The general research procedure was the most dominating method in the teaching experiment and was characterised by steps that were repeated over and over in different versions. The steps were: *What are we researching? What do we know and what do we not know about our research area? How can we formulate and visualise in models the relation between the central concepts of our research area? What methods do we have to explore what we do not know? How does what we get to know fit into our model of the problem area? Should the model be revised?*

  An important aspect of quality teaching was that the methods that characterised the subject domains, transformed into personal thinking strategies so that the students could use them to formulate goals, and to research and reflect on a subject domain (see Table 11.1 for how this was evaluated).

- *In using procedures advocating children's active explorations and their development of motive.* Inside the cultural–historical approach, the motives are conceptualised as dialectically related to the person's cognition (Elkonin, 1999). Motives develop in institutional practice and can be seen as the dynamic that characterise a person in different activities. Motive development takes place in activities where a shared engagement and orientation in social interaction exists between the participants in the situation. When a teacher creates a learning motive the task is to identify the activities that are engaging for the students and these, in turn, reduce the demands on the teacher (see Hedegaard, 2002, Chapter 5).

One example of this was when each group of four children in the first teaching session performed a play of their research activity in history. This task was solved differently by each group, but was enjoyed by performers and audience. This activity gave a foundation for a discussion in the class about how one does research in history, and how the class could research history.

Figure 11.2 A child's (from 3rd grade) first model of what one can research.

A child's motive (i.e. for playing) has to be seen as part of the bigger totality of motives that characterise the child's personality (Leontiev, 1978). A change in a child's leading motive can be seen as a developmental change, for instance, as a change from play to learning. In middle childhood one should expect the learning motive to develop and become a leading motive, since teaching in schools should play a dominant role in middle childhood. An important way to support the development of the learning motive is to create engagement and shared experiences among the students by letting the class participate together in events. In the educational experiment of history teaching presented here, several shared events became part of the teaching: a visit to, and participating in, activities in an open air museum, role playing, picture and film analyses and teacher reading stories aloud and creating a shared library of children's books:

- *Stages in the teaching and their relations to phases in learning.* The double move in teaching is based on the assumption that there should be stages in the teaching process and that these stages should be dialectically linked to phases in the learning process.
    1   The first main stage in the teaching is to help the children to formulate goals about the thematic relationships that comprise the main problem, i.e. to formulate the initial relations to be researched.
    2   The second main stage is characterised by the formulation and expansion of the initial relations into a core model for

the problem area being investigated, where the relationships within the core model are explored through various assignments.

3   The third main stage in the teaching has, as its goal, that the children should learn how to take a critical standpoint with respect to how well they master the conceptual relationships being investigated, as related to the content of the teaching being used to shape the core-cell model.

Each of these three phases can be seen as a cyclic event, where each phase becomes further differentiated through the next cycle.

In our teaching project, we have emphasised that the relationship between the overall formulation of the problem, its themes and its intermediate goals had to be discussed at regular intervals. An important factor in the process of building up the children's understanding of the concepts involved here is that each activity is placed within, and understood as, an element in this larger context of the main problem they were being asked to solve.

Teaching activity in 12th session 4th grade

In the example, students are building models to depict the concepts in the conditions for historical changes of society. They are using a scientific procedure that has been part of teaching from their first year. At the 12th session in 4th grade the children are at a point where they can start to use this procedure in the process of developing, evaluating and extending their core model from the 3rd grade.

The children had already been through a cycle of problem formulation, using the general research method, formulating models and extending the models. They had already acquired the first form of the model of historical change of society (see Figure 11.3). When the teacher introduced the task of creating models for the history of human development, the children already had an understanding of the time dimension in history and that humans lived differently in different societies, and have lived differently in different historical periods. They have made analyses of an ethnographic movie of the way Kung people from the Kalahari desert in Africa were living around the 1950s. We have visited a historical outdoor museum with reconstruction of farmhouses and tools from the Iron Age. This museum also contained the originals of Middle Age farms and tools. Through a class library the children had access to several picture books of historically different periods in Danish society. They gained an understanding of how changes in tools and technology led to changes in the way of living in a society. They had begun to focus on the concept of society, and this was where the teaching headed in the 12th session onwards.

Figure 11.3 A child's model of society.

Extract from observation of the 12th session in 4th grade

The session starts as usual with the teacher writing the plan of the day on the blackboard

- Summary for our goal–result board in the class
- Work with a text and questions about society
- Expanding models
- Sorting pictures from different societies showing ecology of living places, housing, forms of living conditions, types of tool use and work.

The teaching in this session is focused on formulating an overview of what children have learned from summer until now and what they were supposed to do from now until Christmas. The conceptual relations that were focused on were: society and how this relates to what children already had worked with: nature, tool use and living conditions.

In the classroom, the results of the earlier activities were written on cardboard as a goal–result board. On this board, the teachers had concretised the principles from the general research strategy in relation to what they already had worked with and condensed their results.

The class dialogue between the teacher and the students began with the teacher announcing that something was missing in the goal–result board and that the children should know more than was written on the board. The children made suggestions and the teacher wrote them on the blackboard (not yet on the goal–results board).

First they suggested 'what they know' and then 'what they do not know yet'.

On the blackboard the teacher wrote in response to the children's suggestions:

What do we know about?

- Evolution of animals
  - That humans developed from apes

- The difference between life in Iron Age and life today
  - Difference in tool use
  - Living quarters
  - Beliefs

What do we not know about?

- Society
- Different periods in history

> *A student* said: We have started to find out about society.

> *A second student:* It is not the Iron Age we explore now, it is society.

> *A third student:* It is [society] in the different periods [meaning historical].

> *The teacher* then asked if there was something else they would like to explore. He gave them a sheet of paper and asked each of them to draw what they think should be put into the goal–result board in the classroom. They were given a task to draw so that if a 'stranger' visited the class she could see what they had been doing. Several of the children started to *write* what they did not know about but wanted to learn; the teacher intervened and asked them to *draw* this instead.

> *Morten* drew the development of humans that they did not know about.

> *Loke* drew the development of plants, clothes and tools.

After the drawing task the teacher wanted to go to the next point on the agenda – to read a text about society.

Cecilie redirects the activity and asks if they now could be allowed to show the models they were supposed to prepare as homework about the development of society. Cecilie and some of the other children were eager to show their homework, so the teacher made it the next point of the agenda, but they had to finish what they had started.

Not all the children had done their homework because, as *Derek* says: It is difficult.

Morten and Cecilie were allowed to draw their models on the blackboard.

At this point *Susanne* starts a discussion about whether Denmark has always been called Denmark.

Derek doesn't think it has always been called Denmark because as he says: In the Iron Age there were no borders.

Susanne adds that the World was just the World at that time.

Cecilie then tells a saga of who became the first king in Denmark: A baby was found lying on a shield at the beach, the ones who found him could see that he was from a noble family and they thought it was a sign that he was placed there. He then became the first Danish king and was named King Shield. [This story had not been brought up in the teaching, it was her own contribution.]

The children start to discuss how it can be that people speak different languages in different countries. They discuss if somebody decides what language should be spoken in a country.

Sanne says that the spoken language develops through sign language.

The observer reminds them about the film of the Kung people which showed how they used sign language.

[The teacher always supported discussion when children anticipate content of relevance for the problem investigated; here they are exploring their understanding of the origin of society.]

The teacher then moved on in relation to the agenda and gave the children another drawing task: to draw what they know about and have learned about in this class last year and until now. The children got so engaged in this drawing task that they did not want to stop and go out to play during the break. Instead, most of them kept on drawing.

[The result of their activity went into four posters that were finished a couple of weeks later. These posters became the goal–results boards. One showed what they explored last year (3rd grade): evolution of animals. A second showed what they had explored the first month in 4th grade: How people lived different in different countries. A third showed what they were researching recently when designing posters: Living conditions in different societies. A fourth showed what they were going to research after Christmas: The historical changes in Danish society.]

The last activity on the agenda was for the children to analyse and discuss a series of pictures from the Iron Age and the Viking Age. These pictures were a starting point to introduce changes to the Danish society. The children were asked to analyse and discuss with each other in groups of four [these groups lasted for some months] what the pictures could show about the societies in the two age periods].

After 10 minutes the teacher tried to start a class dialogue about how people in the Viking Age lived and worked differently from people in the Iron Age and what this meant for their society. There was only a very short time for discussion and the children did not have much to say in the time they had.

Finally, the children evaluated the class activity in a class dialogue about the different points on the agenda for the day. [The purpose of the evaluation was to help the children to reflect on their own activity.]

The main critique came from *Derek* who said if the task about analysing the pictures had been a little harder, he did not think they could have done it.

Evaluation of the children's learning activity

In this presentation the focus is on Cecilie, one of three focus children who were followed closely over years. The two categories of social interaction and motivation are combined along with the categories of development of thinking and of concept formation.

Motivation and social interaction

During the 12th session, Cecilie's motivation for the content of the teaching increases. In the previous session, the children were given a homework assignment of making a model for changes in societies. Now Cecilie is 'dying' to show her model and asks the teacher to move this up as item no. 2 on the class agenda. The first item is the problem formulation and construction of a goal–results board that shows (1) *what they have investigated last year*, (2) *what they have investigated this year until now*, (3) *what they are investigating and will be investigating until Christmas* and (4) *what they are to investigate in the future*. However, Cecilie's presentation of her homework is not allowed to follow immediately after this, but has to wait until the item is actually on the agenda. Each of the four groups has been given the assignment of drawing one of the main themes: the evolution of species; the evolution of man; the way in which humans live; and changes in society. During the subsequent work on the goal–results board, Cecilie becomes very involved in the issue and again when this work continues in sessions 13 and 14.

Cecilie is eager to put forward her own ideas, but nevertheless still manages to show due consideration to the work of the other children. For instance, she wonders whether they should start to draw their model in the group, when one of the members Allan is absent. Also when some of the children are standing round the table of their group, she offers Louis her chair because Louis says that he does not want to stand up anymore. A parallel group states that they do not know what to do. Cecilie says that she will tell them what to do and she draws and explains to Jette, who, however, is not the most attentive listener.

When Cecilie's own group works on their task of a model about changes in society (session 13), she takes the lead but makes sure on several occasions that they all agree with her suggestions before moving on to the next point. For instance, she suggests that they use the model for the evolution of species as their basis for making the model for changes in society.

Development of thinking and concepts

During the presentation of the goal–result boards, Cecilie makes various critical contributions and, when they look at the board for *human ways of living*, she wants to categorise the way of living both as 'something we know' and as 'something to investigate'. As a consequence of this, several of the concepts of the model are categorised more than once on the research charts. Cecilie has made notes of the following areas as being those the class does not know anything about: 'periods of time', 'environmental developments on Earth', 'developments of societies', and 'ways of living'.

In the 13th session, her group's assignment is to illustrate the area of investigation and to make a model for historical changes in societies. The model is to be placed on the chart concerning 'that which we are investigating'. She suggests they change the model for the evolution of species, which is relevant, though rather a constrictive point of departure. She starts by drawing climate as an element of the model. Allan refers to Jens' drawing of an oasis as the symbol of nature in his model for the evolution of species, but then objects saying that their assignment is to draw something representative of 'society'. Cecilie says that society also includes climate. She goes and asks the teacher and returns with the explanation that climate is related to nature and hence also to society. She also wants to include 'food' and 'cohabitation' in the model and later 'the care of offspring' and 'defence against enemies', i.e. the categories from the evolution-of-species model. The other children's contributions in her group are more relevant for a model of society. Allan draws two hands holding each other, as the symbol of 'cohabitation' (as opposed to the cohabitation of animals). This probably inspires Cecilie to propose that they draw a mother holding a baby as the symbol for 'the care of offspring'. She has not yet, though, developed a model of society of her own, but the group's model can, however, be regarded as one.

Demands for conducting an educational experiment within the cultural–historical tradition

An educational experiment needs to be conducted within some form of societal practice, such as school teaching. But it can also take place within all other forms of practice where the aim is to facilitate learning possibilities.

The experiment implies a cooperation between researchers and educators. In this cooperation, a theoretical foundation for teaching, learning and development is essential. The educational experiment should be based on the theoretical conceptions of where to lead the students – that is, from a subject matter perspective and from a personal developmental perspective.

What makes the educational experiment different from action research is, first, the cooperation that exists between two or more professionals (in the case presented here, the researcher and the teacher) and, second, the theoretical conceptions that frame the intervention. In the concrete case discussed in this chapter, the research focused on how 'the double move' approach in teaching can influence those involved in the learning activity. Therefore the explication of theoretical principles for conducting an educational experiment is essential.

The teaching should relate to:

- What in society and in the community are seen as important subject areas. These areas should be taught so that the students get an integrated coherent understanding of the central relations in the subject area. These relations can be analysed. Teaching should not only be about introducing problems but it should be about problems that focus on what matters in the children's community and society.
- The teaching practice should give children the opportunity to be active and explorative. Explorations should be in the general sense of learning activity and also when supporting the child's initiative in being explorative.
- The structure of the teaching practice should support cooperation within the group activity, in class discussions, and in individual activity.

Children's learning should be seen in relation to:

- How well they can work independently and cooperatively when analysing and solving problems, formulating new learning goals and evaluating their own activity.
- How they develop their learning motive and engagement in explorative activities.
- How they develop a coherent understanding of the subject matter.
- How they appropriate thinking strategies for approaching problems.

12   The role of the researcher

Mariane Hedegaard

The researcher as a participant in the activities being researched

In Chapter 3, I discussed the methodological aspects of being a researcher, drawing on Alfred Schutz's conception of the social scientist as someone who has two roles. One of the roles a researcher takes is where she is a partner in the activity settings being researched. She enters into a social situation with other persons where she has to *understand* what is going on as a participant in everyday practice. But she is also entering the activity setting as a researcher *researching* the activities. This means that the social scientist both participates in activities in everyday settings paying attention to others' needs and motives and, at the same time, includes these activities as her object of study – with the focus on the participants' motives, projects and intentions. Therefore the researcher as a scientist has to conceptualise her own participation (motives, project and intentions) as part of the researched activities. This means that the researcher always has to keep the aim of the research in mind when entering the research setting.

The cooperation with children's caregivers

In all practices, the researcher enters the research setting as a professional and presents herself as a professional. The first task is to give a clear orientation of the research both orally as well as in a short written introduction when making contact with the children and their caregivers. A written introduction has to be given to parents, to the kindergarten or to the school. My recommendation is also to begin the research with an orienting meeting, where involved partners such as parents, pedagogues or teachers can meet and questions can be asked. In relation to this, it is preferable to make a contract for all partners that contains a project description and overview of time and numbers of meetings. When making observations or interviews in the home, kindergarten and school, the adult caregivers in these settings must feel sure that the researcher does not take over their roles or responsibilities. This goes two ways so that, by way of contrast, it is not being expected that the researcher steps into the activities as a teacher – or a pedagogue's assistant or a psychological consultant.

In Chapter 5, Marilyn Fleer describes how she introduced the aim and theoretical foundation of the research project she has planned and wanted to do in the City Early Learning Centre. The staff then had the opportunity to gain insight into the ideas behind the research project. This implied that it was the educational process that was the focus. This perhaps influenced the practice in the centre but when the objective is to follow how the 'small novelties' become 'great novelty', as described by Jytte Bang in Chapter 8, it is not the reflection of a specific practice but through analysing the concrete setting that the researcher gains insight into developmental pathways and what the educational practice means for the children's learning and development.

The cooperation with children entering an activity setting

One has to introduce the research project orally so that it can be also understood by the children in the project. This procedure can be repeated by short narratives as I have shown below, by reading or showing material to the children. The introduction has to explain the aim of the research so that it can be understood why the researchers will repeatedly come back into the activity setting or ask the children to talk to them. The introduction also has to contain a presentation of those who are participating and when they will be there.

Participating in activities in kindergarten or school means that the observer does not take the teacher's role. But this does not mean that the researcher cannot react as a person in the setting and intervene or help. The researcher and her research assistants have to participate as responsible adults. Entering into a research setting such as kindergarten, school and home the researcher is also a guest. How they should manage the two roles of undertaking research and being a guest depends both on the setting and on the aim of the research. It is a balancing act to make clear these two roles to the involved partners, researchers, adult caregivers and children.

In observation, for example, when children come rushing to the researcher asking about 'What are you writing?', one can tell them that: 'Later I will read some of what I had written, but for now I am working so it has to wait.' Also, if one is using a computer and the children would like to try to use the keyboard, I let them do this for a short period and then again tell them that I have to do my work. When a child has difficulties and it is obvious for the researcher that the child needs support, the researchers have to intervene, otherwise the child or children will lose respect for the researcher. This does not mean that she solves the problem but perhaps suggests to the child someone who can help. It is important to acknowledge the children's interest and let them try things or help them for a little while and then tell them that, as a researcher, one has to go back to work. Participating over long intervals as we do – between two and four hours across several settings – what the researcher does not catch in one situation because she helps a child who is having difficulties, she is likely to observe later.

When undertaking *video observations or tape-recording* children, it is likely that in the beginning children will be eager to look at the video view reflecting the situation, or would like to hear their own voice recorded. Again it is worth while for a short period to let them look and listen and perhaps later in the process show them short video clips or let them hear the recording of the situation. As illustrated in the research presented in Chapter 9, the children's interests in the research activity helped Pernille Hviid in the after-school setting to extend her interviews.

The role of being a researcher is a balancing act because the children become aware that the researcher does not have the authority of the caregivers. For example, in school it can happen when a researcher tells a child 'don't do that', i.e. turning another child's school bag upside down so that things fall out, or other such events, a child will tell her that the researcher does not decide here, it is the teacher. Here the researcher has to be firm so that she maintains respect as an adult. But in other situations the researcher does not interfere when she does not want to be seen as an authority. The relationship between the researcher and the children has to be a trusted relationship. It is a personal relation where the researcher is experienced as a person. In Hviid's interview in Chapter 9, pp. 152–153, it is clear that Jonathan wants a relationship with the researcher where she should also share some knowledge about herself.

How far the children will let the researcher go depends not only on their relationship with her but also on the stage they have reached developmentally. Children aged 12 years and older often become tired of having an observer following them, as they may have secrets. They wish to make decisions about, and wish to decide if and when they want to share their secrets. But mostly they do not mind talking to the researcher in an interview. Younger children aged 5 and 6 years usually do not mind if an adult is around them making observations, as they like the attention. During this age period children often do not want to sit and talk for long intervals with an adult, and often express this as boring by asking when will they be finished. This can be solved when talking to the children in situations where it seems relevant. Children when approached as equals have the right to be curious and when given the opportunity to determine how or when they are to be observed or interviewed. In these situations, the researcher has to be aware of how she positions the child in relation to the research situation. The researcher needs to act and talk to the child in relation to the aims of the research, because the children will make up their own minds about the researcher, the activity settings and the actions expected.

A practice I have been using in my research in kindergarten schools, and also in homes, is to establish a period in the kindergarten or school where I read for 5 minutes from an earlier observation that I have made. For example, when in a kindergarten I will sit together with a group of children and read to them or in school I will do this at a time appointed by the teacher, often at the beginning of a class setting. In families, I have used one meeting after a period of several observations where I bring snacks and read for an hour to the family. Even small kindergarten children love to hear about their own activities. In each of these cases, one has to pick observations that do not expose problems to the children or adults that would be hurtful.

Interpretation of the researcher's role in the research activities

Earlier I have argued that, in building on Schutz's work, the social scientist's interactions and construction of meanings are of a different kind than the meaning constructions of the actors in their specific everyday practices (2005, p. 25). Researchers explicitly seek coherence and try to systematise events, constructing meaning through relating these events into meaningful conceptual relations.

The double-ness of the researcher in the research situation – both as a researcher and as having a personal relationship to children and adults in the settings – can also be viewed in the same way when making interpretation of the protocols, where the researcher seeks meaning in relation to both roles. How the researcher is seen from the children's and caregivers' perspective is an important theme but very few researchers in child psychology and research into childhood have focused on this theme. Corsaro (Corsaro and Molinaro, 1999) is one of the few researchers who have written about his relationship with the children he observed. He writes about how the children's conception of him was as neither adult nor as child. He also actively tried to construct a role with the children that was different from that of the teachers. What is important in Corsaro's article is that he reflects about his role. Researchers should take this one step further and try to be aware of the researcher's role both as participant in the research settings and also as the analyst of the protocol and follow how the researcher is contributing to the activities in the setting she is entering.

The children and adult continue to engage in everyday activities but at the same time they are also relating to the researcher. She is somebody doing research in their everyday activities. Part of the interpretation should be to follow how these relations develop. Therefore, in the interpretation of the material it would be wise to follow how the children and adult caregiver relate to the researcher.

One aspect we have found when we focus on specific children in an activity setting is that the children come to see the researcher as *their* researcher and take a kind of ownership and responsibility for her. In Hviid's interview research it is clear that the children feel responsibility in relation to the researcher when they offer to help her to collect interviews. In other cases I have seen, the focus child does not like it when other children attract the researcher's attention or use her time.

The researcher also influences the children's activity. In the example in Chapter 3 of the preschool child Jens, it is obvious that the researcher's writing activity inspired Jens to write. In this setting the researcher advised him to write his name and helps him to accomplish this task.

Researcher's relation to other professionals

In the experimental research cooperation between the teacher and the researcher is essential for the study. Therefore it is important that the adult partners know both the theoretical background and the aim of the research and that cooperation through the experiment takes place in such a way that the teacher has access to the researcher's observations. This is essential because the teacher and the researcher have to model the research in relation to the aim as conducted over time. It is important to arrange a meeting prior to starting the research. Here the meeting should begin with a general discussion about the aim and theory of the research. But this has to be followed by settings where the partners discuss implemented practice. These follow-up meetings must occur close to the research setting, where the experimental interventions is realised so that these can be easily reviewed and changes can be made on the basis of joint decisions (see p. 188). Cooperation between professionals in the education system and the researcher is essential in experimental teaching where each partner respects the other but can discuss the process and interventions in the experimental activity. In this cooperation, one needs to relate the observations to the theoretical conceptual relations. The central relations preferably have to be formulated as a model. The concepts in such a model always have to be related to the concrete lived activity of the person being studied. The scientific demands imply a combination of general categories with concrete practices and events in children's social situation. As Schutz points out, there has to be consistency between the constructions and the social reality.

Conclusion

The main point in focusing on the researcher as a participant in the research activity, both in protocol collections and interpretation, is to get insight into the ethical aspects of the research as well as the reliability and validity of the research.

The researcher has to communicate her research goal clearly to the researched person. The researcher with her aim and theoretical approach intervenes into a person's everyday life in the research setting. It should be possible for both adults and children to approve being participants in research and to decide on how much they want to tell and how close by they want the researcher to look into their activities. Because children cannot directly give their acceptance, as adults do, it is important to be respectful and to be attentive to the children's expressions of inclinations or restraints in participation.

To keep reliability we have to make clear the object of the researcher's goal in order to distinguish this from the researched person's intentions and motives. To keep the research valid it is important to foreground, in the interpretations of the results, the researcher's theoretical conceptions of the theme as well as her conceptions of children's development.

References

Abbott, L. and Langston, A. (2005). Ethical research with very young children. In A. Farrell (ed.), *Ethical Research with Children* (pp. 37–48). Buckingham: Open University Press.

Alanen, L. (1992). Modern childhood? Exploring the chid question in sociology, *Research Report 5*. Jyvaskyla, Finland: University of Jyvaskyla.

Alderson, P. (2000). Children as researchers: The effect of participation rights on research methodology. In P.H. Christensen and A. James (eds), *Research with Children – Perspectives and Practices* (pp. 241–257). London: Palmer Press.

Andenæs, A. (1991). Livsforminterview med 4–5 åringer: Motivasjon, kontrakt og felles fokus. [Life-form-interview with four- to five-year-old children: Motivation, contract and shared focus]. *BARN. Nytt fra Forskning om barn i Norge* (pp. 93–111). Trondheim, Norway: Norsk senter for barneforskning.

Andenæs, A. (1997). Fra undersøkelsesobjekt til medforsker? Livsforminterviu med 4–5-åringer. [From object of investigation to co-researcher? Life-form-interview with four- to five-year-old children.] In P. Schultz Jørgensen (ed.), *Kvalitative meninger – som almengørelse af det sociale* (pp. 112–128). Copenhagen: Nordisk Psykologi/Hans Reitzel.

Aronsson K. and Hundeide, K. (2002). Relational rationality and children's interview responses. *Human Development, 45*, 174–186.

Bakhurst, D. (2007). Vygotsky's demons. In H. Daniels, M. Cole and J.V. Wertsch (eds), *The Cambridge Companion to Vygotsky* (pp. 50–76). New York: Cambridge University Press.

Baldwin, J.M. (1899/1973). *Social and Ethical Interpretations in Mental Development*. New York: Arno Press.

Bang, J. (1996). *Tænkning og Forståelse – En Undersøgelse af Elevers Lærehandlinger I Fysik*; IMFUFA. Roskilde: Roskilde University Center.

Barker, R.G. and Wright, H.F. (1966). *One Boy's Day – A Specimen Record of Behavior*. New York: Harper & Brothers Publishers.

Barker, R. and Wright, H. (1971). *Midwest and Its Children – The Psychological Ecology of an American Town*. Archon Books.

Bateson, G. (1976). A theory of play and fantasy. In J.S. Bruner, A. Jolly and K. Sylvia (eds), *Play: Its Role in Development and Evolution* (pp. 119–129). New York: Basic Books.

Berk, L.E. (2006). *Child Development*, 7th edition. Boston, MA.: Allyn & Bacon.

Bliss, J., Monk, M. and Ogborn, J. (1983). *Qualitative Data Analysis for Educational Research: A Guide to Uses of Systemic Networks.* London: Croom Helm.

Brazelton, B. and Nugent, K. (2000). *Neonatal Behaviour Assessment Scale,* 3rd edition. Cambridge: Cambridge University Press.

Brennan, D. (1994). *The Politics of Australian Child Care. From Philanthropy to Feminism.* Australia: Cambridge University Press.

Bronfenbronner, U. (1977). Toward an experimental ecology of human development. *American Psychologist, 32*(7), 513–531.

Bronfenbronner, U. (1995). Development ecology through space and time: A future perspective. In P.M. Moen, G.H. Elder Jr. and K. Lüsher (eds), *Examining Lives in Context. Perspective on the Ecology of Human Development* (pp. 619–639). Washington, DC: American Psychological Association.

Bruner, J. (1972). *Processes of Cognitive Growth: Infancy* (vol. 3). Heninz Werner Lecture Series. Wouster, MA.: Clark University Press.

Bruner, J. (1999). Infancy and culture. A story. In S. Chaiklin, M. Hedegaard and U.J. Jensen (eds), *Activity Theory and Social Practice* (pp. 225–234). Aarhus, Denmark: Aarhus University Press.

Burman, E. (1994). *Deconstructing Developmental Psychology.* London: Routledge.

Campell, M.M. (2001). Ethics in early childhood research. In G. Mac-Naughton, S.A. Rolfe and I. Siraj-Blatchford (eds), *Doing Early Childhood Research – International Perspectives on Theory and Practice* (pp. 64–72). Buckingham: Open University Press.

Christensen, P. and James, A. (1999). Childhood diversity and commonality. Some methodological insights. In A. James (ed.), *Research and Children: Perspectives and Practices* (pp. 160–178) London: Falmer Press.

Christensen, P. and James, A. (2000). Researching children and childhood: cultures of communication. In P.H. Christensen and A. James (eds), *Research with Children – Perspectives and Practices* (pp. 1–8). London: Falmer Press.

Cole, M., Cole, S. and Lightfoot, C. (2005). *The Development of Children.* New York: Worth Publishers.

Cole, M. and Scribner, S. (1974). *Culture and Thought: A Psychological Introduction.* New York: Wiley.

Corsaro, W.A. (1997). *The Sociology of Childhood.* Thousand Oaks, CA: Pine Forge Press.

Corsaro, W.A. and Molinari, L. (1999). Entering and observing in children's worlds: A reflection of a longitudinal ethnograpy of early education in Italy. In A. James (ed.), *Researching with Children: Perspectives and Practices* (pp. 179–200). London: Falmer Press.

Dansk socialhistorie. [Danish social history] (1979–1980). Copenhagen: Gyldendal.

Davydov, V.V. (1982). Ausbildung der Lerntätigkeit. [Development of Learning Activity.] In V.V. Davydov, J. Lompscher and A.K. Markova (eds), *Ausbildung der Lerntätigkeit bei Schülern* (pp. 14–27). Berlin: Volk und Wissen.

Davydov, V.V. (1988a). Problems of developmental teaching. *Soviet Education,* 30(8), 15–97.

Davydov, V.V. (1988b). Problems of developmental teaching, *Soviet Education,* 30(9), 3–83.

Davydov, V.V. (1988c). Problems of developmental teaching, *Soviet Education,* 30(10), 3–77.

Davydov, V.V. (1990). *Types of Generalization in Instruction: Logical and Psychological Problems in the Structuring of School Curricula* (Soviet studies in mathematics education, Vol. 2; J. Kilpatrick, ed.; J. Teller, trans.). Reston, VA: National Council of Teachers of Mathematics. (Original work published 1972.)

Davydov, V.V. (1999). What is real learning activity? In M. Hedegaard and J. Lompscher (eds), *Learning Activity and Development* (pp. 123–138). Aarhus, Denmark: Aarhus University Press.

Davydov, V.V. and Markova, A.K. (1983). A concept of educational activity for school children *Soviet Psychology, 21,* 50–76.

Elder, G.H. (1997). The life course of human development. In R. Damon and R.M. Learner (eds), *Handbook of Child Psychology* (pp. 939–991). New York: Wiley.

Elder, G.H. (1998). The life course of developmental theory. *Child Development, 69,* 1–12.

Elkonin, D.B. (1999). Toward the problem of stages in the mental development of children. *Journal of Russian and East European Psychology, 37,* 11–29.

EMU/Danmarks Undervisningsportal: https://www.retsinformation.dk/Forms/R0710.aspx?id=25528#K1.

Erikson, E.H. (1950). *Childhood and Society.* New York: Norton.

Flick, U. (2002). *An Introduction to Qualitative Research,* 2nd edition. London: Sage.

Fog, J. (2004). *Med samtalen som udgangspunkt.* [With the conversation as basis.] Copenhagen: Akademisk Forlag.

Gibson, J.J. (1966). *The Senses Considered as Perceptual Systems.* Boston, MA: Houghton Mifflin Company.

Gould, S. (1977). *Ever Since Darwin*. London: Penguin.

Graue, M.E. and Walsh, D.J. (1998). Studying children in context. *Theories, Methods, and Ethics*. London: Sage.

Gulløv, E. and Højlund, S. (2003). *Feltarbejde blandt born. Metodology og etik i etnografisk børneforskning*. [Field work among children. Methodolgy and ethics in ethnographical research.] Copenhagen: Gyldendal.

Hammersley, M. and Atkinson, P. (1983). *Ethnography. Principles in Practice*. London: Tavistock.

Hedegaard, M. (1984). Interaktionsbaseret beskrivelse af småbørn og børnehaveklasse–børn i deres dagligdag. *Psykologisk Skriftserie*. Department of Psychology, Aarhus University, 9 (4).

Hedegaard, M. (1987). Methodology in evaluative research on teaching and Learning. In F. van Zuuren, B. Mook and F. Wertz (eds), *Advances in Qualitative Psychology*. Lisse, The Netherlands: Swets Publishing.

Hedegaard, M. (1988). *Skolebørns personlighedsudvikling set gennem orienterings-fagene*. [Personality development in schoolchildren, exemplified by instruction in the social sciences.] Aarhus, Denmark: Aarhus University Press.

Hedegaard, M. (1990). The zone of proximal development as basis for instruction. In L.C. Moll (ed.), *Vygotsky and Education. Instructional implications and applications of socio-historical psychology*. Cambridge: Cambridge University Press.

Hedegaard. M. (1995). *Beskrivelse af småbørn*. Aarhus, Denmark: Aarhus University Press.

Hedegaard, M. (1999). Institutional practice, cultural positions, and personal motives: Immigrant Turkish parents' conception about their children's school life. In S. Chaiklin, M. Hedegaard and U. Juul Jensen (eds), *Activity Theory and Social Practice*. Aarhus, Denmark: Aarhus University Press.

Hedegaard, M. (2002). *Learning and Child Development*. Aarhus, Denmark: Aarhus University Press.

Hedegaard, M. (2003). *At blive fremmed i Danmark: Den modsætningsfyldte skoletid*. [To become a stranger in Denmark: The contradiction in school.] Aarhus, Denmark: Klim.

Hedegaard, M. (2004). A cultural–historical approach to learning in classrooms. Paper presented at the International Society for Cultural and Activity Research, Regional Conference, University of Wollongong, 12–13 July 2004.

Hedegaard, M. (2008) Child development from a cultural–historical approach: Children's activity in everyday local settings as foundation for their development. *Mind Culture and Activity, 16* (4).

Hedegaard, M., Bang, J. and Egelund, N. (2007). *Elevens alsidige personlige udvikling – et dialogredskab*. [Children's general personal development: A dialogical tool.] Lærervejledning. Virum, Denmark: Dansk Psykologisk Forlag.

Hedegaard, M. and Chaiklin, S. (2005). *Radical-Local Teaching and Learning. A Cultural–Historical Approach*. Aarhus, Denmark: Aarhus University Press.

Hedegaard, M., Frost, S. and Larsen, I. (2004). *Krigsramte børn i eksil*. [Children of war in exile.] Aarhus, Denmark: Klim.

Hedegaard, M. and Hakkarainen, P. (1986). Qualitative research as instruction and intervention. In P. Ashworth, A. Giorgi and A. de Koning (eds), *Qualitative Research in Psychology*. Pittsburgh, PA. Duquesne University Press.

Heft, H. (1988). Affordances of children's environments: A functional approach to environmental description. *Children's Environments Quarterly*, 57(2): 29–37.

Hendrick, H. (2000). The child as social actor in historical sources. Problems of identification and interpretation. In P. Christensen and A. James (eds), *Research with Children. Perspectives and Practices* (pp. 36–61). London: Falmer Press.

Hundeide, K. (1989). *Barns livsverden*. [Children's life-worlds.] Oslo: Cappelens Forlag.

Hundeide, K. (2004). *Børns livsverden og sociokulturelle rammer*. [Children's life world and socio-cultural frames.] Copenhagen: Akademisk Forlag.

Hviid, P. (2002). *Børneliv i udvikling – om børns engagementer i deres hverdagsliv i skole og fritidsinstitution*. [Development of children's lives – on children's engagement in their everyday life in school and after school care.] Unpublished PhD thesis. Copenhagen: Copenhagens University.

Hviid, P. (2008). 'Next year we are small, right?' Different times in children's development. *European Journal of Psychology of Education*. **23**, (pp. 183–198).

Hydén, M. (2000). Forskingsintervjun som relationell praktik. [The researchinterview as a relational practice.] In H. Haavind (ed.), *Køn og fortolkende metode – metodiske muligheter i kvalitativ forskning* (pp. 130–154). Oslo: Gyldendal Norsk Forlag.

Iljenkov, E.V. (1977). The concept of the ideal. In *Philosphy in the USSR*. Moscow: Progress Publishers.

James, A., Jenks, C. and Prout, A. (1997). *Theorizing Childhood*. Cambridge and Southern Oaks, CA: Polity Press.

James, A. and Prout, A. (1993). *Childhood Identifies: Self and Social Relationships in the Experience of the Child*. Edinburgh: Edinburgh University Press.

Jensen, U.J. (1999). Categories in activity theory: Marx's philosophy. Just in time. In S. Chaiklin, M. Hedegaard and U.J. Jensen (eds), *Activity Theory and Social Practice*. Aarhus, Denmark: Aarhus University Press.

Kaye, H.J. (1990). E.P. Thompson, the British Marxist historical tradition and the contemporary crisis. In H.J. Kaye and K. McClelland (eds), *E. P. Thompson: Critical Perspectives*. Cambridge: Polity Press.

Kjelstadli, K. (1992). *Fortida er ikke hva den en gang var.* [The past is not what it used to be.] Oslo: University Press.

Klaus, M.H., Jerauld, R., Kreger, N.C., McAlpine, W., Steffa, M. and Kennel, J.H. (1972). Maternal attachment: Of the importance of the first post-partum days. *New England Journal of Medicine, 286,* 460–463.

Kvale, S. (1997). *Interview – En introduktion til det kvalitative forskningsinterview.* [Interview – An introduction to the qualitative research interview.] Copenhagen: Hans Reitzel.

Kvale, S. (2006). Dominance through interviews and dialogues. *Qualitative Inquiry, XX,* 1–21.

Latour, B. (2003). Do you believe in reality? News from the trenches of the science war. In Robert C. Scharff and Val Dusek (eds), *Philosophy of Technology. The Technological Condition. An Anthology* (pp 126–137). Victoria, Australia: Blackwell Publishing.

Leontiev, A.N. (1977). *Problemer I det psykiskes udvikling.* [Problems in the development of psyche.] Copenhagen: Rhodos.

Leontiev, A.N. (1978). *Activity, Consciousness, and Personality.* Englewood Cliffs, NJ: Prentice-Hall.

Lewin, K. (1946) Behaviour and development as a function of the total situation. In L. Carmichael (ed.), *Manual of Child Psychology* (pp. 791–844. New York: Wiley.

Lewis, A. and Lindsay, G. (eds) (2000). *Researching Children's Perspectives.* Buckingham: Open University Press.

Lewis, O. (1964). *The Children of Sanchez.* Hammondsworth: Penguin.

Lompscher, J. (1984). Problems and results of experimental research on the formation of theoretical thinking through instruction. In M. Hedegaard, P. Hakkarainen and Y. Engeström (eds), *Learning and Teaching on a Scientific Basis.* Aarhus: Aarhus University, Department of Psychology.

Lompscher, J. (1985). Formation of learning activity – A fundamental condition of cognitive development. In E. Bol, J.P.P. Haenen and M. Wolters (eds), *Education for Cognitive Development. Proceedings of the Third International Symposium on Activity Theory.* Den Haag, Netherlands: SVO/SOO.

Lompscher, J. (1999) Learning activity and its formation. In M. Hedegaard and J. Lompscher (eds), *Learning Activity and Development* (pp. 139–166). Aarhus, Denmark: Aarhus University Press.

Lübcke, P. (ed.) (1999). *Vor tids filosofi; Engagement og forståelse.* [Philosophy of our time; Engagement and understanding.] Copenhagen: Politikens Forlag.

Luria, A.R. (1976). *Cognitive Development and Social Foundations*. Cambridge, MA: Harvard University Press.

Luria, A.R. and Yudovich, F. Ia. (1959). *Speech and the Development of Mental Processes in the Child*. London: Stable Press.

Markova, A.K. (1978–79). The teaching and mastery of language. *Soviet Education, XXI*, no. 2-3-4.

Markowa [Markova], A.K. (1982). Das ausbildende Experiment in der psychologishe Erforschung der Lerntätigkeit. In W.W. Davydow, J. Lompscher and A.K. Markowa (eds) *Ausbildung der Lerntätigkeit bei Schülern*. [Formation of students' learning activity.] (pp. 74–83). Berlin: Volk und Wissen.

Mayr, E. (1980). *Evolution and the Diversity of Life*. Cambridge, MA: Harvard University Press.

McNeil, L. (1988). *Contradictions of Control: School Structure and School Knowledge*. New York: Routledge & Kegan Paul.

Mead, M. (2001, orig 1956). *New Lives for Old. Cultural Transformation–Manus 1928–1956*. New York: Perennial, Harper & Row.

Medinnus, G.R. (1976). *Child Study: an Observation Guide*. New York: Wiley.

Miles, M.B. and Huberman, A.M. (1994). *An Expanded Sourcebook: Qualitative Data Analysis*. London: Sage.

Mishler, E.G. (1986). *Research Interviewing. Context and Narrative*. Cambridge, MA: Harvard University Press.

Nelson, K. and Seidman, S. (1984). Playing with scripts. In I. Bretherton (ed.), *Symbolic Play* (pp. 45–71). London: Academic Press

Nsamenang, A.B. and Lamb, M.E. (1998). Socialization of Nso children in the Bamenda Grassfields of Northwest Cameroon. In M. Woodhead, D. Faulkner and K. Littleton, (eds), *Cultural Worlds of Early Childhood* (pp. 250–260). London: Routledge.

Pelligrini, A.D., Symons, F. and Hoch, J. (2004). *Observing Children in their Natural Worlds: A Methodological Primer*. Mahwah, NJ: Erlbaum.

Penn, H. (2005). *Understanding Early Childhood. Issues and Controversies*. Buckingham: Open University Press.

Piaget, J. (1929). *The Child's Conception of the World*. London: Routledge & Kegan Paul.

Piaget, P. (1968). *Barnets psykiske udvikling*. [Six studies of psychology.] Copenhagen: Hans Reitzel.

Riegel, Klaus F. (1975). Toward a dialectical theory of development. *Human Development, 18*, 50–64.

Roberts, H. (2000). Listening to children and hearing them. In P.H. Christensen and A. James (eds), *Research with Children – Perspectives and Practices* (pp. 225–240). London: Falmer Press.

Rogoff, B. (1990). *Apprenticeship in Thinking: Cognitive Development in Social Context*. New York: Oxford University Press.

Rogoff, B. (2003). *The Cultural Nature of Human Development.* Oxford: Oxford University Press.

Rose, N. (1999). *Powers of Freedom – Reframing Political Thought.* Cambridge: Cambridge University Press.

Sarason, S.B. (1976). The unfortunate fate of Alfred Binet and school psychology. *Teachers College Record, 77,* 579–592.

Schaffer, R. (1979). *Spædbarnsomsorg* (transl. from *Mothering*). Copenhagen: Hans Reitzel.

Schaffer, R. (1998). *Making Decisions about Children.* Oxford: Blackwell.

Shutz, A. (1970). *On Phenomenology and Social Relations.* Chicago: Chicago University Press.

Schutz, A. (2005). *Hverdagslivets sociology* (transl. from *Collected Works* , vol. 1, 1972). Copenhagen: Hans Reitzel.

Scribner, S. and Cole, M. (1981). *The Psychology of Literacy.* Cambridge, MA: Harvard University Press.

Shotter, J. (2000). Seeing historically: Goethe and Vygotsky's 'enabling theory-method'. *Culture and Psychology, 6*(2), 233–252.

Smith, E.D. (205). *Institutional Ethnography. A Sociology for Peole.* Lanham, MD: AltaMira Press.

Taylor, A.S. (2000). The UN Convention on the Rights of the Child: Giving children a voice. In A. Lewis and G. Lindsay (eds), *Researching Children's Perspectives* (pp. 21–33). Buckingham: Open University Press.

Tiller, P.O. (1988). Barn som sakkyndige informanter. [Children as competent informants.] In M.K. Jensen (ed.), *Interview med born* (pp. 41–72). Copenhagen: Socialforsknings Instituttet.

Ullstadius, E. (2001). The development of conflicts in mother–child interaction. Paper presented at VII European Congress of Psychology, London 1–6 July.

Valsiner, J. (1987). *Culture and the Development of Children's Action.* New York: Wiley.

Valsiner, J. (1997). *Culture and the Development of Children's Actions. A Theory of Human Development.* New York: Wiley.

Vygotsky, L.S. (1978). Mind in society. In M. Cole, V. John-Steiner, S. Scribner and E. Sauberman (eds) *The Development of Higher Psychological Processes.* Cambridge, MA: Harvard University Press.

Vygotsky, L. (1982). Legen og dens rolle I barnets psykiske undvikling. [Play and its role in the child's development.] In *Om barnets psykiske udvikling* (pp. 50–71). Copenhagen: Nyt Nordisk Forlag.

Vygotsky, L.S. (1987a). *Thought and Language.* Cambridge, MA: MIT Press.

Vygotsky, L.S. (1987b). *Problems of General Psychology. The Collected Works of L.S. Vygotsky,* Vol. 1. R.W. Rieber and A.S. Carton (eds.); N. Minick (trans.). New York: Plenum Press.

Vygotsky, L.S. (1998). *The Collected Works of L.S. Vygotsky. Child Psychology, Vol 5*. New York: Plenum Press.

Vygotsky, L. and Luria, A. (1994). Tool and symbol in child development. In R. van der Veer and J. Valsiner (eds), *The Vygotsky Reader* (pp. 99–174). Oxford: Blackwell.

Vygtosky, L.V. (1997). *The History of the Development of Higher Mental Functions. The Collected Works of L.S. Vygotsky, Vol. 4*, R. W. Rieber (trans. by Marie J. Hall). New York: Plenum Press.

Wartofsky, M. (1983). The child's construction of the world and the world's construction of the child. From historical epistemology to historical psychology. In F.S. Kessel and A.W. Siegel (eds), *The Child and Other Cultural Inventions*. New York: Praeger.

Zuckerman, G. (1999). Diagnosing learning initiative. In M. Hedegaard and J. Lompscher (eds), *Learning Activity and Development* (pp. 335–348). Aarhus, Denmark: Aarhus University Press.

INDEX